CREATIN
GRA
REPORTING SYSTEMS

GET SET,
GO!

THOMAS R. GUSKEY

Solution Tree | Press
a division of
Solution Tree

555 North Morton Street
Bloomington, IN 47404
800.733.6786 (toll free) / 812.336.7700
FAX: 812.336.7790

email: info@SolutionTree.com
SolutionTree.com

Visit **go.SolutionTree.com/assessment** to download the free reproducibles in this book.

Printed in the United States of America

Library of Congress Cataloging-in-Publication Data

Names: Guskey, Thomas R., author. | Solution Tree.
Title: Get set, go: creating successful grading and reporting systems /
    Thomas R. Guskey.
Other titles: Creating a successful grading and reporting system
Description: Bloomington, Indiana : Solution Tree Press, 2020. | Includes
    bibliographical references and index.
Identifiers: LCCN 2019033748 (print) | ISBN 9781949539455 (Paperback) |
    ISBN 9781949539462 (eBook)
Subjects: LCSH: Grading and marking (Students)--United States. | School
    reports--United States. | Educational evaluation--United States.
Classification: LCC LB3060.37 .G893 2020 (print) | LCC LB3060.37 (ebook)
    | DDC 371.27/2--dc23
LC record available at https://lccn.loc.gov/2019033748
LC ebook record available at https://lccn.loc.gov/2019033749

Solution Tree
Jeffrey C. Jones, CEO
Edmund M. Ackerman, President

Solution Tree Press
President and Publisher: Douglas M. Rife
Associate Publisher: Sarah Payne-Mills
Art Director: Rian Anderson
Managing Production Editor: Kendra Slayton
Senior Production Editor: Christine Hood
Content Development Specialist: Amy Rubenstein
Copy Editor: Jessi Finn
Proofreader: Kate St. Ives
Text and Cover Designer: Laura Cox
Editorial Assistant: Sarah Ludwig

Acknowledgments

To be kind to all, to like many and love a few, to be needed and wanted by those we love, is certainly the nearest we can come to happiness.

—Mary Roberts Rinehart

This book is dedicated to the people I love and who always make me happy. They inspired the forerunner to this book, *On Your Mark*, and I'm even more indebted to them now than I was then.

First are my family and friends, who show me more kindness, love, and patience than I deserve. They see my faults as temporary conditions rather than permanent traits, help me become a better person, and are infinitely forgiving. They lift me up in my darkest times and tell me I'm wanted and loved when I need it most. What grace I have comes from them.

Second are the amazing teachers and school leaders with whom I've had the privilege of working. These dedicated educators love what they do; find tremendous joy in helping students learn; and have the courage to challenge any policies, rules, traditions, or persons that stand in their way. What hope I have comes from them.

And third are my former students, who helped me discover the joy in teaching, but whom I inadvertently hurt through my poor grading practices before I knew better. I hope they know I'm truly sorry for what I did, and I am doing my best to ensure that other teachers don't repeat the mistakes I made. What inspiration I have comes from them.

Solution Tree Press would like to thank the following reviewers:

Mike Carpenter
Fifth-Grade High Ability Teacher
Aboite Elementary
Fort Wayne, Indiana

Brian Cinnamon
Chief Academic Officer
Kingsport City Schools
Kingsport, Tennessee

Martha Koch
Assistant Professor
University of Manitoba
Winnipeg, Manitoba, Canada

Laura Link
Assistant Professor of Educational Leadership and Policy
University of Houston–Downtown
Houston, Texas

Michelle Marrillia
Assistant Principal
Fern Creek High School
Louisville, Kentucky

Alexis Wiggins
Founder and Director
Cohort of Educators for Essential Learning
The Woodlands, Texas

Table of Contents

About the Author

Thomas R. Guskey, PhD, is Senior Research Scholar at the University of Louisville and Professor Emeritus in the College of Education at the University of Kentucky, where he served as department chair, head of the Educational Psychology Area Committee, and president of the Faculty Council. He has been a visiting professor at ten other universities in the United States and a visiting scholar at universities in Australia, Canada, and New Zealand.

Dr. Guskey began his career in education as a middle school teacher and earned his doctorate at the University of Chicago under the direction of Professor Benjamin S. Bloom. He served as an administrator in Chicago Public Schools before becoming the first director of the Center for the Improvement of Teaching and Learning, a national research center.

Dr. Guskey is the author or editor of 25 award-winning books and more than 250 book chapters, articles, and professional papers on educational measurement, evaluation, assessment, grading, and professional learning. His articles have appeared in prominent research journals, including the *American Educational Research Journal, Educational Researcher*, and the *Review of Educational Research*, as well as practitioner publications such as *Education Week, Educational Leadership, Phi Delta Kappan, The Learning Professional*, and *School Administrator*. He served on the Policy Research Team of the National Commission on Teaching and America's Future and on the task force to develop the

National Standards for Professional Development. He also has been featured on the National Public Radio programs *Talk of the Nation* and *Morning Edition*.

Dr. Guskey has won numerous awards for his work in education. For his outstanding scholarship, he was named a fellow of the American Educational Research Association, the association's highest honor. He also received the association's prestigious Relating Research to Practice Award. He was awarded the Contribution to the Field Award by Learning Forward, the Jason Millman Award by the Consortium for Research on Educational Assessment and Teaching Effectiveness, the Distinguished Achievement Award by the Association of Educational Publishers, and the Albert Nelson Marquis Lifetime Achievement Award. Perhaps most uniquely, he is one of only three individuals in the 154-year history of his undergraduate institution, Thiel College, to receive the Outstanding Alumnus Award and be inducted into the Thiel College Athletic Hall of Fame.

Dr. Guskey's work is dedicated to helping teachers and school leaders use quality educational research to help all their students learn well and gain the many valuable benefits of that success.

To learn more about Dr. Guskey's work, visit http://tguskey.com or follow him @tguskey on Twitter.

To book Dr. Tom Guskey for professional development, contact pd@ SolutionTree.com.

Introduction

Some books are to be tasted, others to be swallowed,
and some few to be chewed and digested.

—Francis Bacon

You just opened what I hope will be the most helpful book you can read on grading and reporting reform. I developed this book as a sequel to *On Your Mark: Challenging the Conventions of Grading and Reporting* (Guskey, 2015). That book describes the policies and practices we, as educators, need to reform to make grading and reporting more honest, accurate, meaningful, and fair. *On Your Mark* sets forth *what* we need to change in grading and *why*. This book, *Get Set, Go: Creating Successful Grading and Reporting Systems*, describes the next important step: *how* to make those changes in ways that succeed and endure. It explains essential elements in the change process, identifies pitfalls to avoid, outlines procedures for gaining input and support from various stakeholders, and presents implementation strategies for ensuring success.

In the introduction to *On Your Mark*, I warned readers that the ideas presented were likely to prompt controversy and disagreement. I cautioned them not to read the book if they didn't have the stomach for conflict and contention. I told them that questioning the way we grade and report student learning means confronting some of education's deepest and longest-held traditions. Perhaps most important, I stressed that changing the way we grade and report student learning

1

will require a level of courage, commitment, and dedication uncommon in education today.

So, if you're reading this book, the sequel to *On Your Mark*, then one of two things must be true. Either you're a person who enjoys controversy, relishes discontent, and revels in the turmoil that comes with challenging the status quo, or you are one of those rare individuals with the requisite courage, commitment, and dedication to challenge those long-held traditions and do what we know is better for our students. I hope it's the latter. Maybe it's some of both.

The central theme of *On Your Mark* is that grading is one of education's most challenging and problematic areas. What makes it particularly problematic is that most current grading policies and practices are based more on tradition than on evidence of effectiveness. Most teachers grade the way they do not because they've deeply thought about it or thoroughly considered the intended and unintended consequences of their practices but simply because "We've always done it that way" (Olsen & Buchanan, 2019). Teachers seem bound more by tradition in grading than by evidence or truth.

Admittedly, not everyone who read *On Your Mark* found it valuable. Upon learning it had become a bestseller, a colleague of mine remarked, "Not bad for a book that says nothing new." Initially, I was deeply hurt by the comment. I'd worked hard developing the book, trying my best to clearly explain complex grading issues and offer specific, evidence-based strategies to guide improvements. How could anyone describe it as "nothing new," especially someone I counted as a friend?

The more I thought about her comment, however, the more I realized there was some truth in it. Scholars and researchers have written about grading issues for decades. And I had, indeed, written about grading issues before and offered suggestions for improvement. At the same time, I believed it important to describe the most current research evidence on those issues, offer more specific recommendations for change, and make a more forceful call to action. When it comes to grading, the stakes are high for students and their families, and the need for change is more important than ever. *On Your Mark* identified precisely the changes that we need to make.

Knowing what to change is important. But without a deep understanding of *how* to implement change, nothing improves. In this book, *Get Set, Go*, we take that next important step and focus on implementation. Together, we will explore what can be learned from well-intentioned grading reform initiatives that ended in disappointing failure. We will consider procedures for gaining input and support from diverse stakeholder groups through coalitions for change. We will examine the change process, what prompts change, and what impedes it. We will look again at the purpose of grading and reporting and the importance of recording multiple grades to reflect both cognitive and noncognitive student learning goals. We will delve into assessments of student learning and clarify several prevalent misunderstandings about effective assessment practices. Finally, we will describe how to develop an effective grading and reporting system that enhances communication and provides a framework for improving student learning.

The Relationship Between *On Your Mark* and *Get Set, Go*

In *On Your Mark*, I challenged a number of common grading policies and practices. I described why these policies and practices don't work and showed how, in some instances, they can be harmful to students. In particular, *On Your Mark* challenges:

- The purpose of grades
- Percentage grades
- Plus and minus grades and half-grade increments
- Grade distributions
- Class rank calculation
- Use of a single grade
- Use of mathematical algorithms to calculate grades
- Practices that confound the meaning of grades

Of course, it's easy to simply challenge policies and practices, to criticize, or to find fault. The harder part is coming up with meaningful and effective alternatives. *On Your Mark* takes that important step by presenting specific strategies for making grading and reporting better, offering explicit alternatives to these policies and practices that not only address their shortcomings but also provide notable advantages. *On Your Mark* also presents sound evidence to support the recommended changes.

Now, however, an even more daunting challenge lies before us: *How* do we make these changes? Knowing what policies and practices we need to change and having ideas about the specific changes to make, how do we go about implementation? How do we make the alternatives described in *On Your Mark* a reality in states or provinces, districts, schools, and classrooms? What needs to come first, and why? What kinds of resources and support are required? And most important, what evidence supports these steps? Can we go forward with the confidence that carefully conducted studies or thoughtful evaluations offer evidence that supports what we are doing? Can we rely on more than just conjecture and persuasively argued opinions? These are the issues *Get Set, Go* addresses.

As I state in *On Your Mark*, "There is much about grading and reporting we still don't know" (Guskey, 2015, p. 109). Despite all the research on grading conducted since the latter part of the 19th century until today, and despite what some writers and consultants claim, we don't yet have sufficiently conclusive evidence to identify what is truly "best practice." Grading and reporting remain an area of education ripe for careful study and thoughtful investigation.

Nevertheless, there is much we do know about grading and reporting. We have a rich and well-established knowledge base on grading and reporting derived from carefully designed investigations (Brookhart et al., 2016; Guskey & Brookhart, 2019). This research has helped us recognize that some practices are clearly *better* than others. We've also learned a great deal about the negative effects different grading policies have on students, particularly those that diminish motivation and confound the meaning of grades. Even more important, we're learning more each day about how to put that knowledge into practice in modern classrooms. That is the specific focus of this book.

The Importance of Research in Grading and Reporting Reforms

My friend and colleague Susan Brookhart and I recently coedited the book *What We Know About Grading* (Guskey & Brookhart, 2019). In developing that book, we brought together a team of distinguished scholars to examine the vast body of research on grading and reporting conducted since the late 1800s. Our team consisted of individuals who not only are intimately familiar with the research but also have contributed to it. Their summaries describe an astonishing history of investigations on what works and what doesn't work in grading and reporting student learning. We found the knowledge gained from this far-reaching and highly diverse collection of studies truly incredible.

What we found even more incredible, however, is that the extensive knowledge base derived from this research is rarely considered when crafting modern reforms in grading and reporting. When questions about effective policies and practices arise, reliable sources of research or evaluation evidence are seldom the first places educators look. They don't look for well-designed studies that have been published in reputable journals. They don't even consult resources from scholarly professional organizations like the American Educational Research Association, the National Council on Measurement in Education, or the American Psychological Association. Instead, they take their guidance from education books, blogs, and chats.

Overworked school leaders and dedicated teachers struggling to improve grading and reporting frequently turn to one of the more than a dozen books on grading published since 2005. They assume the authors of these books have conducted systematic investigations or carefully planned evaluations of grading reform initiatives. They think that these authors, if not researchers themselves, have studied the research on grading to gain a deep understanding of this extensive body of evidence. The practices they suggest and the strategies they recommend for reform, therefore, must surely come from reliable evidence that readers can examine and confirm.

Unfortunately, that is seldom the case. Some authors fail to cite any significant research on grading. Others cite studies they haven't read but instead rely on another author's summary of the research, which may or may not be accurate.

Other reform leaders bypass the books and begin their inquiry into grading and reporting with an internet search where they find numerous blogs posted by individuals expressing their opinions about grading. Occasionally, they restrict their search to scholarly articles, but that's relatively rare. Still others skip the internet search and start their inquiry by posting questions on Facebook or Twitter chats where they receive a myriad of responses from individuals whose opinions and recommendations may or may not be based on verifiable evidence. Sometimes, Facebook and Twitter chat responders preface their comments with "In my opinion . . . " or "I believe . . . ," but their authoritative tone gives the impression their recommendations are indisputable truths.

I'm not suggesting that educators shouldn't consider books, blogs, and social media. I've personally written books, posted blogs, and occasionally participate in Facebook discussions and Twitter chats. But we must recognize these resources for what they are and, more important, what they are *not*. They are, at best, forums for discussion. They are *not* authoritative or trustworthy sources of information on which to base education policies or practices.

Basing policies and practices on opinions gathered from books, blogs, and social media can become a sure ticket to disaster. Education leaders who do this often find themselves confronted by board members or parent groups who hold opposing opinions and stand prepared to squelch reforms. Because these opposing stakeholders typically have greater credibility in their communities than the book writers, bloggers, or social media consultants, their opinions frequently prevail. As a result, school leaders are forced to abandon grading reforms, and the school or district returns to its traditional grading practices.

The commitment and passion of writers, bloggers, Facebook contributors, and Twitter chatters is certainly commendable. Their efforts help bring grading issues to the forefront in discussions of education reform. But policies and practices based on these sources often do more to extend naiveté and perpetuate myths than they do to promote truth. They also slow advances in our field and make meaningful change more difficult.

Ironically, no teacher would allow students to conduct inquiry on any topic in this manner. When teachers show students how to investigate a problem and conduct systematic inquiry, they explain that after defining the problem, students must establish what is currently known about that problem. This requires examining previous research, determining the quality of that research, and summarizing the results. In formal inquires for research papers, theses, or dissertations, this is referred to as a *review of the literature.*

To ensure accuracy, teachers stress that the evidence students gather must come from reputable sources, not conjecture or opinion. Blogs, Facebook discussions, and Twitter chats are rarely considered acceptable. These sources fail to meet the most modest criteria of credibility or reliability.

When investigating policies and practices related to grading and reporting, educators must do the same. They should consult established research bases such as the following.

- **Education Resources Information Center (ERIC; https:// eric.ed.gov):** The U.S. Department of Education's Institute of Education Sciences sponsors this online library of education research and information.

- **What Works Clearinghouse (https://ies.ed.gov/ncee/wwc):** This online review of existing research on different education programs, products, practices, and policies is managed by the U.S. Department of Education's Institute of Education Sciences.

- **Journal Storage (JSTOR; www.jstor.org):** This vast digital library consists of academic journals, books, and primary sources.

- **ProQuest Research Library (www.proquest.com):** This multidisciplinary resource features a mix of scholarly journals, trade publications, magazines, and other sources.

- **Google Scholar (https://scholar.google.com):** This search engine indexes scholarly literature across an array of publishing formats and disciplines.

> "Although grades should never be the only information about learning students and families receive, they can be a meaningful part of that information."

To succeed in grading and reporting reform, education leaders must be more thoughtful in their approach. They must address the process more carefully and proceed with the same judicious inquiry skills that teachers encourage students to develop. The result will not only be better and more effective policies and practices; it will also help make education the evidence-based profession we want it to be.

Essential Steps for Reform Implementation

Efforts to make grading and reporting more effective can take many different approaches, but those that succeed typically include the same essential steps. Although these steps do not guarantee success, experience shows that reform efforts that proceed without them have significant problems and often end in failure.

Essential Steps of Reform Implementation

1. Learn from failures.

2. Form a Coalition for Change.

3. Understand the change process.

4. Clarify the purpose of grading and reporting.

5. Report multiple grades for cognitive and noncognitive outcomes.

6. Get assessment policies and practices right.

7. Develop a systematic plan for implementation.

The chapters in this book detail how to implement these essential steps to grading and reporting reform. They are outlined in the following sections.

Learn From Failures

Not every attempt at grading and reporting reform has been successful. Despite dedicated efforts and commitments on the part of school and district leaders, some programs have been dismal failures. Analyzing what happened in these schools and districts and the difficulties they encountered provides unique insights that can guide efforts with greater likelihood of success. Chapter 1 (page 17) focuses on such an analysis.

Form a Coalition for Change

After considering the reasons so many reform efforts fail, chapter 2 (page 35) focuses attention on the second essential step in implementing successful grading and reporting reforms: forming a Coalition for Change. A single individual cannot accomplish reforms in grading and reporting, regardless of that person's position, commitment, charisma, power, or influence. A dynamic school superintendent or head of schools cannot do it alone, nor can a single committed school principal or solitary teacher. Grading and reporting reform requires a Coalition of dedicated individuals who will take on different tasks in the process, share responsibilities, and collaborate for success.

Understand the Change Process

Chapter 3 (page 61) addresses the third step of grading and reporting reform: developing a thorough understanding of the change process. Many enthusiastic and dedicated leaders desperately want to do the right thing but don't know how to negotiate the change required to successfully implement grading and reporting reform initiatives. As a result, their well-intentioned efforts meet with predictable resistance and pushback from different stakeholder groups to which the leaders have no idea how to respond. Chapter 3 explores how understanding the change process can help guarantee more successful implementation efforts.

Clarify the Purpose of Grading and Reporting

The fourth essential step entails clarifying the purpose of grading and reporting at the district, school, and classroom levels (Brookhart, 2011b). Chapter 4 (page 83) details the process of establishing a unifying purpose and offers specific examples emphasizing why the meaning of grades must be clearly stated, transparent to everyone, and consistently implemented by all teachers. Chapter 4 also discusses why any policies or practices that misalign with the stated purpose must be revised or completely abandoned. For grading and reporting reforms to succeed, teachers at all levels must reach consensus about what grades mean, for whom they are intended, and what results or actions should stem from those involved in the grading and reporting process. Until we clarify our purpose, no change in grading method or reporting format will make much difference (Guskey & Bailey, 2001, 2010).

Report Multiple Grades for Cognitive and Noncognitive Outcomes

The fifth essential step in grading and reporting reform involves using multiple grades to ensure grading policies and practices align with our stated purpose. Grades should communicate multiple dimensions of students' performance in school. To combine evidence on all those dimensions into a single grade, however, confounds the meaning of grades and defies effective interpretation. Instead, we must report multiple grades, offering a "dashboard" of information to reflect these qualitatively different dimensions of performance. Chapters 5 and 6 focus on how we can report multiple grades to enhance communication of student learning outcomes. Chapter 5 (page 117) addresses reporting on cognitive outcomes, and chapter 6 (page 143) turns to reporting important noncognitive outcomes.

Get Assessment Policies and Practices Right

The sixth step entails getting assessments right. The use of classroom assessments to facilitate and enhance learning, rather than simply to evaluate performance, has a long history in education coupled with significant research. Too often, however, that history is ignored, and the research is misinterpreted. These misinterpretations have resulted in educators getting bad advice about what is effective assessment practices and how to successfully implement effective practices in modern classrooms. Chapter 7 (page 181) sets the record straight by tracing this distinguished history and reviewing specific research-based implications for effective practice.

Develop a Systematic Plan for Implementation

The final step in grading and reporting reform is to develop a systematic implementation plan aligned with established evidence of better practices. Successful reforms don't come from opinion, conjecture, speculation, or hearsay. They also can't be initiated based on what everyone else is doing or even what others have done. Too often in education, we refuse to try something new until we see examples of other schools or teachers who have already done it. We are afraid to do what is right until we are assured that others have gone before us, tested the waters, and came away unscathed. But advances in education don't come from imitation; they come from informed innovation.

Revisions in grading and reporting should emanate from careful examination of the research evidence and our accumulated knowledge base of what works best for students (Brookhart et al., 2016; Guskey & Brookhart, 2019). Chapter 8 (page 219) focuses on basing change on trustworthy research evidence and taking steps to gather additional evidence of the effects of change at every step of the implementation process.

Proceed With Caution

To base grading and reporting reforms on validated evidence also requires caution, not only in what we read in books, blogs, and social media posts, but in what we hear from well-intentioned consultants as well. The ideas espoused by some consultants on grading and reporting today are based more on personal beliefs than on a careful analysis of the research. Their presentations focus mostly on opinions and anecdotes rather than on verifiable evidence of effects. Battle-scarred education leaders know, however, that opinions and anecdotes are an inadequate substitute for evidence when challenges and opposition arise.

Being cautious means when charismatic consultants preface their statements with phrases like, "Research shows . . . ," or "According to the research . . . ," we should immediately ask, "*What* research?" And we should expect them to offer specific, verifiable citations of quality research studies published in reputable journals, not simply the books or blogs of other consultants.

Sometimes consultants skirt these questions by asking, "Where is the evidence to support current practices?" But while this tactic may sidetrack some opponents, it seldom proves acceptable to honest critics or concerned skeptics. It also does little to deter those with genuine doubts.

Ironically, critics of grading reform are often the first to acknowledge that current grading policies and practices may not be based on solid research evidence. They readily admit, as described earlier, that those policies and practices are based on some of education's longest-held traditions. They believe, however, those traditions worked well in the past and still work well today. Why abandon those traditions for ideas they consider speculative at best?

> "Nothing dies harder than a bad idea."
>
> —Julie Cameron

Successfully challenging the many old traditions associated with grading and reporting requires creating new traditions to take their place. Furthermore, we must ensure those new traditions come from solid evidence documenting their effectiveness in supporting student learning and enhancing students' perceptions of themselves as competent learners (Guskey, 2011). If we lack such evidence, we must be prepared to gather it as an integral part of the implementation process.

As I described in *On Your Mark*, there is much about grading and reporting we still don't know. But that shouldn't keep us from basing reforms on what we do know. Although we may not yet have sufficient evidence to identify what is truly *best* practice, we have lots of evidence to show that some practices are clearly better than others.

Do We Even Need Grades?

In numerous newspapers, magazines, and journals, you can read articles about the evils of grading. Writers tell us that grades warp student motivation, destroy the morale of teachers, and corrupt the education process (Barnes, 2014, 2018; Blum, 2017; Kohn, 1993; Lamb-Sinclair, 2017; Long, 2015). To get students to focus more on learning instead of grades, most of these writers recommend we eliminate grades completely (Barnes, 2018; Harris-Perry, 2012). We're told that we need to "go gradeless" (Nagel, 2016).

But while the pursuit of high grades can divert some students' attention from the true purpose of education, abandoning grades will not solve the problem (Guskey, 2017a). Some suggest eliminating grades may even be harmful to students, especially those who are poor or disadvantaged (Rampell, 2017).

In many ways, grades are at the same place today that tests were in the 1990s. Back then, as accountability advocates pressed for an increased emphasis on students' test scores, writers began to criticize tests. They said, and rightly so, that the multiple-choice format and restricted content of the tests used in most schools confined the curriculum and diminished valid learning opportunities for students. They described tests as evil and corrupt and suggested we get rid of them.

Educational measurement experts tried to point out that these criticisms were true for only a narrow range of tests. They stressed that other forms of tests, such as demonstrations, exhibits, and performance events, expanded students' response options, tapped higher-level cognitive skills, and more closely resembled learning in real-world contexts (Guskey, 1994d). But these reasoned voices were drowned out by critics who found it easy to gain public support with their outcries, even though such outcries were based on only partial truths.

Unable to counter these narrow interpretations of tests and gain an audience in the public media for an alternative view, the educational measurement community took a different approach: they changed the name. Regardless of their form, measures of student learning were no longer called *tests*. Instead, they were labeled *assessments*.

Changing the name changed the entire tone of the conversation. Assessments seemed friendlier, less harsh, and far less threatening. Assessment experts further enhanced the appeal by attaching the adjective *authentic* to their descriptions of assessments.

The same is happening with grades. Writers portray grades as evil and corrupt, and say we need to get rid of them. If teachers no longer give grades, critics argue that students and families will magically shift their attention to learning instead of the status of high grades.

Some experts suggest that as we did with tests, we should simply change the name. Efforts in this direction have already begun. Some consultants advocate using *marks* to convey something less stigmatizing. Others recommend using *proficiency levels* or *progress indicators* to infer a temporary level of performance rather than a permanent achievement status. A more difficult but far more productive approach, however, would be for educators to clarify the meaning of grades and then radically alter the consequences of grades.

Clarify the Meaning of Grades

As to their meaning, grades are really nothing more than labels attached to different levels of student performance. They identify how well students performed and answer the question students always ask: "How am I doing?" These labels can be letters, numbers, words, or symbols. They serve an important formative purpose by helping students know where they are in meeting particular learning goals. When paired with individualized guidance and direction for improvement, they also help direct students' learning progress.

Radically Alter Grades' Consequences

To serve this formative purpose of grades, two essential consequences of grades must be changed.

1. **We must help students and their families understand that grades do not reflect *who* students are as learners but *where* they are in their learning journey—and where is always temporary:** Knowing where you are is essential to improvement. Informed judgments from teachers about the quality of students' performance can help students become more thoughtful judges of their own work (Chappuis & Stiggins, 2017). Granted, a grade in the form of a number, letter, phrase, or symbol offers only a shorthand description of where students are, and additional information is essential to direct progress. But when accompanied by guidance on how to do better, a grade provides the basis for improvement.

2. **We must never use grades to sort, select, or rank students:** Too often, schools use grades to represent a student's relative standing among classmates. In many schools, for example, grades provide the basis for determining class rank and selecting the class valedictorian. When grades are used for these sorting and ranking purposes, students see grades as scarce rewards offered to a select few rather than as recognition of learning success attainable by all. With this sorting and ranking, doing well does not mean learning excellently—it means outdoing one's classmates. Helping others is discouraged because for one student to move up in rank, another student must move down.

> *"Grades do not reflect who students are as learners but where they are in their learning journey—and where is always temporary."*

Students need honest information from their teachers about the quality and adequacy of their performance in school. Parents need to know how well their children are doing and whether or not grade-level or course expectations are being met. Although grades should never be the *only* information about learning students and families receive, they can be a meaningful part of that information. When combined with guidance to students and families on how to improve, grades become a valuable tool in facilitating students' learning success.

Summary

Questioning the long-held traditions of grading and reporting will not win you friends or make you popular. In fact, those who ask these questions are often labeled as troublemakers. Being a true leader and doing what's right in these efforts sometimes requires sacrificing popularity. A tough road may lie ahead.

But leading grading reform is also not about wishful thinking. It's not about emotional pleas, logical appeals, or philosophical justifications. It's especially not about engaging school board members or concerned parents in public debates or launching social media campaigns to discredit naysayers. Such activities divert attention, damage credibility, waste energy, and subvert goodwill.

Rather, leading grading reform is about knowing what you want to accomplish, why you want to do it, and how you can get it done. It's about anticipating the concerns and possible objections of different stakeholders and addressing those up front. It's about being thoughtfully proactive rather than chaotically reactive. The changes involved in grading reform cannot be accomplished haphazardly or by chance. They must be systematically planned, strategically implemented, and guided by a positive sense of optimism that you can and will succeed.

This book is about how to put that strategic optimism into action. It's about understanding the change process and using that understanding in purposeful and intentional ways. Moving schools toward more effective grading policies and practices requires more than bold and courageous leadership; it requires smart leadership. For those bold enough and smart enough to take on this challenge and to press for thoughtfully reasoned, purposeful change, I hope this book helps. Results won't come easy, but they are important and worthwhile, and they could make school a better and more positive experience for *every* student.

CHAPTER 1

Learn From Failures

Mistakes are a fact of life. It is the response to error that counts.

—Nikki Giovanni

o find examples of districts or schools that failed in their efforts to reform grading and reporting, you don't have to look far. As described in the introduction, the road to grading reform is cluttered with the wreckage of those who took on the challenge and were soundly defeated in their efforts (Rado, 2016; St. George, 2017).

The leaders of these failed attempts—committed educators convinced they were doing the right thing—intended to improve grading and reporting with new policies and practices that benefit students and enhance communication with families. Most sought advice from prominent consultants who offered specific guidance on implementation. And all believed that changing grading and reporting was their professional responsibility.

But often, shortly after initiating the change, these reform leaders encountered unanticipated problems and organized resistance. When attempts to address the problems and calm the resistance failed, many of these leaders were forced to abandon their efforts. The districts and schools they led then returned to traditional grading and reporting methods, leaving reform leaders' credibility in doubt and reliance on

Portions of this chapter appear in "Class Rank Weighs Down True Learning" (Guskey, 2014a) and "Standards-Based Learning: Why Do Educators Make It So Complex?" (Guskey, 2016b).

traditions more firmly entrenched than ever (Field, 2019; Moody, 2018). In a few instances, the reform efforts so damaged the good standing of these leaders that they lost their jobs and had to move to another district or retire from the profession (Brochu, 2013; Cregan, 2013).

To succeed in grading and reporting reforms, we need to understand why these particular efforts failed. What did these districts and schools do or not do that led to their downfall? And more important, what could they have done differently that would have given them a better chance at success? This chapter considers how districts typically go about reforming grading and reporting practices, what lessons we can learn from efforts that failed, and how we can more successfully implement grading and reporting reforms.

How Most Districts Approach Grading and Reporting Reform

Many districts and schools approach grading and reporting reform in similar ways, but most of those approaches are unsuccessful.

Most begin by appointing a report card committee to address the many problems different stakeholder groups voice regarding grading and reporting. Teachers, building leaders, district administrators, and occasionally a few parents typically make up this committee. In some instances, student representatives are included as well.

At the first committee meeting, members discuss their dissatisfaction with the current report card. Typically, they don't like its structure and believe it offers inadequate information about students' learning progress in school. They acknowledge the constraints imposed by the computerized grading program the district purchased, and they wish it was more flexible. They are especially upset that district leaders did not recognize these limitations before investing such a large sum of money in the program.

After discussing what they don't like, a few committee members are assigned the task of searching the internet for examples of report cards that other districts or schools have developed. After all, why go to the trouble of creating an entirely new form if someone else has already developed something useful and effective? These members dutifully conduct their search and assemble a collection of report cards used in other districts. They then present their collection of examples to the other committee members for review.

Committee members study the assorted examples and discuss what they like and don't like about each. Based on their discussion, they develop a hybrid report card, combining the elements they favor from the examples. They discuss and revise their hybrid report card and then present it to district and building leaders, who offer their input. After another round of revisions, they present the new report card to the faculty, along with plans for implementation.

What committee members don't realize throughout this process is that nearly every example report card they gathered in their internet search was developed in exactly this same way. Districts and schools typically don't base their forms on careful examination of evidence about what works in grading and reporting. Nor do they develop them based on pilot versions and trials that include surveys or interviews with various stakeholders (for example, parents, students, teachers, and school leaders). This search-adapt-implement process, therefore, doesn't result in shared knowledge and expanded expertise. Instead, it often leads to shared naiveté or, in the worst cases, shared ignorance.

Typical but Unsuccessful Steps in Grading and Reporting Reform

1. Appoint a report card committee.

2. The committee meets to discuss problems and concerns.

3. Selected committee members search the internet for examples of report cards from other districts or schools.

4. Committee members review examples, choose what they like, and combine elements to create a "hybrid" report card.

5. Committee members present their work to fellow teachers and make plans for implementation.

What We Can Learn From This Approach

We can learn two important lessons from the lack of success districts and schools have had with this approach.

1. **Don't initiate reforms in grading and reporting with the report card. First, decide the *what* and the *why*, and**

then decide the *how*: Because of their vital role in communicating information about students' learning to parents and families, report cards must be considered in the reform process. But that's not the place to start. Before deciding *how* to report, you must first decide *what* information is most important to report and *why* you want to report it. The following sections of this chapter describe the many important decisions schools and districts need to make and critical issues they must address *before* considering the structure and content of the report card.

2. **Don't guide reform of any aspect of grading and reporting with a haphazard internet search. Use substantiated evidence from quality research:** With rare exceptions, anyone with an idea about anything can post their idea on the internet. Few critical checks exist to confirm the validity or authenticity of information found on the internet. Reforms in grading and reporting must be guided instead by quality research studies, well-designed evaluation reports, or substantiated evidence gathered from verifiably successful programs. Grading and reporting are too important and the consequences far too serious for reforms to be guided by guesswork, opinions, and speculation.

To succeed in grading and reporting reform, education leaders need to find a better approach. They need to be much more thoughtful about the process and proceed with the same judicious inquiry skills we encourage students to develop. Specifically, their planning efforts must be purposeful, systemic, informed, and strategic.

How to Learn From Mistakes

The following story was posted on a grading social media site. It describes one school district's unsuccessful attempt to revise grading and reporting. The name of the person who posted the story and the district name are omitted to protect their anonymity. The story has also been paraphrased.

This kind of heartbreaking tale is far too common. This district clearly had dedicated educators at all levels who supported reform efforts. They

A Sad but Not Uncommon Story

Our district had been trying to transition to standards-based grading. We started implementation with high school freshmen. The entire district followed the next school year. We experienced significant resistance from parents the first couple of years, but that eventually settled as students adjusted and most of the complaining stopped. In my opinion, however, we did not provide our faculty with the needed professional development. Teachers were simply given a book by a prominent consultant and asked to read it. We had a handful of presenters on standards-based grading and formed a couple of committees to guide implementation at each school level. Although a few teachers took the time to read the book, most never opened it. Most of our teachers had little understanding of standards-based learning, and few bought into standards-based grading.

Three new superintendents and four high school principals later, coupled with a great deal of teacher turnover, standards-based learning and standards-based grading have become a thing of the past in our district. It's both sad and frustrating for those of us who worked hard to fully make the transition to standards-based grading. None of us has the desire or energy to try again.

read books on grading and reporting reform and invited several consultants to the district to share ideas and offer advice on needed change. They developed a gradual approach to implementation in order to ease the transition to new grading and reporting methods. Yet despite their planning and hard work, the result was a frustrating experience for all.

No one reason accounts for failures such as this in grading and reporting reform efforts. Nevertheless, a quick review of troubled programs and failed efforts reveals that most made the same or quite similar mistakes. In addition, in nearly every case, school and district leaders could have anticipated and avoided these mistakes. Taking the following steps will help schools and districts avoid these reform-killing mistakes. If thoughtfully planned and carefully executed, these steps can dramatically increase the likelihood of success in any grading and reporting reform initiative.

Keep the Process Simple

> ### Keys to Successful Grading and Reporting Reform
>
> 1. Keep the process simple.
> 2. Complete tasks in order.
> 3. Address *why* before *what*.
> 4. Understand the importance of tradition.
> 5. Anticipate opposition.

Educators often take simple ideas and make them inexplicably complicated. Granted, there are always subtleties and nuances in education related to the varied contexts in which teaching and learning occur. But adding complexity to simple ideas typically yields confusion rather than clarity. It can confound implementation efforts and often results in the demise of potentially good ideas. A classic example is what often happens when educators involved in grading reform move toward standards-based learning.

> "Making the simple complicated is commonplace; making the complicated simple, awesomely simple, that's creativity."
>
> —Charles Mingus

The simple idea of standards-based learning is to *ensure transparency in all elements of the teaching and learning process: curriculum, instruction, assessment, and grading and reporting.* This means that each of these elements must be carefully described, completely transparent, and clearly understood by everyone involved: teachers, students, parents, school leaders, and board members. There can be no exceptions and no excuses.

Curriculum

Standards-based learning requires educators to *articulate clear learning goals that identify what students should learn (content) and be able to do (cognitive behaviors).* Effective learning goals always include both of these components (Guskey, 2016b). In other words, you can't have curriculum content without an accompanying description of what students are expected to do with it. Separating content from process within a curriculum makes no sense.

For example, should students simply know and be able to recall the content? Or should they comprehend and understand it in sufficient depth to explain it in their own words? Should they be able to apply it or transfer it to a new and different context? Once articulated, these goals should be shared so they become well known by everyone involved: students, families, teachers, school leaders, and community members.

Typically, we organize learning goals in grade levels at the elementary level and in courses at the secondary level. But organizational structures associated with continuous progress, learning progressions, individualized programs, or personalized learning could be equally valid.

Clear learning goals bring meaning to discussions about curriculum rigor, college and career readiness, and global citizenship. They clarify the difference between memorizing factual information and developing enduring understandings. An emphasis on *essential questions* or *power standards* similarly shifts the focus to deeper, more complex, and higher-level cognitive skills.

Instruction

Educators implementing standards-based learning must develop instructional activities that help *all* students achieve those learning goals. Here, discussions of students' entry-level skills, interests, and cultural differences; learning modalities; differentiated instruction; project-based learning; cooperative learning; online learning opportunities; flipped classrooms; and alternative forms of instruction become vitally important.

Assessment

Standards-based educators must *identify what evidence best reflects students' achievement of those learning goals.* This integrates important issues related to formative and summative assessments, assessments *for* and *of* learning, multiple ways for students to demonstrate mastery, authentic and performance-based assessments, meaningful feedback, and student self-regulation.

Grading and Reporting

Finally, standards-based learning requires educators to *use grading and reporting strategies that meaningfully communicate students' achievement of those learning goals.* This brings attention to gradebook, report card, and transcript design; multiple grades reflecting product, process, and progress criteria; reporting on citizenship, work habits, social and emotional learning, and other noncognitive skills; and grading and reporting policies and practices.

Standards-based learning simply requires transparency and consistency in these elements. In other words, we must have clarity and reliability in what we teach, how we teach it, how we evaluate student learning, and how we report students' learning progress.

> "Simplicity is complex. It's never simple to keep things simple. Simple solutions require the most advanced thinking."
> —Richie Norton

Given this simple purpose of transparency, on what basis would anyone oppose standards-based learning? Admittedly, not everyone agrees on what content students most need to learn and what skills they should develop. Differences abound in our education philosophies and what we most value as a society. But once we make these decisions, would anyone suggest that we keep these decisions secret from students and their families? Does anyone think we should not teach students what we consider most important for them to learn or not assess students based on what they were taught? Would anyone advocate a reporting system that fails to accurately inform parents and families of what students have learned? Of course not! This defining characteristic of standards-based learning is essential to effective teaching and learning at any level and in any context (Guskey, 2016b).

The more complicated we make the simple process of standards-based learning, the easier it is to lose track of the primary and indispensable importance of transparency in these essential elements. Establishing and maintaining transparency in these elements must be kept at the center of this important work. It is vital to success.

Complete Tasks in Order

Occasionally, reformers make the mistake of not addressing the essential elements of curriculum, instruction, assessment, and reporting in order. As discussed earlier, problems always arise when educators change grading practices or the report card and move ahead with standards-based reporting without first addressing curriculum, instruction, and assessment. This can lead to frustration, inconsistent implementation, and eventual abandonment of the entire reform process. We must always address issues regarding what we teach, how we teach it, and how we assess learning *before* we consider how best to grade and report student learning progress.

Implementing standards-based grading without first addressing these other elements is like trying to put the roof on a house before constructing the foundation and building the walls. We lose the central purpose of transparency in reporting if we do not have clarity on what we are being transparent about.

Simplifying our focus also means putting off other issues until we establish purpose and transparency in these essential elements. Appropriate and effective homework policies, multiple opportunities for students to demonstrate mastery or redo assessments, common formative assessments, the consequences for not turning in assignments on time, and so on are all important issues. But they are *not essential elements of standards-based learning.* Taking on all these issues at the beginning of the reform process seriously complicates implementation. It also drastically increases the magnitude of change required for most teachers. If we establish purpose and transparency first, discussions of these other issues will naturally evolve and can be dealt with in a more focused and decisive way.

> *"Have a bias toward action—let's see something happen now. You can break that big plan into small steps and take the first step right away."*
> —Indira Gandhi

Standards-based learning is a simple idea. Complexity comes in its implementation. To successfully implement standards-based learning requires that we keep the simple purpose of transparency in mind and do things in order while adapting to the unique and complex contextual characteristics of different schools and classrooms. Implementation efforts will succeed not by making this simple idea more complex but by finding new and better ways to adapt and apply the idea in widely varied and highly diverse school settings (Guskey, 2016b).

Address *Why* Before What

As previously discussed, many attempts to reform grading and reporting begin by revising the report card. Reformers start by changing what they include on the report card, the report card's structure, how they determine grades, and numerous other policies related to report card grades. Some educators work with the developer of their computerized grading program to make specific adaptations. Others launch organized efforts to explain the planned changes to various stakeholder groups, including students, teachers, parents and families, administrators, board members, and community leaders.

These committed educators fail to recognize, however, that stakeholders' initial concerns are not so much about *what* is changing but about *why* it needs to change. Stakeholders don't see the grading- or reporting-related problems that reformers may consider obvious. They don't understand, for example, the reporting complications associated with percentage grades, plus and minus grades, class rank, the use of a single grade to describe students' performance, or the misguided use of mathematical algorithms to calculate grades (Guskey, 2015). Stakeholders experienced all these aspects of grading when they were in school. They see little reason to change something that they know and believe has always worked well.

For this reason, explanations of reform initiatives must always begin with *why* rather than *what*. In challenging percentage grades, for example, reformers must start by explaining how difficult teachers find it to reliably apply a grading scale that includes 101 discrete levels of performance, two-thirds of which denote levels of failure (Guskey, 2009, 2013; Guskey & Brookhart, 2019). Discussions of class rank should begin with descriptions of the impact this process has on students and how, in many instances, it actually hurts students' chances of admission to highly selective colleges and universities (Boccella, 2016).

In explaining the shift to multiple grades, reformers should describe how combining aspects of achievement, behavior, responsibility, and effort into a single grade makes the grade impossible to interpret and diminishes the value of grades in efforts to help students improve (Guskey, 2018a). To move away from the use of mathematical algorithms in determining students' grades, educators must show parents examples of how these mindless calculations often falsely depict what students have learned and are able to do (Guskey & Jung, 2016; Rose, 2016).

Stakeholders in the grading and reporting process are generally reasonable people who sincerely want what is best for students. They hang on to traditions because they see nothing wrong with them. Providing these different stakeholder groups with a sound rationale for change, a thorough explanation of *why* the change is important, and specific evidence to support the change can drastically improve their openness to and acceptance of change.

Understand the Importance of Tradition

Traditions have an important role in every society. They are the way we transmit customs, beliefs, or ways of acting from one generation to the next. All our traditions have some origin in the past, and they provide a sense of stability and consistency as we move forward in time. Traditions give us security in a world filled with change and uncertainty. But maintaining traditions that have long outlived their purpose and usefulness can also stifle progress.

> *"It is necessary for us to learn from others' mistakes. You will not live long enough to make them all yourself."*
> —Hyman G. Rickover

As discussed in the introduction, many grading policies and practices are based more on tradition rather than evidence of effectiveness. Educators do this not because they know it works well but simply because "we've always done it that way." Changing the way we grade and report student learning means challenging these traditions with the knowledge and confidence that we can do better. But challenging time-honored traditions also means disrupting the security those traditions provide. It means pushing people away from something they find comfortable and familiar and toward a place of uncertainty and anxiety.

Some reform leaders and consultants try to do this through confrontation. They describe these long-held traditions in grading as evil and indefensible. To these reform advocates and consultants, changing such traditions is not just the duty of responsible educators—it is a moral imperative.

But confrontation rarely succeeds. Instead, it causes discussions of change to degenerate into battles of opposing opinions that divert attention and diminish reform efforts. Evidence indicates that to debate another's opinions often serves only to deepen the other's attachment to those opinions (Maeli, 2016). Thus, even when confrontation leads to change, that change tends to be short-lived. It lasts only as long as it takes for opponents of the change to get organized, gather support, and press those in charge to return to the traditional policies and practices they believe to be tried, true, and still valuable.

To succeed in reform efforts, leaders must be sensitive to the loss of security, the intense anxiety, and the extreme discomfort that accompany abandoning established traditions. They must clearly understand the historical importance of these traditions and why educators have maintained them despite the lack of substantiating evidence. Most important, leaders must be ready to offer new, evidence-based traditions to take their place.

"Tradition becomes our security, and when the mind is secure, it is in decay."

—Jiddu Krishnamurti

Consider, for example, the earlier discussion about challenging the traditions of calculating class rank and selecting the class valedictorian (Guskey, 2014a). In most high schools throughout North America, graduating students are ranked according to their cumulative grade point average, or GPA. Many high school educators feel compelled to rank-order graduating students because selective colleges and universities require this information as part of the application process. But while those colleges and universities might have required that information in the past, that requirement is not nearly as prevalent today.

A survey by Eric Hoover (2012) found that only 19 percent of colleges and universities say class rank has considerable importance in the application process, and since then that percentage has dropped even further since 2012 (O'Brien, 2014). Most admissions officers actually express serious skepticism about the meaningfulness of class rank (McKibben, 2017). Schools maintain the practice of calculating class rank primarily because it is a long-held tradition.

Using class rank to select the class valedictorian is also a prevalent tradition in U.S. high schools. This tradition is particularly ironic because the term *valedictorian* has nothing to do with academic achievement. It comes from the Latin *vale dicere*, which means "to say farewell" (Wikipedia, 2019). It is the individual selected from the graduating class to deliver a farewell address at the commencement ceremony called a *valedictory*.

Suppose we wanted to challenge these traditions of class rank and class valedictorian selection. First, we would need to address why we want to do this. What is wrong with recognizing academic excellence?

Why not honor those students who work hard and make earning high grades a priority? Doesn't this process motivate students to do their best? And how else would you select the class valedictorian?

There is nothing wrong, of course, with recognizing excellent academic performance. All educators champion the idea of acknowledging students' outstanding scholastic achievements. Educators also want to provide students with incentives to work hard and do their very best. But ranking students based on their cumulative GPA and using that ranking to determine the class valedictorian pits students against each other to attain that singular distinction. The process often results in aggressive and sometimes bitter competition among high-achieving students to be that top-ranked individual. Gaining the honor requires not simply becoming a high achiever; it requires outdoing everyone else in the class. And sometimes the difference among these top-achieving students is as little as one-hundred-thousandth of a decimal point in their weighted GPA. For one student's poignant portrayal of this process, see the YouTube video "Valedictorian Shocks World With Brutally Honest Graduation Speech" (www.youtube.com /watch?v=a5uqNhfNHL8; Tolley, 2016), which has had more than six million views.

Some high schools address this issue by identifying the ten top-ranked students in the class, rather than picking a single top-ranked individual. But while this policy may ease the tension among those ten students, it does little for the student ranked eleventh. Plus the choice of ten is quite arbitrary. Why not twelve? Or twenty? Or the top 10 percent so the number varies depending on class enrollment? Regardless of the number or percentage chosen, the result is the same. This policy defines excellence not in terms of challenging and rigorous learning criteria but in terms of a student's relative standing among classmates (Guskey, 2014a).

> "The less there is to justify a traditional custom, the harder it is to get rid of it."
> —Mark Twain

To successfully challenge this tradition and change the system, we need to have another system to take its place. The criterion-based Latin system most colleges and universities use to honor high-achieving students, for example, is a useful alternative to the competitive ranking system. At these institutions, students graduate *cum laude* (with honor), *magna cum laude* (with great honor), and *summa cum laude* (with highest honor). Schools award such status based on students' cumulative GPAs, typically 3.50–3.74 for *cum laude*, 3.75–3.99 for *magna cum laude*, and 4.0 for *summa cum laude*.

In turn, we could adopt the procedures that colleges and universities use for selecting the student commencement speaker or valedictorian (Guskey, 2011). Depending on the institution, high-achieving college or university graduates might vote to determine who will represent them as valedictorian at the commencement ceremony. In some cases, the entire graduating class nominates and then votes for the person who best represents the class ideals. Sometimes, the faculty appoint the valedictorian based on a merit system that takes into account not only grades but also involvement in meaningful service projects and extracurricular activities. At some institutions, students compete in an essay contest to give the valedictory speech, while at other schools, a committee composed of students and faculty nominates students for the honor (Guskey, 2014a).

Would a system like this work at the high school level? As described in *On Your Mark* (Guskey, 2015), it works at Wilson High School in Reading, Pennsylvania. Wilson High School made this change after hearing from past valedictorians that they felt victimized by the competition to maintain the highest GPA. Some students reported that it made high school a repressive, unpleasant experience. Under the changed policy, Wilson rewards students for academic achievement measured against rigorous standards of excellence instead of comparing them to their peers (Heesen, 2013). Both parents and students have had an overwhelmingly positive response to the change at Wilson High School. In describing the change, one high-achieving Wilson student said, "I feel that the new system puts the focus on your education instead of competing for a name" (Heesen, 2013). And who delivers the valedictory at the graduation ceremony? A committee made up of faculty members chooses that student, and any senior can audition. Redmond High School in Redmond, Oregon, has implemented a similar program (Tribune, 2013).

These schools succeeded in challenging long-held traditions because they focused on *why* issues first. They addressed stakeholders' concerns and then implemented evidence-based alternatives that were better for students. They replaced a tradition that had long outlived its usefulness with a new tradition that has proven better for everyone involved. They were purposeful, systematic, informed, and strategic.

Anticipate Opposition

Educators typically make two major mistakes regarding opposition to their proposed grading and reporting reforms. First, they don't anticipate opposition. Based on what they've read and what charismatic consultants have told them, they believe everyone will recognize that they are doing the right thing. As a result, it surprises them when anyone doubts the value and reasonableness of their actions. Second, they view the opposition as antagonistic. They see those opposed to these changes as opponents of progress who are stuck in old ways of thinking and misguided about what is truly best for students.

Let's be clear about this: there will always be opposition. As described earlier, challenging long-held traditions evokes uncertainty and anxiety. It threatens the security we feel in things we have known and believed to work. It also goes against what we have experienced. Change is hard under any circumstances, and when it flies in the face of tradition, it is all the more difficult.

> "We must not confuse dissent with disloyalty. When the loyal opposition dies, I think the soul of America dies with it."
> —Edward R. Murrow

But those who oppose reforms in grading and reporting are generally not antagonistic. They don't oppose the reform just because it means change. Their opposition stems from genuine care for students' well-being, especially when those students are their children (Franklin, Buckmiller, & Kruse, 2016).

To succeed in reforming grading and reporting, therefore, educators must understand three things about those who may oppose the change.

1. **New reforms challenge a system that opponents know and believe they understand:** Grading and reporting have remained relatively unchanged since the early part of the 20th century. The grading policies and practices teachers currently use are much the same as teachers used when

most parents, board members, school leaders, and community members were in school. These stakeholders have personal experience with the current system, see nothing wrong with it, and don't understand why it is inadequate for students. They need to be convinced that change is even necessary before they can consider the specific reforms educators propose.

2. **Opponents not only know the traditional grading and reporting systems of the past but also often thrived within them:** In many cases, these individuals succeeded in school because they figured out the grading system and knew what they needed to do to earn high grades. They behaved well in class. They did their homework. They turned in assignments on time. They took advantage of every extra-credit opportunity their teachers offered. In other words, they learned the rules and played by those rules. They mastered the grading system, inadequate as it may have been, and feel well qualified to pass along their wisdom to others, especially their children. Phillip Jackson (1986) refers to this as *a presumption of shared identity bias* that reinforces the status quo. They believe that if the system worked for them, it will also work well for their children.

Educators who press for more meaningful and accurate grading and reporting must help these stakeholders understand that previous grading practices often miscommunicated actual school achievement. In fact, the same policies and practices that benefited them may have harmed other students, especially those who were less privileged and had fewer advantages. These stakeholders need to know that the proposed reforms will result in grades that more accurately reflect what students have learned and are able to do, rather than how well students abided by the teacher's rules and manipulated the grading system. They need to understand that grades are temporary markers of learning progress, not judgments of students as individuals. Most important, they must recognize that grading and reporting serve primarily as a communication tool between teachers and families to guide and coordinate efforts to help all students succeed.

3. **Opponents of reform often fear the proposed changes will have a detrimental effect on their own children:** These individuals believe the reforms may alter their children's motivation to do well in school and their commitment to hard work. Sometimes, they believe the changes will put their children at a disadvantage when it comes to the college admissions process, earning scholarships, or getting the best jobs. In the absence of solid, confirming evidence, they are unwilling to accept reform leaders' opinions that these damaging effects will not occur, and they refuse to sacrifice their children's future and well-being for the sake of untested innovation.

To counter such concerns, reformers must be prepared to support proposed changes with verifiable evidence. They must offer specific research that investigates the effects of grading reforms on student motivation (Stan, 2012). They should review the results of evaluation reports that discuss college admissions officers' acceptance of new reporting forms (Achieve, 2014; Buckmiller & Peters, 2018; Great Schools Partnership, 2018; Hanover Research, 2011; Riede, 2018). They should provide evidence from surveys of students, teachers, and parents regarding their satisfaction with current grading policies and practices (Guskey & Link, 2019c; Guskey, Swan, & Jung, 2011a). Most important, they should make plans to gather evidence from different stakeholder groups throughout the implementation process and use that evidence to guide any adaptations or revisions that may be needed to improve results.

No reform in education goes forward without some level of opposition. In many instances, however, we can anticipate that opposition. With grading and reporting reforms, we can anticipate that opposition will come from concerned stakeholders, especially parents and families who sincerely want what is best for their children. They simply are not yet convinced the advocated reforms are necessarily better, especially when they run counter to well-established traditions.

We cannot ignore such opposition. We also can't address it through argument or confrontation. Instead, we must anticipate opposition and address it directly with patience, purpose, and resolve. It is far easier to disarm a potential opponent before a conflict begins than in the midst of a battle. By anticipating opponents' concerns and addressing those immediately as part of introducing change, reformers can guarantee less troublesome implementation and a far greater chance of success.

> "Better to be wise by the misfortunes of others than by your own."
>
> —Aesop

Summary

No one knows exactly how many grading and reporting reform efforts have succeeded or failed. This is especially true of efforts to implement standards-based approaches to grading and reporting, both because these programs vary so widely and because success is hard to define. Is reporting on specific standards or strands of standards in each subject area or class enough, or must we also tie proficiency to specific student work samples? Is changing the report card in grades K–5 sufficient, or must the change include the middle school and high school report cards as well?

Regardless of the criteria for success, it's clear that many grading and reporting reform efforts don't get very far. A few years into the process, opponents gather support and call for a return to traditional grading and reporting policies and practices; and eventually, reforms are cast aside.

Because every district and school is different, no single approach to reform will always work. But reform efforts that simplify the process, take things in order, address *why* before *what*, understand the importance of traditions like those associated with class rank and valedictorian selection, and anticipate opposition have a far greater chance of success. To bring about meaningful and enduring change, reform efforts must be purposeful, systematic, informed, and strategic. The next chapter turns to an important initial step in this strategic reform process: forming a Coalition for Change.

CHAPTER 2

Form a Coalition for Change

No one can whistle a symphony. It takes a whole orchestra to play it.

—H. E. Luccock

Watching the wildlife on the Maasai Mara in Kenya, Africa, is an incredible experience. It's especially striking to see how these amazing animals have learned to collaborate. Experience has taught them that they are better off when they work together and are in greatest danger when they are alone. Strength, security, and effectiveness come with numbers, while isolation leaves you vulnerable and weak. Your chances of success and sustainability dramatically improve when you collaborate with others, even when they are different from you.

In Africa, the gazelle, impala, topi, wildebeest, and zebra all travel together. They know that when it comes to spotting danger, twenty eyes are better than two. While one set of eyes looks for food, numerous other sets of eyes look out for danger. If a threat is spotted, the alert goes out to all, and together, they escape to safety.

Cheetahs and lions have likewise learned that they are stronger and more effective together than alone. When they form coalitions and work collaboratively, they are far more successful in capturing prey. Coalitions of cheetahs and prides of lions are also able to pursue a wider variety of prey than they can as individuals. Animals that a single cheetah or lion could not take on alone, a coalition of cheetahs or pride of lions can. When they coordinate their efforts, take on different roles and responsibilities, and help each other, they significantly increase their chances of success.

Similarly, in grading and reporting reform, success requires collaborative effort. Dynamic leaders working alone may make a big splash, attract lots of attention, stir things up, and get people talking. But when it comes to the difficult work of putting new ideas into practice, adapting those ideas to unique school contexts, gaining the support of increasingly diverse stakeholder groups, and sustaining support for implementation over multiple years, they quickly discover they can't do it alone. Despite their commitment, hard work, and determination, they lack the knowledge, skill, time, and energy to do it. Alone and without support, they are vulnerable and ineffectual. When the results they promised do not come to fruition, whatever support leaders garnered begins to wane, and they are forced to abandon their efforts. The grading and reporting reforms they advocated never become an integral part of the district's or school's culture and traditions. Instead, old traditions are maintained, and the status quo becomes more firmly entrenched than ever before.

Leaders of successful reforms work differently. Like the animals on the Maasai Mara, they recognize they can't be effective alone. So instead, they surround themselves with the best, smartest, and most thoughtful people they can find. In particular, they look for people who will bring different perspectives to problems and are willing to work hard to find meaningful solutions. They want people who will listen to others' views, challenge long-held traditions when necessary, and collaborate to make things better.

"Whatever you do in life, surround yourself with smart people who'll argue with you."

—John Wooden

Grading and reporting reform is far too complex and highly nuanced for any single person to accomplish. Just as is true among the animals on the Maasai Mara, alone you are vulnerable, weak, and ineffective. Success in this challenging work requires collaboration. It requires a coalition of dedicated individuals united for a specific purpose, committed to fundamental change, prepared to act, and confident they can succeed.

This chapter addresses the first crucial step of grading and reporting reform: forming a Coalition for Change that will plan and lead the implementation of more effective grading policies and practices. Change theorist John Kotter (2012) refers to such a group as a *Guiding Coalition*. After developing a knowledge base from solid evidence on effective grading and reporting, this coalition of leaders from different stakeholder groups fashions the changes to be made and organizes efforts to implement these policy and practice changes.

This chapter describes who should be part of the Coalition for Change, what roles they will have, what principles they will follow, and what issues they will need to address. These issues include the elements required for successful implementation, the crucial questions the Coalition members need to answer, and the best order for addressing those questions. All Coalition members must have a deep understanding of these elements, address the crucial questions, and be ready to support implementation through purposeful, systematic, informed, and strategic collaborative actions. Without a strong Coalition for Change ready to plan and take action to implement new grading and reporting policies and practices, reform efforts will go nowhere.

Coalitions Versus Committees

Some educators believe the best way to facilitate collaboration and gain broad-based support for any reform initiative is to establish a committee that will guide the process. A *committee* is "a body of persons delegated to consider, investigate, take action on, or report on some matter" (Merriam-Webster, 2020b). Committees are normally formed in districts and schools to provide various stakeholders with a "voice" in addressing problems or issues. The best committees function as think tanks, in which people share different perspectives and understandings merge. But in some instances, committees actually stifle progress. They can divert the focus of reform initiatives and delay vital action (Corcoran, Fuhrman, & Belcher, 2001). In the worst cases, committees become places where good ideas go to die.

Savvy leaders know that when new ideas for reform prompt controversy and disagreement, the best approach is to appoint a committee to study the ideas. If the ideas are particularly thorny and troublesome, they label the committee a *task force*. Committee members are asked to address the idea, come to consensus, and make recommendations for decision makers to consider at a later date. Turning a controversial idea

over to a committee takes it out of the public spotlight, at least tempo-
rarily, and buys the leader crucial time in making decisions regarding
the idea. As one school leader privately confessed, "I've never met a
problem so immediate, so pressing, or so contentious that I couldn't
appoint a committee to study it." Especially shrewd leaders include both
advocates and opponents on the committee because they know that
this will extend the debate, prolong discussions, and delay any decision
that they must make. They also know that putting advocates and opponents together will ensure people perceive their leadership to be fair-
minded and impartial.

By the time committee members meet, get organized, plan agendas,
negotiate consensus, and report their recommendations, sufficient time
has usually passed for the ideas to lose their volatility. Reaching consensus frequently requires watering down poten-
tially controversial ideas and softening their most
contentious elements so that key aspects of fidelity
are lost. The passage of time also means that stakeholder groups have probably turned their attention
to new issues, and decision makers are involved in
other, more pressing matters. So when stakeholders
finally consider the committee's recommendations, discussions are calm
and unemotional. The changes the district or school finally enact tend
to be uninspiring and modest at best (Morrow, 1979).

> "A committee is a cul-de-sac down which ideas are lured and then quietly strangled."
>
> —Barnett Cocks

Coalitions differ from committees in both purpose and function. A
coalition is "a temporary alliance of distinct parties, persons, or states
for joint action" (Merriam-Webster, 2020a). For example, in countries
with many political parties, none of which gets a majority of the citizens'
votes, the only way to establish an effective government is by forming
a coalition of parties. This coalition unites different parties in a collaborative effort to move the government forward. What distinguishes
definitions of *coalition* from definitions of *committee* is inclusion of
the word *action*. While committees offer recommendations *for* actions,
coalitions *take* action. Coalitions shoulder responsibility for making
change and putting new ideas into practice.

Coalitions as the Avant-Garde

In many ways, coalitions function as the avant-garde. Originally a military term used to describe the front line of an infantry unit, *avant-garde* came to be used in the early 1900s to describe artists who were the pioneers or innovators of a particular period. Members of an avant-garde rebel against old ways and traditions and press for innovation. They introduce new ideas and new ways of thinking.

Similarly, Coalitions for Change are the avant-garde in grading and reporting reform. They, too, rebel against traditions, introduce new ways of thinking, and press for innovation. They are the frontline leaders in reform, united in their efforts and committed to significant and meaningful improvement.

Forming Coalitions for Change

Coalitions for Change are typically launched by a person or group of individuals in the district or school who have leadership responsibilities. It could be a superintendent or head of schools, assistant superintendent or district coordinator, building leader, or group of leaders at any level, including lead teachers. We will refer to this person or group as the *initiators*.

The initiators must have a comprehensive understanding of pertinent grading and reporting issues gained from broad reading and study of the topic. In many cases, the initiators will have attended conferences or seminars focused on grading and reporting reforms. These experiences may have caused them to develop a healthy sense of skepticism and doubt, recognizing that much of what they've read and heard is more opinion-based than evidence-based or research-based. Still, they understand the need for change and *why* reforms in current policies and practices are important. In addition, they must be willing to enlist other stakeholders' help in planning and implementing change, and they must have confidence the reforms they implement together will yield important benefits for everyone involved.

With this understanding and confidence, the initiators next must consider the wide range of stakeholders in the grading and reporting process and whom within each stakeholder group to enlist in developing reforms. In order to be successful, Coalition for Change members should be:

- Excited to take on the work and understand the difficulties involved in challenging long-held traditions
- Aware of the need and urgency for change
- Open to new ideas and willing to seek out strong and verifiable evidence that supports change
- Respected within their stakeholder group
- Ready to collaborate with others outside their group to develop the reforms
- Prepared to publicly advocate for recommended reforms
- Eager to take action that will ensure high-quality implementation of those reforms
- Share the belief that grading and reporting not only communicate information about learning but also can and should purposefully enhance student learning

In other words, they will be powerful in terms of their positions, information and expertise, reputations and relationships, and capacity for leadership (Kotter, 2012).

With these criteria in mind, initiators must choose or arrange for the choice of members of various stakeholder groups who will participate in the Coalition for Change. In some cases, the choice will be obvious (for example, superintendent or head of schools, district administrator, or school principal). In other cases, however, they may ask stakeholder organizations (for example, teacher associations, parent associations, or student organizations) to choose volunteers. Initiators must next schedule a time and place for the Coalition's meeting, describe the Coalition's purpose, and make a preliminary list of tasks for the Coalition to take on. An invitation to potential Coalition members like the following might be helpful.

**Invitation to Join the Coalition for Change
in Grading and Reporting**

We would like to invite you to be a member of our Coalition for Change that will examine our district and school policies regarding grading and reporting student learning. The Coalition will include leaders from a variety of important stakeholder groups in the grading and reporting process. Our goal is to learn what current research reveals about effective grading and reporting, review our current policies and practices in light of that research, recommend revisions in policy and practice if needed, and ensure consistent and successful implementation of those revisions.

The first meeting of the Coalition for Change will be [when and where]. Your input and contribution to this important work will be particularly valuable. We look forward to seeing you at the meeting and to working together.

If you have questions or need additional information, please contact [email and phone number].

Sincerely,

[Initiators]

Coalitions for Change Members and Their Roles

Coalitions for Change should include representatives from different stakeholder groups. Each of these individuals brings a unique perspective to the work of the Coalition and offers an important contribution to the reform process. These stakeholder individuals and groups include the following.

- Superintendent or head of schools
- District administrators
- School principals
- Lead teachers
- Special staff members
- Parents and families
- Students

In addition to describing each individual or group, the following sections include procedures for selecting these Coalition members and detail the vital nature of their explicit support.

Superintendent or Head of Schools

In most cases, the superintendent or head of schools (the equivalent of superintendent in international school contexts) is a vital member of the Coalition for Change. The superintendent is the most public and visible leader in a school system. But the position of superintendent is also the most political. Superintendents must strike a critical balance between being a strong advocate for students and teachers and having direct accountability to a board of education or board of directors that provides citizen oversight of the school system to ensure responsiveness to the local community.

Although superintendents may not be the initiators or even the primary Coalition leaders, their input and engagement in developing grading and reporting reforms is essential. Superintendents must actively participate in Coalition discussions, come ready to offer their perspectives, and listen to and consider other stakeholders' perspectives. They must be genuinely knowledgeable of the reforms that the Coalition advocates, and they must be well prepared to describe the value and importance of those reforms to any constituency.

> **Momentum-*Killing* Statements**
>
> - "Rest assured, we're going forward *very slowly* in this process."
> - "We're proceeding with *guarded optimism*."
> - "We *think* we're doing the right thing."
> - "We're *cautiously* moving ahead, gathering data as we go."
> - "This is a pilot effort *only*, and we've not yet made plans to expand implementation."

Being the primary spokespersons for school districts, superintendents also must make their support of the Coalition's work evident to all. In particular, they must make their support clear when they explain the purpose of the Coalition's work to board members and other community leaders. Furthermore, they must avoid momentum-*killing* statements.

Leaders sometimes say these things believing such statements convey thoughtfulness, care, and due diligence in the reform process. But more often, statements like these communicate timidity, lack of confidence, and uncertainty of the value of change. They severely dampen motivation for any reform initiative and drastically reduce the chances of success. Such statements often cause building leaders, teachers, and especially parents to think, "If the superintendent isn't confident these reforms are better, why should we be?" While superintendents and heads of schools cannot successfully initiate reforms in grading and reporting alone, they can effectively squelch reform efforts with their words, their actions, or their inaction.

As part of the Coalition for Change, superintendents must know they are not alone in their support of grading and reporting reform initiatives. An entire team of committed individuals, all leaders in their respective stakeholder groups, stands with them. Superintendents can advocate for the reform process much more clearly and directly with momentum-*enhancing* statements.

The superintendent's role in the Coalition for Change can vary depending on the district's size. In larger school districts, particularly those that include multiple high schools, grading and reporting reform often takes place at the school level rather than the district level. Fayette County Public Schools in Lexington, Kentucky, for example, enrolls approximately forty-three thousand students and has six comprehensive high schools. Two of the district's high schools (Bryan Station High School and Paul Laurence Dunbar High School) have initiated major grading and reporting reforms aligned with standards-based grading, while the other high schools have maintained more traditional grading policies and practices (Spears, 2017; Yaffe, 2017). Although the

> ### Momentum-*Enhancing* Statements
>
> - "We planned carefully and considered many different options."
>
> - "We developed these changes based on input from important stakeholders throughout our district and schools."
>
> - "We are confident this is better for our students."
>
> - "We are committed to improving communication between schools and families."
>
> - "Our goal is to help *all* our students succeed!"

district superintendent is knowledgeable and supportive of the reforms, progressive high school principals and forward-thinking curriculum and instruction coordinators at these two high schools initiated the change efforts.

In smaller districts that include a single comprehensive high school, however, superintendents usually have more direct involvement in school operations. This is also true of heads of schools in most international school settings. Furthermore, smaller districts and international schools tend to have systemwide grading and reporting policies rather than individual school policies. In these contexts, it is essential that the superintendent or head of school be directly involved and actively participate in the Coalition for Change.

District Administrators

In most school districts, district-level administrators initiate and often lead grading and reporting reforms. A district administrator may be an assistant superintendent, curriculum and instruction coordinator, or program director. District administrators represent the first contact for assistance when problems arise at any school. They are also the primary source of information about programs or regulations sponsored by federal, state, provincial, or local governments.

District administrators bring broad-based perspectives to the work of Coalitions for Change. Because of their districtwide responsibilities, they see beyond the context of individual schools to the implications that reforms have for the entire school system. Typically, their work also involves initiatives that have implications for instructional programs at all levels, from preschool through high school. As a result, they can offer important insights for linking grading and reporting reforms across school levels and for easing students' transitions between levels. Their involvement in the Coalition is crucial.

School Principals

School principals and assistant principals probably play the most important part in the success of Coalitions for Change. A growing body of research evidence shows that principals have profound influence on the reforms initiated, the quality of the reforms' implementation, parents' and families' support of reforms, and how well reforms are sustained (Bottoms & O'Neill, 2001; DuFour & Mattos, 2013; Kraft

& Papay, 2014; Liebowitz & Porter, 2019; Papay & Kraft, 2016). A study by Garth Larson (2017), for example, looked specifically at the implementation of standards-based grading reforms and found the one common element in all successful efforts was a strong, well-informed, purposefully engaged school principal. Another comprehensive research review on leadership in grading reforms by Laura Link (2019) showed the same. The compelling nature of this evidence and its consistency across studies indicates that the success of grading and reporting reforms at all school levels largely depends on the strong and active support of school principals.

In many unified school districts and international schools, grading and reporting reforms begin at the elementary level with plans to phase in implementation at the middle school and high school levels as students advance to upper grades. In other districts and schools, however, secondary educators initiate reforms after discovering striking inconsistencies in grading policies and practices among teachers, even those who teach in the same academic department (Taketa, 2019). No current evidence indicates that one approach to implementation is better or more effective than the other. With each approach, however, principals' active support is crucial to success. In addition, because grading and reporting policy reforms are generally implemented schoolwide, especially those that involve changes in report card structure or format, it is vitally important that school principals at all levels—elementary, middle, and high school—actively engage in Coalitions for Change.

The importance of principals' personal involvement and support in grading and reporting reforms cannot be overemphasized. Not only is their input needed to structure and implement reforms, but their public support of reforms to teachers, parents, and community members is crucial. Principals and assistant principals must be able to explain the rationale for change; why the reforms are important; and how these reforms will benefit students, families, and the school. They also must work collaboratively with other stakeholder leaders in the Coalition to ensure shared advocacy of the change.

Lead Teachers

As the persons most directly responsible for implementing grading and reporting reforms, lead teachers must be involved in Coalitions for Change. Even the most modest changes in grading and reporting require additional work for teachers. Evidence indicates, however, that teachers are generally willing to take on the extra work associated with these changes when:

- Tasks are made manageable within their current professional responsibilities

- The changes yield observable benefits for students and their families

- Their extra efforts are recognized and appreciated by district and school leaders (Swan, Guskey, & Jung, 2014)

Ensuring that discussions of reforms and implementation plans include, value, and honor teachers' perspectives helps guarantee these conditions are met.

The challenge and extra work involved in implementing grading and reporting reforms varies depending on the grade level, mostly due to school structures and curriculum differentiation (McMillan, 2019). Most elementary teachers, for example, have responsibility for grading and reporting the learning progress of twenty-five to thirty students in multiple subjects, while most middle school and high school teachers must judge the performance of more than one hundred students in a single academic discipline. In addition, while all second-grade students are usually learning the same things, that is not true of all tenth-grade students. Because of these differences, Coalitions should include lead teachers representing both elementary and secondary school levels. When possible, Coalitions should involve teachers from different academic disciplines as well. Although these lead teachers need not be senior staff members, they should have a few years of experience in the school so they are familiar with current grading and reporting policies and practices. Knowledge of the school's computerized grading program is also helpful. Finally, because people will look to them for leadership in implementation efforts, the lead teachers should also be well respected by their colleagues.

A Growth Mindset

Some advocates of grading and reporting reform believe that for implementation efforts to succeed, school leaders and teachers must think about grades similarly and share certain dispositional characteristics. In particular, they contend school leaders and all teachers in a school must share a *growth mindset* or *mastery orientation*. Teachers with a growth mindset believe that their talents, as well as the talents of their students, can be developed through dedication and hard work. They see challenges and occasional setbacks as opportunities to improve their skills and performance (Dweck, 2006). Similarly, teachers who hold a mastery orientation have specific learning goals for both themselves and their students, and they enjoy new challenges. They believe that they and their students can always get better and that effort influences success more than does innate ability (Ames, 1992).

According to these advocates, school leaders and teachers must share a growth mindset or mastery orientation in order to create a school culture that is amenable to change and ready to consider reforms.

> "It takes more than one person to make a path."
> —African proverb

Therefore, change efforts must begin with activities designed to ensure all teachers develop this common mindset or orientation. Reforms in grading and reporting can then grow from the inside, based on collective ideals, aspirations, and paradigms (O'Connor, 2013; Schimmer, 2016). As grading and reporting reforms evolve, school leaders can then disseminate them to other districts and schools with similar cultures and like-minded school leaders and teachers.

Although the concept is inspiring and intuitively appealing, no research evidence confirms that all school leaders and teachers need such a shared mindset or orientation to successfully implement grading and reporting reforms. Furthermore, no evidence shows that the lack of a shared mindset or orientation causes reform efforts to fail. In fact, given what we know about the variation in beliefs and perceptions that typically exists among teachers in the same school (Raudenbush, Rowan, & Cheong, 1992; Sabers, Cushing, & Berliner, 1991), it seems highly improbable that all school leaders and teachers will share a common mindset or orientation at any time. Not only is this unlikely to exist in any school; it may be impossible to attain.

What is true, however, is that all Coalition for Change members, including school leaders and lead teachers, *must* share a growth mindset and mastery orientation. They *must* believe that improvements are possible, and they *must* have confidence that with careful planning, their district, schools, and classrooms can successfully implement the changes needed to bring about those improvements. So although it may not be necessary for all school leaders and teachers to share these dispositions in order to begin reform efforts, those involved in leading the reform efforts clearly must.

Special Staff Members

In addition to lead teachers, Coalitions for Change often include special staff members whose work bears directly on grading and reporting. Guidance counselors are the most frequently involved special staff members because of their work with students' grade reports, transcripts, and college admissions procedures. Teachers of exceptional learners—including students who are gifted and talented, English learners, and students with identified learning disabilities—can have especially valuable insights as well. Because grading and reporting policies can have profound effects on how teachers communicate these students' learning progress to their families and others (Jung & Guskey, 2012), these special staff members' input can be especially important in developing and implementing reforms.

Parents and Families

Parents and families have a powerful influence on how students feel about learning, how they regard themselves as learners, and how well they perform in school (Hill & Taylor, 2004; Jeynes, 2012; Pomerantz, Moorman, & Litwack, 2007). As primary recipients of the information included in report cards and other reporting tools, parents and families have an important role in Coalitions for Change.

Among all stakeholder groups, parents and families are undoubtedly the most diverse. In most districts and schools, the parents and families of the students enrolled vary widely in their economic, ethnic, racial, language, educational, and social characteristics. Although this variability enriches the school and community, it sometimes affects parents' and families' ability to be involved in Coalition work. Despite strong interest in their children's education and particularly in grading and reporting, work schedules, childcare responsibilities, language differences, and transportation complications prevent some parents and family members from taking part. Because of these difficulties, Coalitions must make efforts to gain insights from a broad range of parents and families as their work proceeds.

In districts and schools where parents' and families' professional or personal responsibilities preclude their involvement in Coalition meetings, Coalition members can conduct surveys to gather information on parents' and families' perspectives and concerns. Some districts and schools organize focus groups at times convenient for parents and family members to attend. Translators or bilingual persons are included when language differences exist. In other instances, grading and reporting issues are discussed during home visits to inform parents and families of the purposes of grading and reporting and the important role of families in the process. Coalitions can also use these occasions to collect parents' and families' perceptions and ideas for improvement.

Students

Because grading and reporting reforms affect them most directly, Coalitions for Change sometimes include student members. In most cases, these are high school students who have experience with current grading policies and practices and for whom the information on report cards and transcripts has important consequences. Students must be assured, however, that their honest input in Coalition discussions will not have detrimental repercussions.

Like parents and families, students represent a highly diverse stakeholder group. Deliberate efforts must be made, therefore, to ensure students represent the broad spectrum of diversity in the district or school. In particular, the Coalition should include both high-achieving, successful students and low-achieving, struggling students so their potentially different perspectives on grading policies and practices are understood. If concerns arise about the adequacy of student representation, then focus groups designed to target specific subgroups of students can be formed and results shared with Coalition members. When the Coalition considers and values students' perspectives in planning grading and reporting reforms, not only will students better understand the reasons for change, but they will be far more likely to support implementation.

Operating Principles of Coalitions for Change

The operating principles of successful Coalitions for Change resemble those that characterize any effective professional learning environment (Papay & Kraft, 2016). Coalition members should discuss these principles at the first Coalition meeting so all members understand the purpose of their work and how to accomplish it. A quick review at the beginning of each Coalition meeting can also serve to keep members mindful of the agreed-on working procedures.

The six essential operating principles of Coalitions for Change include the following.

1. Engage in foundational reading.

2. Provide supportive leadership.

3. Foster a culture of trust.

4. Find opportunities for collaboration.

5. Disagree and commit.

6. Gather meaningful feedback.

Engage in Foundational Reading

To begin their work in reforming grading and reporting, Coalition members must have a shared understanding of the issues involved, the problems to be addressed, and the evidence supporting change. Beginning Coalition conversations with a shared knowledge base, rather than individual members' opinions and speculations, is essential to progress. Building this common knowledge base can be accomplished by developing a list of readings that outline those critical issues and describe the associated evidence. Many books and authors offer recommendations for change. The following works, however, relate directly to the ideas this book presents, principally due to their consistent approach and shared emphasis on solid evidence.

- *On Your Mark: Challenging the Conventions of Grading and Reporting* (Guskey, 2015), the prequel to this book, describes grading and reporting conventions that have long outlived their usefulness and need to be challenged. It also offers meaningful alternatives to these common practices, accompanied by pertinent evidence supporting the change.

- *What We Know About Grading: What Works, What Doesn't, and What's Next* (Guskey & Brookhart, 2019) summarizes the research on grading and reporting gathered since the latter part of the 19th century. It also presents guidelines for using this extensive body of evidence to direct improvements in grading policies and practice.

- *Answers to Essential Questions About Standards, Assessments, Grading, and Reporting* (Guskey & Jung, 2013) provides simplified definitions and clear explanations of these popular education concepts. It also offers numerous practical examples and illustrations to clarify relationships among these important aspects of education.

> "Authors who speak about their own books are almost as bad as mothers who talk about their own children."
>
> —Benjamin Disraeli

Of course, other works also offer valuable ideas and provide a basis for informed conversations.

Provide Supportive Leadership

The Coalition will need one or two persons to serve as Coalition leaders. Sometimes, the initiator who brought the Coalition together serves as a leader. But other individuals selected at the first meeting could take on leadership tasks for the Coalition.

The Coalition leaders have four major responsibilities.

1. **Schedule Coalition meetings and prepare the agenda for each meeting:** This involves finding a convenient time and place for the different stakeholders to meet and outlining the issues to be addressed and goals to be accomplished at each meeting and between meetings.

2. **Facilitate Coalition meetings, manage discussions, ensure items on the agenda are addressed, and arrange for someone to take the minutes:** These procedural matters may seem trivial, but they are essential to the efficiency and productivity of the Coalition.

3. **Secure and sustain the support of district and school leaders:** As described earlier, a Coalition's reform efforts in grading and reporting will unlikely go forward or endure without superintendents', heads of schools', and building principals' active involvement and public support. While district and school leaders' active support alone will not guarantee success, important evidence indicates their lack of support pretty much dooms reform efforts to failure (Larson, 2017; Link, 2019).

4. **Coordinate Coalition members' actions in implementing grading and reporting reforms:** The leaders' role, however, is not necessarily to direct or supervise these actions. Rather, the leaders facilitate reform development and organize collaborative procedures for putting the reforms into practice.

Foster a Culture of Trust

The various stakeholders involved in the Coalition for Change usually have not had opportunities to work together before and often don't know each other well. In addition, the work they will do involves addressing long-held school traditions about which many people have strong opinions. Therefore, to succeed at this work, a culture of openness and trust must permeate all Coalition activities.

The following three types of trust are essential in Coalition work.

1. **Coalition members must trust each other:** They must know that they can be honest and forthcoming in all discussions without fear of reprisal. They must be confident that their perspectives will be valued and weighed in developing reforms. And most important, they must honor the perspectives of others, even when strikingly different from their own, and stay open to the possibility that their own perspectives might change in light of new evidence.

2. **Coalition members must support their decisions with trustworthy evidence:** They must know that trustworthy research evidence—not the persuasively argued opinions of authors, bloggers, social media contributors, or

consultants—will serve as their primary guide in developing grading and reporting reforms. When asked to defend a particular new policy or practice, they should be able to offer specific evidence, rather than simply replying, "We were told by so-and-so."

Coalition members should also plan to gather specific evidence throughout the implementation process to verify that the reforms are yielding the desired results. This formative evaluation evidence helps ensure that if the reforms have unanticipated shortcomings or are not producing expected results, Coalition members can make purposeful revisions.

3. **Coalition members must trust and work to ensure that the reforms they develop and implement will benefit students and their families:** They must trust that all the stakeholders involved in these grading and reporting reforms share a common desire to do what is best for students. They should know that all the stakeholders are dedicated to implementing policies and practices that not only enhance communication between school and home but also help improve student learning.

Find Opportunities for Collaboration

Coalitions for Change provide participants with unique opportunities to work with stakeholders in the grading and reporting process with whom they may rarely interact. District leaders and principals may learn about unforeseen problems teachers face in trying to develop grading policies that are fair and equitable to all students. Teachers may discover unexpected difficulties that parents experience in trying to understand grades and report cards. Students may reveal interpretations of grading policies and practices that neither teachers nor parents considered. Coalition discussions that take place in an open, trusting, and collaborative atmosphere allow all stakeholders to see critical grading and reporting issues from different perspectives, hear concerns they may not have considered, and develop reforms that will benefit all.

Disagree and Commit

Coalition for Change members must follow the principle of *disagree and commit*. This planning and management principle not only allows but also encourages individuals to disagree while they are making decisions and planning strategies. Once a decision is made, however, everyone must commit to it. This principle is based on the idea that conflict and disagreement are useful in the early stages of decision making. They allow people to consider multiple options and weigh the merits of various strategies. But after the decision is made, disagreement diverts attention, weakens efforts, and seriously hinders the chances of success.

The principle of disagree and commit is typically credited to leaders of highly successful modern corporations, Amazon and Intel in particular (Emanuele, n.d.; Lencioni, 2012; Szamko, 2016). But its roots can be traced to much earlier times as a way of planning military campaigns. The Allied Forces used the principle of disagree and commit in planning the D-Day invasion during World War II. U.S. Army General Dwight D. Eisenhower and British General Bernard Montgomery brought together their top military strategists in an allied command team to plan an immense operation to cross the English Channel and liberate France. Initially, team members disagreed on the best strategy. But after considering the merits and drawbacks of various options, all agreed to one coordinated plan of attack.

Coalition for Change members similarly should expect disagreements during the early planning stages. Even when they base decisions on the best evidence available, stakeholders may disagree on their interpretations of that evidence, the best strategy for implementation, or an optimal timeline. After discussing and fairly considering various options, however, all stakeholders involved must commit to and actively support a unified implementation plan.

This does not imply that the Coalition can't make changes as a plan unfolds and new evidence is gathered on its effects. Adaptations to the best-laid plans are sometimes needed. Nevertheless, *commit means commit*! It means that in discussions during implementation, Coalition members should not make statements such as "I always thought it would be better if we . . . ," "Despite my objections, we decided to . . . ," or "I said early on we should . . . ." Coalition members must make their commitment to and support for the plan and any adaptations to it clear and evident to all.

Gather Meaningful Feedback

Implementing reforms in any context always involves some experimentation. Despite careful planning, unanticipated difficulties or snags often occur. For this reason, Coalitions for Change must plan specific follow-up activities as part of the implementation process that include gathering feedback from stakeholders closest to the reform effort. With grading and reporting reforms, this typically means collecting detailed information from school principals, teachers, students, and parents.

The Coalition can gather formative feedback formally through surveys, focus groups, or staff meetings. These more formal techniques can target specific issues by asking direct questions or addressing specific concerns. But important feedback can also be collected informally through brief hallway conversations or simply asking various stakeholders, "How's it going?" or "What's happening with . . . ?"

Feedback should be gathered at regular intervals throughout the implementation process and especially at important grading and reporting junctures in the academic year—for example, after distribution of the first report card, during parent-teacher conferences, and at the end of the academic term or semester. Coalition members can then summarize this feedback to determine what successes they have achieved, what problems remain, what changes they will make to address those problems, and how they will determine the results of those changes.

Crucial Questions for Coalitions for Change

To successfully reform grading and reporting policies and practices, Coalitions for Change must address a series of crucial questions. These most basic questions of grading and reporting reform are the same as those used in all forms of information gathering and problem solving: the five Ws—*who, what, where, when,* and *why*—and *how.*

Just as important as the questions themselves is the order in which Coalition members address these questions. Districts and schools that encounter difficulties in implementing grading and reporting reforms often consider the right questions but address those questions in the wrong order. As a result, they find themselves caught in disputes and entangled in controversies that could have been avoided. For success in grading and reporting reform, the optimal order for addressing these questions is (1) *why*, (2) *what*, (3) *how*, (4) *when*, and (5) *who*. The *where* is important but usually evident—that is, in our district or school.

Why

After Coalitions for Change members do foundational reading and develop a shared knowledge base, the first and most important questions they must consider all relate to *why*. Why is change necessary? Why is the current system not working? Why infringe on teachers' professional freedom and discretion when it comes to grading? Why take on grading and reporting when other issues seem more pertinent? In fact, the question foremost in most stakeholders' minds regarding grading and reporting will be, "Why do we need to change?" Failure to effectively address these *why* questions is the major reason so many grading and reporting reform efforts encounter resistance and pushback.

Before considering specific changes in grading and reporting policies and practices, stakeholders must clarify why change is needed. They need to recognize that most current grading and reporting policies and practices are based on tradition rather than careful consideration of what actually benefits students. They should know that a significant research base on grading and reporting exists and can guide improvements and lead to better practices. Most important, they need to understand that grading and reporting are about more than merely communicating information on student learning. Rather, they represent a primary means to help all students reach higher levels of learning success and gain the many benefits of that success.

As described in chapter 1 (page 17), many grading and reporting reform efforts fail simply because reform leaders move directly to *what* they want to change without adequately clarifying *why* change is needed. Consequently, when stakeholders raise *why* questions with regard to the proposed change, these leaders feel ill prepared to answer the questions, and reform efforts fall apart. *Why* questions must always come first. In chapter 4 (page 83), we will explore this rationale in greater depth.

What

After clarifying *why* issues, reform leaders are ready to consider *what* needs to change. What particular aspects of grading and reporting will be addressed? What specific policies and practices need to be revised? What adaptations to gradebooks, report cards, and permanent records or transcripts will be involved? What evidence justifies these changes? After the reasons for grading and reporting reform are clearly explained and generally accepted, discussions of what needs to change always go more smoothly.

The most serious objections and pushback from stakeholders typically occur when reformers describe what they are going to change without providing a clear and well-reasoned argument as to why. Introductions of grading and reporting reforms that begin with clear explanations about why change is needed help resolve stakeholders' concerns and focus their attention on what potential benefits the new policies and practices will bring to students and families.

How

After describing the reasons for change and what specific changes they will make, Coalitions for Change can turn their attention to *how* questions. Specifically, they can address, How will they implement changes in grading and reporting policies and practices? How will they ensure school principals and teachers have support in their efforts? How will they gather feedback on the responses of school principals, teachers, students, and parents? How will they identify implementation problems and difficulties, and how will they help resolve them?

> "It's not the will to win that matters—everyone has that. It's the will to prepare to win that matters."
>
> —Bear Bryant

Addressing *how* questions clarifies the implementation process and identifies the specific elements needed for success. These questions compel Coalition members to think practically and strategically about implementation and consider a variety of what-if scenarios so they can anticipate potential problems and take steps to avoid them. *How* questions also relate to impact and determining the effects of reforms. For example, How will the reforms affect various stakeholders in the grading and reporting process? What data will be gathered to determine those effects, and how will those data be gathered? How will Coalition members use that information to improve implementation and gain higher levels of success? Although contextual differences across schools and classrooms may influence implementation strategies to some extent, applying general guidelines across settings helps ensure consistency and fidelity in implementation efforts.

When

Closely tied to *how* issues are questions related to *when*. Addressing *when* questions requires Coalition members to consider the optimal order of events for the implementation process. For example, When will they survey stakeholders? When will professional learning opportunities be provided? When will they implement pilot programs? When will follow-up assistance be offered? When will they collect formative information from various stakeholders, share results, and refine implementation strategies so they sustain support?

Most important, when constructing this implementation timeline, Coalition members must recognize this is not a one-year event. They can't accomplish everything in a single year. Changing grading and reporting is a multiyear process that must be supported and sustained over a two- to five-year period. In addition, some policy and practice reforms must be phased in as more teachers are involved and implementation spreads across grade levels and schools. Still, constructing a multiyear timeline for implementation, even if the Coalition members adjust it along the way, provides focus at every stage and keeps reform efforts on track.

Who

The last important questions that Coalition members must address relate to *who*. Coalition members need to decide: Who will lead every step in the implementation process? Who will explain to the various stakeholder groups why particular changes are being made, what is involved, and how success will be determined? Who will help new district and school leaders become familiar with the planned reforms? Who will guide newly hired teachers to implement the reforms in their classrooms? In too many instances, well-designed reform efforts have fallen apart because key individuals left the district or school, and the new leaders didn't understand why changes were being made or what role they had in the implementation process.

Summary

No one person can accomplish grading and reporting reform alone. Reform requires the collaborative efforts of a Coalition of dedicated individuals committed to making improvements that benefit students. As they take on these challenging tasks, however, Coalition members need to know that other like-minded individuals have their back and stand ready to help them through any difficulties that may arise. Grading and reporting reform is a complex process that requires the collaborative efforts of a team of leaders committed to improvement.

A Coalition for Change unites leaders from different stakeholder groups for the purpose of guiding fundamental change. Coalition members must be powerful in their positions, their information and expertise, their reputations and relationships, and especially their capacity for leadership (Kotter, 2012). They will plan and lead the implementation of more effective grading and reporting policies and practices by fashioning the changes to be made, coordinating implementation efforts, and organizing the follow-up and support necessary to sustain implementation.

Although they represent different stakeholders in the reform process, all Coalition members must share a deep understanding of the key issues involved; know the essential questions that need to be addressed; and be ready to support implementation through collaborative actions that are purposeful, systematic, informed, strategic, and ultimately successful. The next chapter discusses another essential trait of Coalition members and of all leaders in grading and reporting reform: thorough knowledge of the change process.

CHAPTER 3

Understand the Change Process

You never change things by fighting the existing reality. To change something, build a new model that makes the existing model obsolete.

—R. Buckminster Fuller

To bring about meaningful and lasting change, you need to understand the change process. You must know what prompts change, what limits change, and what inhibits change. You also need to understand what approaches to change don't work so you can avoid them from the start.

It's vital that all Coalition members share a deep understanding of the change process. Their success in implementing grading and reporting reforms depends on it. Knowledge of the change process not only informs their approach to reform; it also guides the implementation strategies and the procedures used to gather evidence on results.

This chapter explores the change process in depth. First, we explain which approaches to change don't work and consider evidence of the inadequacy of these approaches. This will bring added clarity to the discussion in chapter 1 about why so many well-intentioned grading and reporting reform efforts fail. It also will raise serious questions about why so many districts and schools follow pathways that no evidence supports as ever having worked. Then, we explore an alternative model of change

Portions of this chapter appear in "Professional Development and Teacher Change" (Guskey, 2002c) and "Experience Shapes Attitudes and Beliefs" (Guskey, 2016a).

"It is not necessary to change. Survival is not mandatory."

—W. Edwards Deming

and its implications for gaining different stakeholders' acceptance and support. Finally, we turn to applications of this alternative change model and its use in implementing successful grading and reporting reforms in widely varied districts and schools.

What Doesn't Work

Many education leaders, along with many writers and consultants, think they can change people through logical or philosophical arguments. They believe a well-structured presentation that sets forth their carefully reasoned opinions will win the hearts and minds of educators, regardless of educators' backgrounds or experience. They present their ideas and conjectures in an engaging manner, often pointing out hidden contradictions in many educators' grading practices. They may describe, for example, how educators say that grades reflect student learning, and then point out how many teachers actually raise the grades of students who show exceptional effort or lower the grades of students who misbehave or fail to turn in assignments on time.

These leaders, writers, and consultants are convinced that when educators see these logical and philosophical inconsistencies, they will automatically recognize the errors in their thinking and commit to reform. In essence, they try to create "cognitive dissonance" in educators and trust this dissonance will prompt educators to change.

Cognitive dissonance occurs when individuals are confronted with new information or situations that contradict their current beliefs, ideas, or values. The concept was originated by psychologist Leon Festinger (1957, 1962). He proposed that individuals strive to maintain internal psychological consistency in order to function in their lives.

To deal with the psychological discomfort of this dissonance, individuals do one of three things: (1) avoid the contradictory information or situations that prompt the dissonance; (2) alter their understanding of the new information or situations to reduce the dissonance; or (3) revise their beliefs, ideas, or values to align with the new information or situations. In other words, they can ignore the new, change the new to fit their view, or change their view to align with the new. The most difficult of these to accomplish, either by a person trying to prompt change or by individuals involved in change, is option 3—the revision of personal beliefs, ideas, or values.

Those seeking to initiate reforms generally try to create cognitive dissonance in one of three ways: (1) confrontation, (2) mental manipulation, or (3) emotional appeal.

1. **Confrontation:** The leaders, writers, and consultants who use this approach begin by describing the beliefs or practices they want teachers to change as *traditional*. Initially, they portray the traditional as innocent, innocuous, and generally accepted. But they quickly turn the tables and include under the traditional label every evil, demeaning, student-unfriendly practice that has ever existed in any school or classroom, even if only peripherally related to grading. They then present the practices they advocate in stark contrast to the traditional practices. On slides, they display their ideas in bright and cheery colors and display traditional ideas as dark and menacing. They express their views with such confidence that it seems anyone who might defend the traditional has surely fallen under the influence of the inexcusable and deplorable dark side.

2. **Mental manipulation:** Those using this approach often construct arguments to show educators the wrongness of their thinking, the illogic of their assumptions, or the inappropriateness of their beliefs. These leaders, writers, and consultants attempt to persuade educators through mental entanglement, convincing educators that they cannot justify their beliefs through reason or logic. They then present their own ideas and opinions with seemingly indisputable rationality and challenge others to defend different perspectives with comparable logic or philosophical validation. Their tactic may be described as, "If you cannot defend your perspective, then you must concede that mine is true or at least more appropriate."

3. **Emotional appeal:** The leaders, writers, and consultants who use this approach try to make educators have a highly emotional response to the ideas and opinions they present.

They tell heart-wrenching stories of the hardships students suffer and the alleged devastating effects of the grading policies or practices they want educators to change. They stress that continuing these policies and practices will have dire psychological consequences for students and, as a result, change is not merely an ethical responsibility; it is a moral imperative.

Although confrontation, manipulation, and emotional appeal may prompt temporary reactions, these attempts to create dissonance rarely produce significant and enduring change. People are simply not changed by logical or philosophical arguments. As renowned psychologist Edward de Bono notes, "Logic will never change emotion or perception" (as quoted in Balakrishnan, 2007). People don't form attitudes, beliefs, emotions, and perceptions intellectually, and they do not typically defend them rationally. Instead, attitudes, beliefs, and perceptions stem from what people have previously known and experienced, what they feel, and what they want.

This is not to imply that cognitive dissonance is unimportant in the change process. As human beings, we want harmony in our attitudes, beliefs, and behaviors. We purposefully work to avoid situations that cause conflict or disharmony. This is known as the principle of *cognitive consistency*. However, attempts to persuade people through logical or philosophical arguments seldom succeed simply because they focus on the way people think. These attempts run smack into the wall of *confirmation bias*—the tendency people have to embrace information that supports their beliefs and reject information that contradicts them (Nickerson, 1998). Of the many identified forms of faulty thinking, confirmation bias is among the best catalogued (Kolbert, 2017).

> "When dealing with people, remember you are not dealing with creatures of logic, but with creatures of emotion."
>
> —Dale Carnegie

This idea relates to our discussions in chapter 1 (page 17) and chapter 2 (page 35) about the importance of addressing *why* before *what*. Most articles about grading and reporting reforms, and most presentations by consultants who advocate grading reform, focus on what needs to change. They describe how important it is to revise report cards, change grading scales, and adopt new policies with regard to zeros, homework, and late assignments. They tell educators what they need to fix and how to fix it. Trusting this advice, well-meaning educators launch their efforts, innocent and naive of the many problems that lie ahead because experiences and desires of stakeholders have been ignored. When objections arise and conflicts occur, they are left unprepared to deal with them, and implementation efforts fall apart.

Now that we know what *doesn't* work, what actually *does* work to progress in the change process? How can reformers appeal to stakeholders in a way that addresses their needs, desires, and experiences?

What Does Work

In order to understand the change process and how to facilitate change, reformers must know what stakeholders want and why they want it. In other words, reformers should ask, "What do stakeholders desire, and how can the reforms and innovations we want to implement relate to those desires?" Kotter (2012) describes this as *communicating for buy-in*. It doesn't mean that stakeholders' desires dictate precisely what the reforms will be. Rather, it implies that reformers must acknowledge what stakeholders want, understand it at a deep level, and then use it to frame their approach to change.

One of the most famous quotes in the worlds of business and innovation is attributed to Henry Ford: "If I had asked people what they wanted, they would have said faster horses" (Goodreads, n.d.). These words are attributed to him as support for the idea that we can accomplish true innovation without stakeholder input. If people truly said this, however, Ford probably would have pressed deeper and understood that what people *really* wanted was a faster and more efficient mode of transportation (Roth, 2017). They might not have mentioned the internal combustion engine or the need for the assembly line. But seeing beyond such a shortsighted response is what it means to understand stakeholders' input at a deeper level.

Similarly, if we ask the top stakeholder groups in grading and reporting—parents and families, students, and teachers—what they truly want, it's likely they will give fairly self-evident answers. Parents and families, for example, want their children to be successful in school.

They want them to feel good about school and have self-confidence in learning environments. They want their children to be valued and cared for and have a sense of belonging in school. They want them to have new experiences and opportunities, and to believe the forces that determine their future are under their control. To ensure this sense of belonging and success, parents and families want regular feedback from teachers about how their children are doing in school. They want to know when their children do well and when learning problems or difficulties arise. Most important, they want that information in a form they can easily understand and readily use (Guskey, 2002a).

What students want is not so different from what their parents and families want for them. Students want to feel successful and confident in school. They want to work on engaging and challenging tasks, but they also want to know that success is attainable. They want to see themselves progress, and they want others to recognize their improvement too. They want to feel in control of the conditions that determine their success, and they want to know that help is available when they need it. They want to trust their teachers and believe that teachers are on their side. They also want regular feedback from teachers about how they are doing, and if difficulties occur, they want to know what to do to get better.

Teachers share with parents and students the desire to have students succeed and be confident in themselves as learners. They also want to feel they can influence students' learning and contribute to that success. That's why they chose to become teachers in the first place; it's what brings them their greatest professional satisfaction. As noted in chapter 2 (page 35), teachers are willing to take on extra work to help students achieve greater success if the tasks involved are manageable, if those tasks yield tangible benefits for students and their families, and if their extra efforts are recognized and appreciated.

How, then, can we organize reform efforts to take these stakeholders' desires into consideration? How can we approach the change process in a way that results in more effecting grading and reporting policies and practices *and* provides for the wants of these critical stakeholders? To do so requires a new vision of the change process, a new approach to reform, and an alternative model of change.

Professional Development as the Impetus for Change

For many years, I have been intrigued by the process of change in education, especially in the context of professional development. What prompts educators to change? What conditions facilitate change? What confounds or inhibits change?

Educators generally agree that, despite differences in content and format, nearly all professional development efforts and professional learning activities are designed to bring about change. Most educators also agree on the three major areas of change they hope to impact.

Specifically, professional development efforts set out to change (1) teachers' attitudes and beliefs, (2) teachers' classroom practices, and (3) students' learning outcomes (Learning Forward, 2011).

What interested me most about these areas of change, however, is the *order* in which they occur. In other words, what is the typical sequence of these change events? Clearly, they don't happen simultaneously, and any reform leaders who hope to succeed must consider the order to determine where they should focus attention and what critical needs they must address.

These outcomes have a detailed and highly complex relationship. In addition, numerous factors can snarl the change process, including the innovation involved, the magnitude of change required, and the experiences of participating educators (Fullan, 2016; Guskey, 2002c). Still, professional development activities are deliberate and purposeful endeavors, and changes that reform leaders want to bring about usually can be well defined. Thus, while these outcomes undoubtedly have a reciprocal relationship to some degree, efforts to facilitate change must consider the order of outcomes most likely to result in the desired change and the endurance of that change (Guskey, 2000a).

As noted earlier, professional learning leaders and consultants typically set out to change teachers' attitudes, beliefs, perceptions, and dispositions. With regard to grading and reporting, for example, they may try to change teachers' attitudes about certain aspects of grading or their beliefs about the effectiveness of particular grading policies and practices. They want teachers to see issues differently, believe that a new approach is better, and become committed to innovation and reform. They assume that changing teachers' attitudes and beliefs leads to changes in classroom practices, which, in turn, will result in improved student learning.

This perspective on teacher change can be traced to the work of early change theorists such as Kurt Lewin (1935), who developed many of his ideas about affecting change from psychotherapeutic models in the early 20th century. Modern research on teacher change, however, indicates that the assumptions of this model may be inaccurate, especially with regard to professional learning endeavors involving experienced educators (Guskey & Huberman, 1995; Putnam & Borko, 2000). We need an alternative model for change that re-examines the process of teacher change under these special conditions and to guide the creation of more effective professional learning experiences for educators.

Alternative Model for Change

An alternative approach to the change process is shown in figure 3.1. According to this model, significant change in teachers' attitudes and beliefs takes place only *after* positive changes in student learning outcomes are evident. These changes in student learning result from specific changes teachers have made to their classroom practices. They might, for example, result from a new instructional approach, new materials or curriculums, new classroom policies and practices, or simply some modification in the way teachers grade and report on student learning. Whatever the case, this model indicates that significant change in teachers' attitudes and beliefs is contingent on evidence of change in students' learning outcomes (Guskey, 1985).

The critical point of the model is that professional learning alone rarely yields significant change in teachers' attitudes, beliefs, perceptions, or dispositions. Teachers are not changed by what someone tells or shows them; they change based on what they experience. *Experience shapes their attitudes and beliefs* (Guskey, 2002c). Thus, according to the model, teachers' attitudes and beliefs will significantly change only when they have clear evidence of improvement in the learning outcomes of their students (Guskey, 1986, 2002a). When teachers *see* that a program or innovation works, then they will believe it works.

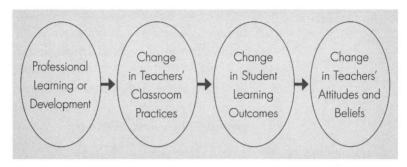

Source: Guskey, 2002c, p. 383.

Figure 3.1: Alternative model for change.

This model broadly defines *learning outcomes* to include not only cognitive and achievement measures but also the wide range of students' affective, behavioral, and noncognitive outcomes. They may consist of evidence of student engagement in class activities; motivation for learning; or attitudes toward school, the class, and themselves as learners. In other words, learning outcomes include whatever evidence teachers use to judge the effectiveness of their teaching, their classroom practices, and their success with students.

This model for change is predicated on the idea that change is primarily an experientially based learning process for teachers. Teachers retain and repeat practices that work—that is, the practices teachers find useful in motivating students, managing student learning, or helping students attain desired learning outcomes. They generally abandon practices that don't work or fail to yield any tangible evidence of improvement. Therefore, the endurance of any change in classroom practices and procedures relies on demonstrable results in student outcomes. (For a video explanation of this model, see Spehar, 2015.)

As any model of a complex phenomenon does, this alternative model for change somewhat oversimplifies the change process, and exceptions to the model certainly exist. For example, teachers must have some modest openness to change and the possibility of improvement before they will consider revising their grading and reporting practices (Guskey, 2002c). Furthermore, the process of teacher change may be more cyclical than linear (Huberman, 1992, 1995). In other words,

> *"Nothing ever becomes real till it is experienced—even a proverb is no proverb to you till your life has experienced it."*
> —John Keats

changes in teachers' attitudes and beliefs will likely spur additional changes in teachers' practice that bring further changes in student learning, and so on (Huberman, 1983, 1985). Still, diverse studies of teacher change have yielded consistent results that provide strong support for the model (Clark & Hollingsworth, 2002; Gatt, 2009; Rogers, 2007).

Similar Models

The sequence of change events this model describes is similar in many ways to a 19th century theoretical change model that described the temporal relationship between emotion and behavioral response. In the late 1800s, psychologist William James (1890) theorized that the critical factor in an emotion is feedback from bodily changes that occur in response to a particular situation. His theory seemed to conflict with commonly held notions about emotion and human behavior. Simply stated, James's theory suggested that we see a bear and run; therefore, we are afraid. Or, if we slip while descending a staircase, we grab for the railing first, and then sense the fear of our near fall. Danish physiologist Carl Lange also proposed this theory, so it is generally known as the James-Lange theory (Cannon, 1927).

This model for change also corresponds with Albert Bandura's social learning theory. Bandura (1977, 1986) theorized there are four major sources of people's attitudes and beliefs, especially their perceptions of self-efficacy: (1) mastery experiences, (2) vicarious experiences, (3) verbal and social persuasion, and (4) emotional and physiological states. Among these, mastery experiences are the most powerful (Guskey & Passaro, 1994; Usher & Pajares, 2008). In other words, teachers' attitudes and beliefs are formed or changed not through logical persuasion or philosophical argument but rather by what they experienced as students and their personal experiences in teaching others. Change in teachers' attitudes and beliefs, therefore, is primarily a result, rather than a cause, of change in student learning outcomes. The model of teacher change suggests that, in the absence of positive change in student learning, significant change in teachers' attitudes and beliefs is unlikely (Guskey, 2002c).

Implications of the Alternative Model for Change

This alternative model for change has widely documented support (Claesgens et al., 2013; Clark & Hollingsworth, 2002; Gatt, 2009; Guskey, 1989, 2002a; Hanson, Pennington, Prusak, & Wilkinson, 2017; Lowden, 2006; Rogers, 2007; Rush & Young, 2011; Sider & Ashun, 2013; Signe, 2016; Whitworth & Chiu, 2015). Most important for reform leaders, however, are the implications of this model for planning and implementing successful reforms that result in significant and sustained improvements in grading policies and practices.

Efforts to Directly Change Attitudes and Beliefs Rarely Succeed

As stressed throughout this chapter, reform leaders who set out to change stakeholders' attitudes and beliefs directly are pretty much doomed to failure. Peoples' attitudes, beliefs, perceptions, or dispositions rarely change in the absence of confirming evidence. Some modest change may be possible, of course, and should definitely be sought. When presented with new ideas and supporting evidence with regard to reforms in grading and reporting, for example, people's attitudes may move from cynical to skeptical. Although not persuaded or convinced, perhaps they will engage in discussions and consider new points of view. But commitment to a new approach, confidence that it will work, and trust that positive results will follow almost never occur up front, prior to implementation. The best that can be hoped for prior to implementation is a tentative "I'm not sure, but let's give it a try." If by giving it a try, stakeholders see tangible evidence of improvements in student outcomes, then, and perhaps only then, will significant change in their attitudes and beliefs occur.

> **Implications of the Alternative Model for Change**
>
> • Efforts to directly change attitudes and beliefs rarely succeed.
>
> • Change is a gradual and difficult process.
>
> • Feedback on results is essential.
>
> • Change requires continuous follow-up, support, and pressure.

The key to success, therefore, rests not in trying to change attitudes and beliefs directly, but in changing the experience. This holds not only for teachers but for parents, families, and students as well.

The film *Remember the Titans*, starring Denzel Washington, provides a classic example of this change process. Based on a true story, the film portrays African American coach Herman Boone's efforts to integrate a high school football team in Alexandria, Virginia, in the early 1970s. Changing the experience of these young athletes completely transformed their attitudes and beliefs. Likewise, if leaders in grading and reporting reform can find ways to meaningfully change individuals' experience, then significant change in their attitudes and beliefs will likely follow.

> *"Faced with the choice between changing one's mind and proving that there is no need to do so, almost everyone gets busy on the proof."*
>
> —John Kenneth Galbraith

Change Is a Gradual and Difficult Process

Becoming proficient at something new and finding meaning in a new way of doing things require time and effort, especially when the change runs counter to long-held traditions. Any change that has great promise for increasing teachers' effectiveness and enhancing student outcomes will likely require extra work, especially at first. The requirements of extra time and energy can significantly add to teachers' workloads, even when they receive support.

In addition, change always comes with a certain amount of anxiety and can feel threatening. Like practitioners in many other fields, teachers are reluctant to adopt new practices or procedures unless they feel sure they can make them work (Lortie, 1975). They know that to change or to try something new means to risk failure. Not only would such failure be highly embarrassing, but it also runs counter to most teachers' strong commitment to student learning (Guskey, 2002c). To change means risking the possibility that students might engage less, have less motivation, and learn less effectively than they do under current practices. Therefore, even when presented with evidence from carefully designed experimental studies, teachers do not easily alter or discard the practices they have developed and refined in their own demanding classroom environments (Goodson, Moore, & Hargreaves, 2006; Hargreaves, 2005).

It is also important to recognize that not every school will implement grading and reporting reforms in exactly the same way. Schools must adapt the implementation of new policies and practices to their situational and contextual differences (Elmore, 1997). Reforms based on assumptions of uniformity in the educational system repeatedly fail (Elmore & McLaughlin, 1988).

For this reason, reform leaders must strike an appropriate balance between program fidelity and contextual conditions. Researchers refer to this process as *mutual adaptation* (McLaughlin, 1976; McLaughlin & Marsh, 1978). This means that when innovations are implemented, change takes place in two directions. First, individuals must adapt in order to implement the new policies and practices. Second, the innovation must be adapted to fit the unique characteristics of the context.

> *"It is not the strongest or the most intelligent who will survive, but those who can best manage change."*
> —Leon C. Megginson

Too much change in either direction can mean disaster. If the innovation requires too much adaptation from individuals, implementation is likely to be mechanical and ineffective. Likewise, adapting the innovation too much may lose elements essential to program impact. Successful implementation of new grading policies and practices requires a critical balance between the teachers' workload requirements and vital dimensions of innovation fidelity.

Feedback on Results Is Essential

For the implementation of new practices to be sustained and changes to endure, those involved need regular feedback on the effects of their efforts. When their actions are successful, people find it reinforcing and are likely to repeat those actions, while actions that are unsuccessful tend to be diminished or halted completely. Similarly, people will accept and retain new and unfamiliar practices when they perceive that those practices increase their competence and effectiveness. And they will likely abandon new practices in the absence of any evidence of their positive effects. This is especially true of teachers, whose primary psychological rewards come from feeling certain about their capacity to affect student growth and development (Guskey, 1989; Huberman, 1992).

This means procedures must be built into reform initiatives to offer teachers specific feedback on results. Teachers need to see that their hard work in implementing the recommended changes makes a difference. With grading reforms, for example, teachers would find it helpful to see students focusing more on learning rather than on simply earning points to attain a high grade. Teachers might also experience greater student engagement in class activities, more student willingness to collaborate with classmates, or different student attitudes toward learning and class assessments.

Whatever feedback is provided, it must be based on evidence that teachers find meaningful and trustworthy. It should address changes teachers would value. As noted earlier, learning outcomes describe a broad range of achievement, affective, behavioral, and other noncognitive outcomes. Among these, however, what specific outcomes would teachers expect the grading and reporting reforms to effect? Might teachers, for example, expect students to focus more on their learning and less on the grade? Do they believe the changes might result in students being more motivated to learn, more actively engaged in learning activities both in and out of school, and more willing take advantage of opportunities to improve their learning? Would they expect students to have more confidence as learners and take greater pride in their learning successes? And equally important, what evidence would verify these changes? In addition, that evidence must come rather quickly (Guskey, 2007a). Teachers won't wait one or two years to see if new strategies or practices work. They want to see evidence of change in their students within a few weeks, or a month or two at most.

Change Requires Continuous Follow-Up, Support, and Pressure

If teachers' attitudes and beliefs changed primarily before the implementation of new practices or innovations, the quality of the initial training on grading and reporting reform would be of utmost importance. But because teachers' attitudes and beliefs change mainly *after* implementation takes place and they gain evidence of improved student outcomes, it is the continuous follow-up, support, and pressure that teachers receive *following* their initial training that is most crucial.

Support coupled with pressure are essential for continuation and sustained implementation. Support helps those engaged in the difficult process of implementation to tolerate the anxiety of occasional setbacks. Pressure is often necessary to initiate change among those who may not have a great self-impetus for change (Corcoran, Fuhrman, & Belcher, 2001; Creemers & Kyriakides, 2010). In addition, pressure provides the encouragement, motivation, and occasional nudging that many practitioners need to persist in the challenging tasks that are intrinsic to all change efforts.

For new grading policies and practices to be implemented well and for reforms to continue and expand, these policies and practices must become a natural part of teachers' repertoire of classroom procedures. Teachers must come to use the new practices almost out of habit. This requires that teachers receive continuous follow-up and support (Guskey, 2002c).

Of all aspects of professional learning experiences, follow-up is perhaps the most neglected. To be successful, professional learning must be seen as a *process*, not an event (Learning Forward, 2011). Learning to be proficient at something new or finding meaning in a new way of doing things is difficult and sometimes painful. Furthermore, any change that holds great promise for increasing individuals' competence or enhancing an organization's effectiveness is likely to be slow and require extra work. It is imperative, therefore, that improvement be seen as a continuous and ongoing endeavor.

Will Changes in Grading and Reporting Improve Student Learning?

Change leaders are often uncertain about what kinds of results can be expected from reforms in grading policies and practices. Many ask if changes in grading and reporting will actually improve student achievement. Writers and consultants frequently relate stories describing remarkable turn-arounds in schools that have reformed their grading practices. But the truth of the matter is that at this time, few well-designed, systematic studies have linked the implementation of grading reforms to specific improvements in student achievement (Brookhart et al., 2016; Guskey & Brookhart, 2019). This is true even of reforms associated with standards-based grading or competency-based models (for noted exceptions, see Pollio & Hochbein, 2015, and the review of research by Welsh, 2019). That is to say there is neither confirmation that such a link exists nor strong evidence to show that it doesn't.

In a larger sense, however, why would we expect changing grading practices or reporting procedures to affect student achievement in any way, positive or negative? Changing the way we evaluate and report information on student learning has no direct or immediate effect on how students are taught or what they learn. Any potential impact on curriculum or instruction would be tangential at best (Guskey & Jung, 2013).

Grading and reporting are more about communicating better, more accurate, and more meaningful information to families and students *in order to provide the basis for improving student learning*. Whether or not this *leads* to specific improvements in student learning depends not on the information itself, but on how that information is used (Guskey, 2008).

We can use a sports analogy to help us think about what moving to a standards-based model of grading might mean for students. Imagine, for example, you were taking part in a sporting event. If someone told you the score of the game while you were playing, would that help you play better? Probably not. That is precisely what a single grade on an assessment or report card offers to students. But if someone told you which things you were doing well and which things you needed to improve, would that improve your play? Maybe not, but at least it would give you some guidance and direction in making improvements.

> "To improve is to change; to be perfect is to change often."
> —Winston Churchill

More detailed forms of grading and reporting, especially those associated with standards-based grading and reporting, are designed to do precisely this. Instead of offering only a nebulous overall indicator of performance, they provide students and families with detailed information on multiple aspects of students' performance in school so that improvement efforts can be better targeted and more effective. So while grading and reporting alone may not improve student achievement, they can be an important and perhaps critical factor in the process.

Leaders, writers, and consultants sometimes tell wonderful stories about the results of the reforms they advocate, and they claim to have seen a stunning impact on students and teachers. But skeptical teachers and honest critics are seldom moved by these third-person accounts. They want direct evidence gathered from students in their classrooms.

This means again returning to *why* questions such as: Why are we doing this? Why do we need to change? Why is it important? And asking additional questions like: What do we hope to accomplish? How will we know if it works? When teachers gain evidence that what they are doing makes a difference and the reforms are actually bringing improvements for their students, change in their attitudes and beliefs can and will follow.

In later chapters, we will consider examples of the specific kinds of learning outcomes and evidence that other stakeholders find particularly meaningful and describe how to include these when evaluating the effectiveness of grading and reporting reforms. Reform leaders should consider, for example, what evidence parents and families, students, and board members find most important and believable. Because different stakeholders trust different types of evidence, multiple sources of evidence on multiple outcomes will need to be considered when evaluating the effects of reforms (Guskey, 2007a).

A Practical Example of the Change Model

Forthcoming chapters will present many examples in which reform leaders used strategies based on the model of change and succeeded in their reform efforts. In the example described here, colleagues and I applied the alternative model of change to gain the support of parents and families in a large-scale grading and reporting reform effort in Kentucky. We also described this program in the article "Grades That Mean Something: Kentucky Develops Standards-Based Report Cards" (Guskey, Swan, & Jung, 2011a) and in a blog prepared for *Education Week* (Guskey, 2016b).

One of the biggest challenges leaders in grading and reporting reform must face is changing families' and students' attitudes about grading and reporting. They want parents to view grades as a means of communication between teachers and families, and not as the currency students need to advance in school and life. They want students to focus on learning instead of simply getting a high grade. Most important, they want parents and families to understand that abandoning some of the traditional grading practices they experienced in school will enhance teachers' and families' efforts to help all students learn better and improve their performance in school.

As described earlier in this chapter, many school leaders, writers, and consultants try to accomplish this change through logic and reason. They expect to move families with quotes from informed authorities or reports from other districts or schools. Others rely on emotional appeals, hoping to persuade families with sincere *I believe* or *In my opinion* statements about new approaches to grading and reporting. But as we explained, neither of these approaches consistently yields significant change in parents', families', or students' attitudes about grading.

The reason these approaches don't work is they run counter to many parents' and students' personal experiences with grading, and their personal experiences profoundly influence their attitudes and beliefs. To change these attitudes and beliefs, therefore, we must find ways to change parents' and students' experiences.

Most parents' experiences with grading happened in classrooms where teachers judged their performance in comparison to classmates' performance. Teachers determined grades not by how well students mastered clearly articulated learning targets or standards, but by how their performance compared to that of other students in the class. A grade of C didn't mean you were at step 3 in a five-step process to mastery. It meant your performance was average or ranked in the middle of the class. Grades communicated little about what students actually learned or were able to do.

In our program in Kentucky, we don't try to directly change the attitudes of parents shaped by these experiences. Instead, we change the *experience*. We introduce new grading and reporting practices and especially newly developed standards-based report cards by allowing parents and families to view two different report cards either online or as hard copies sent home.

The first is the traditional report card parents are accustomed to receiving that lists a single grade for every subject area or course. It is typical of report cards generated by the majority of online grading programs that looks much like the report card most parents received when they were in school. The second is the new standards-based report card that includes grades based on how well students have achieved specific learning standards. This report card offers separate grades for students' performance in different aspects of each subject or course. Instead of a single grade for language arts, for example, students receive separate grades for reading, writing, listening, speaking, and language skills. Important student behaviors related to homework completion, cooperation, respect, punctuality in turning in assignments, and class participation are recorded separately on the report card as well.

After comparing the report cards side by side for at least two grading periods, we survey parents to ask which report card they prefer. Invariably, nearly all parents prefer the standards-based report card. Why? It's simply better. It gives parents the detailed information they need to track their child's performance in school. It offers students valuable feedback regarding their progress on explicit learning goals. In addition, it provides guidance and direction to parents and students in improvement efforts. As a result, parents and students often become our strongest advocates for change (Guskey, 2016a). Experiencing the new form influences their attitudes about the change.

The same holds true for the teachers involved. Few teachers leave the seminars, workshops, or professional learning sessions for our Kentucky program convinced that grading and reporting change will make a difference. It would be an exaggeration to say that professional learning causes teachers to commit to the change process or convinces them that the new grading policies and practices will work. At best, some teachers may feel cautiously hopeful. The majority are probably skeptical but at least willing to give the change a try.

Those attitudes and beliefs start to change when teachers do try and see that the change works. They hear students talking about what they need to do to learn better rather than how they can earn more points. They see students helping each other because the learning goals are clear for everyone. They get fewer questions from parents and families about how a teacher determined a grade and more questions about how parents and families can help with improvements. Although teachers

> "Change can be frightening, and the temptation is often to resist it. But change almost always provides opportunities—to learn new things, to rethink tired processes, and to improve the way we work."
>
> —Klaus Schwab

typically report that the change initially requires extra work, they believe it's worthwhile because of the differences they see in students and their parents and families.

Experience shapes attitudes and beliefs. If we focus on changing the experience so parents, students, and teachers clearly see how new grading and reporting procedures benefit them, a change in attitudes will almost certainly follow.

Summary

To effectively lead change and successfully implement important grading and reporting reforms requires a thorough understanding of the change process. You must know what actions facilitate change and which are likely to be ineffective. You need to know what leads to changes that can be maintained and will endure versus those that will likely be temporary and short-lived. Most important, you must understand the order of change so you know how and where to invest time and energy.

The alternative model for change presented in this chapter is based on the premise that stakeholders' experience and desires shape their attitudes and beliefs. Therefore, efforts to change attitudes and beliefs must focus primarily on changing stakeholders' experience while acknowledging and directly addressing what they want and believe they need.

In implementing reforms that translate what we know about effective grading and reporting into practice, it is imperative that we focus on *working with* stakeholders rather than *working on* them. We must offer stakeholders targeted feedback on results, based on the kinds of evidence they trust and consider meaningful. We must help stakeholders see that the grading and reporting change makes a positive difference. And we need to do this early in the implementation process. Stakeholders' support comes from seeing rather quickly that the reforms work and yield positive results on outcomes they consider important.

The alternative model for change offers a very optimistic perspective on the potential of change efforts and the professional learning opportunities that accompany them. It also illustrates that although the change process is complex, it is not haphazard. Careful attention to this model's order of change events will likely not only facilitate change but also contribute to its endurance. As a result, even reform efforts that challenge some of education's longest-held traditions will likely be far more powerful, much more effective, and more sustainable.

CHAPTER 4

Clarify the Purpose of Grading and Reporting

Efforts and courage are not enough without purpose and direction.

—John F. Kennedy

ducation reforms that bring enduring improvement for educators and students are never arbitrary or haphazard. They are never based on whims or intuition. They are not fads or crazes. Instead, they result from carefully planned and deliberately implemented systemic changes. Reformers guide these changes with a clear purpose and specific direction. They build changes around explicit goals with carefully conceived strategies for achieving those goals.

To bring about meaningful change in grading and reporting, reformers must similarly guide change with a well-defined purpose. This purpose should address important *why* issues related to the changes; it should describe the intended goals and why they are important. As earlier chapters emphasized, we must first decide our destination before we can determine the best route to get there.

This chapter explores the three major elements of a grading system: (1) the gradebook, (2) the report card, and (3) the permanent record or transcript. It identifies differences in the detail of reporting in each element and the specific terminology used in describing each. From there, we turn to identifying the purpose of each element and ways to ensure reporting procedures align with that purpose. Since Coalition for

Change members and the stakeholders they represent may have different opinions about the purpose of each element, this will likely involve the disagree-and-commit principle discussed in chapter 2 (page 54).

To make progress and bring about intended improvements, we need to have consensus on the purpose of grading and reporting. Reform efforts that are unclear about their purpose, lack transparency about their purpose, or completely neglect discussions of purpose invariably fail. When stakeholders understand and agree on that purpose, they find it much easier to make decisions about the best means, strategies, or procedures to achieve it (Stosich & Bae, 2018).

Grading System Elements

As noted previously, all grading systems consist of three major elements: (1) the gradebook, (2) the report card, and (3) the permanent record or transcript (see table 4.1). These elements also form the basis of nearly every computerized grading and reporting program available to educators.

Table 4.1: Grading System Elements

	Gradebook	**Report Card**	**Permanent Record or Transcript**
What it includes	Scores	Grades	Summary grades
What purpose it serves	Ongoing record of performance	Interim summary of performance	Summary judgments of performance
Who has access to it	Teachers, families, and students	Teachers, families, and students	Teachers, families, students, and third parties

Educators generally recognize the need for and importance of each element in a grading and reporting system. Most educators also accept the features that computerized grading program developers build into each element and assume these features are based on thorough knowledge of the field and evidence on best practice. Unfortunately, that is rarely the case.

Software engineers design the features of most computerized grading and reporting programs to make traditional practices easier to implement. This is especially true in report card design (Guskey & Bailey, 2010).

As a result, although they simplify recording tasks for teachers, many computerized grading programs perpetuate grading practices that have long outlived their usefulness. Their inflexible structure also makes it difficult for reform leaders to affect meaningful change. So while grading and reporting stand out as an area of education in which nearly all teachers use technology, they are also an area where available technology frequently poses barriers to the implementation of better and more effective practices.

If these grading system elements are to achieve vital communication goals with families and important learning goals for students, the purpose of each element must be made clear. Additionally, and equally important, the features of each element must align with that purpose. In many cases, this requires overriding the default options built into computerized grading programs—but schools can usually accomplish that with modest effort. To decide what to override in order to effectively use these elements, the purpose of each element must be clearly articulated.

Gradebook

The first and most detailed element in any grading system is the gradebook. Modern gradebooks consist of online forms or spreadsheets where teachers record all types of evidence gathered on students' performance in school. The gradebook's primary purpose is to provide families and students with important information that keeps them abreast of *all* aspects of students' performance in school. Typical gradebooks include data on students' daily work, homework assignments, quiz results, formative assessments, major examinations, projects, and reports. Teachers may also record data on specific student behaviors in the gradebook, such as students' attendance, class participation, collaboration with classmates, and behavior in class. Many gradebooks are linked to student information systems (SIS) that include personal information, such as students' birth dates, home addresses, and contact phone numbers.

Gradebooks provide wide-ranging documentation of all aspects of student performance in school, which teachers can update daily. They help identify areas of strength and areas where students might need additional help or support. Although scores on student behaviors do not reflect learning or achievement per se, they communicate vital information about behaviors that assist learning and are important for both families and students. Data on these behaviors may also help explain achievement scores and offer direction in improvement efforts.

Most modern computerized grading programs allow families and students to access the gradebook online at any time but restrict families' access to only the information on their child. Some programs even provide phone apps that notify parents and students when teachers enter new information. Figure 4.1 shows an example of a typical gradebook.

We will refer to the information recorded in the gradebook as *scores*. These scores may be numbers, letters, symbols, words, comments, or verbal descriptions attached to different levels of student performance. In many grading programs, including the one shown in figure 4.1, scores are color-coded to further distinguish performance levels.

Standards-Based Gradebook

Many computerized grading programs offer a standards-based option for both gradebooks and report cards. The major difference between typical gradebooks and standards-based gradebooks is how the program labels the columns. In the typical gradebook, the columns designate particular assignments, quizzes, exams, or projects, and the scores students attained appear in the columns. In a standards-based gradebook, the columns usually describe specific standards or learning goals. A single quiz or exam, for example, might yield two or three scores in a standards-based gradebook if the items included in that assessment tap two or three different standards. Figure 4.2 (page 88) shows an example of a standards-based gradebook.

Teachers implementing standards-based grading typically use the gradebook to record information about students' progress on *individual learning standards* for each grade level or course. An elementary teacher, for example, might record different scores in the gradebook for students who are *making progress* with and those who have achieved *mastery* of the mathematics standard: *Accurately compares two 2-digit numbers using >, <, and =.*

Some computerized gradebooks allow parents and students to click on a score and access the actual assessment or scoring rubric from which the teacher determined the score. This not only provides important

Teacher Form: English 5   Katrina Mendez ▾

File   Edit   View   Insert   Format   Data   Tools   Help

All changes saved in drive

	Unit					Unit 1.1B					1.2C				1.3D			
Standard	L6 B																	
Assignment Type	Re	Wr	Re	Pr	Br	Quiz	Re	Re	Wr	Pr	Quiz	Re	Wr	Wr	Quiz	Br	Re	Wr
Date	9/2	9/5	9/13	9/19	9/25	10/1	10/5	10/10	Any	Any	10/17	10/23	10/29	11/3	11/8	Any	Any	11/22
Student 1	3	3	4	4	2		3		4	3	3	2	4	4	4			3
Student 2	1	3	3	4	2		1	3	3	2	2	3		4	4	4	4	
Student 3	2	2	3	2	2	2	4	4	3		4	1	2	2	4			4
Student 4	2	4	4	3	3		4	4				3	4		4	3		4
Student 5	3	3		2	2	2	4	4			2	3	3	4	4			
Student 6	3	2	1		4	2		3		2	3	3		4	4			3
Student 7	3	4	4	4	4	4	3	2			4	3	4	4	3	3		
Student 8																		
Student 9	2	2	2	2		3	2	4			3	3	2	2	2			3
Student 10	3	3	3	4	4	3	4	4	4		3	3	2	4	4	2		4
Student 11	1		1	4	4	3	3	4	2	3	1	3	3	2	4			4
Student 12	1	4		4	4	3	3	4			2	3	3	4	4			3
Student 13	1	1	2	2	3	3	3	2			3	3	3	2	3			3
Student 14		2	2	1		2	4	3	1		3	4		4	3		2	4
Student 15		3	1	1		2	2	2			3	3	2	2	3			3
Student 16	3	3	3	4	4	3	4	4			3	3	2	4	4			4
Student 17		1	1	2	1	3	3	3			3	2	4	4	3	2		3
Student 18	1		1	2	2	3		4			3	4	4	4	4			3
Student 19	2	2	1		3	3		3			4	2	2	3	3			4
Student 20	2	4		4	1	2	3	4			2	3	3	2	3			3
Student 21	1		2	3	3	1	3	3				2	4	4	3			3
Student 22	3	2	3	3	4	3	3	4			3	2	4	2	4		3	3
Student 23		2	3	3	4	3	3	3			3	3	4	4	4			3
Student 24	2	2		3	4	4	4	3			4	4	3	3	2			3

Details ▾   Summary ▾   Student List ▾   Summary ▾   Summary Transposed ▾   Details Transposed ▾   Standards ▾   Assign ▾   ▾ ▴

Figure 4.1: Typical gradebook.

| Last | First | Triangles 1 | Volume 1 | Area 1 | Volume 2 | Averages | Area 2 | Triangles 2 | Volume 3 | Calculus 1 | Integers 1 | Calculus 2 | Integers 2 | Triangles 3 | Partial Fractions | Area 3 |
		A1	C1	C2	C3	C4	C5	F1	F2	F3	F4	F5	F6	S1	S2	S3
Student	1	4	4	4	4	4	4	4	4	3	3	4	4	3	4	4
Student	2	3	2	1	1	1	0	2	3	4	3	2	2	0	1	2
Student	3	4	4	4	4	2	2	4	4	4	3	3	1	2	3	3
Student	4	3	3	3	3	4	3	3	2	1	3	3	4	4	3	4
Student	5	1	0	1	2	2	2	4	4	4	4	3	0	2	2	3
Student	6	3	2	1	3	2	4	4	4	2	2		0	1	1	3
Student	7	4	4	4	4	3	3	3	0	3	3	3	4	2	3	2
Student	8	4	4	2	2	1	3	3	3	4	4	4	2	0	1	4
Student	9	4	4	4	4	4	2	4	4	4	4	4	2	2	3	4
Student	10	1	0	1	2	2	4	4	4	3	0	2	3	3	4	4

Figure 4.2: Standards-based gradebook.

details on expectations for student performance but also gives families direct evidence of how teachers determined students' scores and how the families might help students improve.

Purpose of the Gradebook

The primary purpose of the gradebook is to provide families and students with important information that keeps them abreast of *all* aspects of students' performance in school. It helps identify students' areas of strength and areas where additional help or support may be needed. In a standards-based gradebook, these areas typically relate to specific grade-level or course learning goals or standards. Because of the all-inclusive nature of gradebooks, however, they also may include information describing aspects of students' behavior, such as homework completion or class participation. Although scores on these behaviors do not reflect learning or achievement per se, they communicate vital information about behaviors that assist learning and are important for both families and students. Data on these behaviors also may help explain achievement scores and offer direction to improvement efforts.

Critical Gradebook Features Related to Purpose

To support student learning using gradebooks, teachers must understand the following three ideas and clearly communicate them to all families and students: (1) not everything recorded in the gradebook is used to determine student grades, (2) gradebook data are not tallied until the end of the grading period, and (3) gradebook tabulations that don't align with the purpose are eliminated. Misunderstanding the features of online gradebooks can lead to serious communication difficulties between teachers and families and severely impede reform efforts.

Not Everything Recorded in the Gradebook Is Used to Determine Student Grades

Families and students need accurate and meaningful information about *all* aspects of students' performance in school. They especially need teachers' feedback about student achievement of important learning goals and standards. But they also need information about student behaviors that enable learning, such as formative assessment scores, effort and perseverance in learning tasks, punctuality in turning in class assignments, and collaboration with classmates. Gradebook data on these aspects of student performance allow families and students to monitor learning activities more closely and work together with teachers to immediately remedy any learning difficulties that might occur.

All teachers, families, and students must understand, however, that not all the data included in the gradebook will be used to determine students' report card grades. Although many scores recorded in the gradebook reflect learning and achievement, others do not. If the purpose of a report card achievement grade is to accurately communicate what students have learned and are able to do, then data related to nonachievement aspects of student performance *cannot* be included as part of that grade.

This does not imply that these aspects of students' performance are unimportant or that "they don't count." Some behaviors, such as completing homework assignments and performing well on formative assessments, are vitally important in supporting and enabling student learning. Other behaviors, like collaborating with classmates or showing initiative and persistence, represent important nonacademic learning goals. Because of their importance to student success in school and life, information on these aspects of student performance should be summarized and included on the report card. But because they do not represent evidence of academic achievement, they should not be used in determining student achievement grades. Instead, they must be reported separately. Chapter 5 (page 117) offers procedures for providing separate grades for these other aspects of students' performance and describes the benefits that provides for teachers, families, and students.

Gradebook Data Are Not Tallied Until the End of the Grading Period

The purpose of the gradebook is to present comprehensive information on *all* aspects of students' performance in school. It includes data on student learning that teachers will tally and summarize at regular intervals throughout the school year in determining students' report card grades. Some computerized grading programs, however, tabulate data as soon as they are entered by the teacher to generate a current class or course grade. Although designed to be informative and keep families up to date on students' learning status, these immediate tabulations of gradebook data are unnecessary and may be detrimental to students' learning progress.

They can distort students' and family members' understanding of what is important in school and most vital to learning success. In particular, they encourage families and students to focus more on points and grades than on learning. Such immediate tabulations also discourage students from trying new things or taking on challenging assignments because doing so risks damaging their point total.

If students experience learning difficulties, these should be documented in the gradebook with individual assignment or assessment results, or with individual standards in a standards-based format. These special notations should be accompanied by specific suggestions for improvement to students and families so immediate remedial actions can be taken. Most important, these suggestions should offer explicit directions related to students' performance and not be admonitions for students to simply "study more" or "try harder." The key point is that cumulative tallies are unnecessary along the way and should be reserved to end of the grading period when report card grades are determined.

Gradebook Tabulations That Don't Align With the Purpose Are Eliminated

As noted in the previous section, many computerized gradebooks build in certain data tabulations as default functions without thoughtful consideration of their alignment with the gradebook's purpose. Reform leaders must have their technical consultants override, disable, or otherwise eliminate any tabulations they consider ill aligned with the agreed-on purpose of the gradebook, especially tabulations that have potentially negative consequences for students and families, and communicate this action to students and families. Two tabulations that fall into this category include (1) percentage grades and (2) "Current GPA" or "Cumulative GPA."

1. **Percentage grades:** The practical, ethical, and educational problems associated with the percentage grading scale have been well documented and are widely known (Brookhart & Guskey, 2019a; Guskey, 2013, 2015).

   The lack of reliability in a scale that includes 101 distinct levels of student performance (0 percent to 100 percent), two-thirds of which denote levels of failure, makes it impossible to defend percentage grades (Brookhart & Guskey, 2019a,

2019b). Grading scales with fewer, more clearly discernible performance levels have far greater reliability and validity.

Despite these recognized shortcomings, some computerized grading programs compel teachers to use percentage grades and even include algorithms that automatically convert the letters or numbers teachers enter to percentages. Although these programs vary widely in their conversion approach, all yield similar negative consequences. Most programs, for example, convert an A or 4 to 100 percent but differ in how they treat a B or 3. Should it convert to 80 percent, making it 20 percent different from a 4? Would a C or 2 then be 60 percent? Or perhaps a 3 should convert to 75 percent because it represents 3 out of 4, making a 2 equivalent to 50 percent?

Neither approach is appropriate or meaningful. More important from a measurement perspective, scales with fewer levels (for example, 0–4) simply *cannot* be accurately or validly converted to a scale with more levels. In essence, any conversion to percentages is inadequate, inappropriate, and invalid.

Regrettably, some states, provinces, districts, and jurisdictions require teachers to assign percentage grades to students in gradebooks, report cards, and permanent records or transcripts. Teachers certainly must comply with these requirements. Hopefully, however, teachers will always strive to be fair in their procedures for assigning grades and will continue to help policymakers understand the inherent shortcomings of percentage grading scales in accurately describing student performance.

2. **Current GPA or Cumulative GPA:** The second tabulation to override, disable, or eliminate is the immediate calculation of a grade point average or GPA (for example, in PowerSchool). Averages are extremely volatile, especially early in a grading period when teachers have entered only a few scores. In addition, inclusion of a single extreme score (for example, a zero) drastically affects the average and yields

a distorted picture of student performance. Averaging data on student performance over time can also misrepresent students' current level of mastery or proficiency. What students knew or could do days or weeks ago may have no relation to their current level of performance or achievement.

Complicating matters further is tabulation of "Cumulative GPA" or "Your Grade Today." These indices recalculate students' GPAs in classes as soon as teachers enter new data, and then report this number to families and students in the computerized grading program's dashboard program app. Some grading programs add an arrow to indicate whether the new data have raised or lowered students' previously calculated GPA. Parents report that students regularly access this number at lunchtime or after school and use it to measure their worth in comparison to other students. Families similarly use it to compare and rank their child's performance.

This tabulation combines the detriments of both percentages and averages. It also reinforces in students as young as grade 6 that success in school is not about learning but about accumulating points. This can discourage students from venturing into a new area or taking on a new challenge because it could irreparably damage their cumulative grade. Teachers also may fear entering data from an assessment on which students did poorly because it might incite concerns among parents and families.

> "Good leaders organize and align people around what the team needs to do. Great leaders motivate and inspire people with why they're doing it. That's purpose. And that's the key to achieving something truly transformational."
>
> —Marillyn A. Hewson

Given the lack of evidence showing that these two tabulations facilitate learning or enhance communication between teachers and families, it is hard to understand why any computerized grading program would include them. Fortunately, because most programs make them optional, these features can and should be disabled or eliminated completely.

Report Card

The second element in a grading system is the report card. Report cards provide interim summaries of students' performance at specific intervals during the school year. These intervals vary, from six weeks to nine-week quarters to, in some cases, twelve-week trimesters. Nine-week intervals are the most common among U.S. and Canadian schools. Modern grading programs provide families and students with online access to report cards, and most offer hard-copy versions at families' request. Most programs also offer translated versions of the report cards in both online and hard-copy forms for families with limited English language skills.

Some educators suggest that report cards are antiquated and will soon be abandoned in education. They argue that if parents, families, and students have 24/7 access to gradebooks that record all the data teachers gather on students' performance in school, why are report cards necessary? Others counter, however, that teachers use report cards to summarize and evaluate the evidence in a way that helps parents, families, and students understand the adequacy of students' performance. This evidence is especially important if teachers note areas of difficulty or struggle, because that evidence can then be used to provide students with immediate assistance. We will refer to data recorded on report cards as *grades*. These data may include letters, numbers, words, symbols, or any set of descriptors that designate different levels of student performance.

Teachers implementing standards-based grading typically use report cards to summarize students' progress in *strands* or *domains* of standards within a subject or course, rather than reporting on individual standards. In language arts, for example, teachers may provide report card grades representing student proficiency in reading, writing, listening, speaking, and language skills (for example, spelling, grammar, and punctuation). This allows teachers to use the same report card across multiple grade levels, because although the standards change from level to level, the strands or domains in which those standards are grouped do not. Information about the specific standards emphasized during the marking period within each of these strands is provided in the gradebook.

Preliminary Cautions

Before beginning significant report card reform, three preliminary cautions must be kept in mind.

1. **Address purpose and function *before* considering form and structure:** Because the report card is the centerpiece of nearly every grading system, many reform leaders begin by revising its structure and organization. This emphasis on form before purpose, however, almost always leads to trouble. Enamored by the appeal of new technology and the reporting forms generated by new computerized grading software, reformers often neglect vital dimensions of the communication process. In particular, they go forward in their efforts unaware of critical shortcomings inherent in many new reporting formats and the numerous interpretation problems they can create for families and others (as discussed in chapter 3, page 61). As a result, they encounter predictable difficulties that thwart even the most dedicated attempts at reform.

2. **Be mindful of the problems involved in challenging traditions:** As described in chapter 3, many school leaders overlook the powerful influence of tradition and the importance of fully communicating with the broad range of stakeholders involved in the grading and reporting process. They proceed in a politically charged environment with little more than vague conventional wisdom to guide their efforts. The problem with this approach is while conventional wisdom and common sense are important, they often turn out to be wrong or at least simplistic, especially when it comes to grading and reporting (Guskey, 1999).

3. **Focus on a reporting system rather than the report card alone:** Report cards are an indispensable component of grading and reporting at any level of education. But far too often, educators try to accomplish too much and serve too many purposes with this single reporting device. This results in a reporting form that serves no purpose particularly well

and satisfies no one. The report card then quickly becomes a target of criticism and a lightning rod for controversy.

A reporting system includes not only the grading system elements (the gradebook, report card, and permanent record or transcript) but also the wide range of other means educators can use to communicate information about student learning to parents, families, and other stakeholders. The reporting system might include any or all of the following means of reporting (Guskey & Bailey, 2001).

- Report cards
- Notes given with report cards
- Standardized assessment reports
- Weekly or monthly progress reports
- Phone calls
- School open houses
- Newsletters
- Home visits
- Email
- Personal letters
- Homework
- Evaluated assignments or projects
- School webpages
- Homework hotlines
- Parent-teacher conferences
- Student-led conferences

Educators should design and structure each element in a reporting system to achieve a clear and specific purpose. Establishing the purpose makes questions about the most appropriate structure and method much easier to address.

Purpose of the Report Card

Successful efforts to revise the report card always begin by defining the report card's purpose (Brookhart, 2011b; Guskey & Bailey, 2010). This involves addressing the simple but vitally important questions, "Why do we assign grades or marks to students' work?" and "Why do we summarize evidence on students' performance and record those summaries on report cards?"

Researchers who have asked educators these questions generally find their answers can be classified in one of six broad categories (Airasian,

2001; Feldmesser, 1971; Frisbie & Waltman, 1992; Guskey & Bailey, 2001; Linn, 1983). These six major purposes include the following.

1. **To communicate information about students' achievement to families and others:** Grading and reporting provide families (including guardians and relatives) and other interested persons (for example, tutors and coaches) with information about students' achievement, learning progress, and behavior in school. In some instances, grading and reporting also serve to involve students' families in educational processes.

2. **To provide information to students for self-evaluation:** Grading and reporting offer students information about their achievement level and the adequacy of their performance in school. As important feedback devices, grades and report cards can also serve to redirect students' efforts and guide improvements in their academic performance.

3. **To select, identify, or group students for specific educational paths or programs:** Grades and report cards are the primary source of information used to select and group students for education programs. Students must achieve passing grades to be promoted from one grade level to the next. High grades are usually required for entry into gifted education programs and honors or advanced classes, while low grades are often the first indicator of learning problems that result in placement in programs that offer special assistance. Summaries of report card grades on transcripts are typically a major factor in gaining admission to selective colleges and universities.

4. **To provide incentives for students to learn:** Although some educators debate the idea, extensive evidence shows that grades and other reporting tools are important factors in determining the amount of effort students put forth and how seriously they regard any learning or assessment task (Brookhart, 1993; Cameron & Pierce, 1994, 1996; Chastain, 1990; Natriello & Dornbusch, 1984).

5. **To evaluate the effectiveness of instructional programs:**
   Comparisons of grades and other reporting evidence are
   frequently used to judge the value and effectiveness of new
   programs, curriculums, and instructional strategies.

6. **To provide evidence of students' effort or responsibility:**
   Teachers use grades and other reporting devices to document students' effort in learning tasks or demonstrated
   responsibility in learning activities. Teachers may raise the
   grades of students who try hard and behave well in class, or
   lower the grades of students who don't complete homework
   or fail to turn in assignments on time.

Although educators generally agree that all these purposes may be
legitimate, they seldom agree on which purpose is most important.
When asked to rank-order these purposes in terms of their importance,
school leaders and teachers tend to vary widely in their responses—even
when they are staff members from the same school (Link, 2018b).

When educators don't agree on the primary purpose of grades and
the report card, they often try to address *all* these purposes with a single
reporting device, usually a report card, and end up achieving none very
well (Austin & McCann, 1992). The simple truth is that no single
reporting instrument can serve all these purposes well. In fact, some of
these purposes actually counter others.

As described in *On Your Mark* (Guskey, 2015), suppose the educators in a school or district work hard to achieve their goal of having
all students learn well. Suppose, too, that they are highly successful

> *"Definiteness of purpose
> is the starting point
> of all achievement."*
> —W. Clement Stone

in their efforts and, as a result, nearly all their
students attain high levels of achievement and
earn high grades. These positive results pose no
problem if the purpose of grading and reporting
is to communicate students' achievement status to
families or to provide students with self-evaluation
information. This school or district's educators can take pride in what
they accomplished and can look forward to sharing those results with
families, students, board members, and other stakeholders.

This same positive outcome poses major problems, however, if the purpose of grading and reporting is to select students for special educational

paths or to evaluate the effectiveness of instructional programs. Selection and evaluation demand variation in grades. They require that grades be dispersed across all possible categories in order to differentiate among students and programs. How else can selection take place or one program be judged as better than another? If all students learn well and earn the same high grades, there's no variation. Determining differences under such conditions is impossible (Guskey, 2015). Thus, while one purpose was served well, another purpose was not.

This is why defining purpose from the very beginning is so important. All actions and procedures, policies, and practices will be determined by and must align with the agreed-on purpose.

Parents' and Families' Perspectives on the Purpose of the Report Card

When deciding the report card's purpose, educators must consider the perspectives of parents and families. They are, after all, the primary recipients of the information included in the report card. To this end, many districts and schools initiating grading and reporting reforms hold special evening sessions for parents and families on a day that they find convenient to attend. At many of these sessions, parents take part in the same activity described earlier in which they are asked to rank-order the six purposes that report cards serve in terms of importance. Unlike school leaders and teachers, parents tend to be remarkably consistent in their rankings. Overwhelmingly, they rank communicating with families as most important. They believe report cards represent one of the most crucial sources of information they have about how their children are doing in school.

This illustrates the typical but frequently ignored disparity in perspectives between educators and parents or families. If we consider grading and reporting primarily a challenge in effective communication, then such disparities must be recognized and addressed. This means members of the Coalition for Change must take on purpose-related issues and reach consensus before turning to the report card's form and structure. A clear and concise purpose statement makes all other decisions about grading policies and practices easier to make.

> "When you're surrounded by people who share a passionate commitment around a common purpose, anything is possible."
>
> —Howard Schultz

The Purpose Statement

Most of the difficulties schools experience in their efforts to reform grading policies and practices can be traced to the absence of a well-defined and commonly shared purpose. In other words, the lack of clarity and consensus about the purpose of the report card makes any progress difficult. Purpose gives direction to reform efforts. It makes the pathway clear and progress easier to judge.

Remember the adage from architecture that "form *follows* function"? The same holds true in grading and reporting reform: method *follows* purpose. Clarifying the purpose of grades and the report card must always come first (Brookhart, 2011b; Guskey & Bailey, 2010).

This does not imply that clarifying the purpose of grades or the report card is easy. As described earlier, differences abound regarding the purpose of grades—as do explanations for those differences. Some suggest that these differences stem from different groups' conflicting opinions about what grades mean and for whom they are intended. Others argue that such differences run much deeper and arise from fundamental tensions in values and educational philosophies. One side points to the need to differentiate student performance levels in order to make accurate decisions about what students have achieved. The other side emphasizes the desire to treat all students as capable of high levels of performance (Hiner, 1973; Trumbull, 2000). These tensions can be particularly problematic in developing standards-based report cards because the process usually begins from the premise that *all* students can and should learn well (Bloom, 1976; Guskey, 2006b).

In addition, educators sometimes distinguish different purposes for grades on individual assignments or assessments versus grades on report cards. Grades on assignments or regular classroom assessments are often seen as more tentative and formative. These grades may even be subject to change, depending on follow-up actions students take. Teachers typically use individual assignment or assessment grades to inform students about the adequacy of their performance and how well their performance matches specific expectations for their learning. Grades on report cards and transcripts, however, are usually considered more permanent and summative. These grades represent teachers' culminating judgments about students' competence or level of achievement at a particular point in time. If such differences exist, they should be clarified in the purpose statement.

Key Questions in Defining the Purpose of the Report Card

Three key questions need to be answered in defining the purpose of grades on the report card (Guskey & Bailey, 2010). These key questions include (1) What information will be communicated in the report card? (2) Who is the primary audience for that information? and (3) What is the intended goal of that communication? or How should that information be used? After these key questions are answered, critical issues about the report card's form and structure become much easier to address and resolve.

What Will Be Communicated in the Report Card?

While other reporting devices often contain widely varied types of data, a report card includes quite specific information. The best report cards clearly communicate three points: (1) what students are expected to learn and be able to do, (2) how well students are doing those things, and (3) whether that level of performance aligns with learning expectations set for this grade level or course at this time in the school year. The report card should provide information specific enough to communicate the knowledge and skills that teachers expect students to gain, but not so detailed that it overwhelms families and others with data they don't understand and don't know how to use. Families want to know how well their child is doing and whether that performance level is in line with the teacher's and school's expectations. If it's not, then they want to know what they can do to help teachers and students remedy minor learning difficulties before they become major learning problems.

Keep in mind, too, that in most instances, families have access to the gradebook in conjunction with the report card. The detailed information on students' performance included in the gradebook helps clarify the summaries offered on the report card and do not need to be replicated.

Who Is the Primary Audience for That Information?

The second question considered in defining the purpose of the report card is the primary audience for the information. While the audience for other types of reporting devices may vary, a report card's audience is almost always parents or other adults, such as guardians or relatives, and the students themselves, especially in the upper grades.

Elementary educators rarely debate this matter. For them, the primary audience is definitely parents, guardians, and other adults. Because of the nature of most elementary classrooms, teachers regularly communicate with their students about individual learning progress. They let students know when they are doing well and when they might need additional work or study. Report cards are designed to bring parents up to date, summarize the data recorded in the gradebook, and keep parents and families abreast of their child's achievement and learning progress in school.

When asked about the purpose of the report card, parents and families express similar consistency in their perspectives: they believe the report card is for them. As noted earlier, families see report cards as their primary communication link with teachers and the school regarding their child's learning progress. Why else would teachers ask them to sign the report card or otherwise provide notification that they received it?

Middle-grade and secondary-level educators tend to be more divided. Many believe, as elementary educators do, that the primary audience is parents. For these educators, report cards serve to inform parents and other adults about their children's performance in school. Other secondary educators, however, believe that older students should be taking increased responsibility for their own achievement and accomplishments in school (Guskey & Anderman, 2008). For these educators, report cards also serve to inform students about their teachers' formal judgments of how well they have met established learning goals and expectations.

In some cases, educators decide that the primary audience is both families *and* students. While completely appropriate, this heightens the communication challenge. Under these conditions, specific steps must be taken to ensure that families *and* students understand what information is included in the report card, how it relates to the data recorded in the gradebook, and how to use the information to guide improvements when needed.

How Should That Information Be Used?

Finally, the report card's purpose should offer guidance regarding how the information in the report card should be used. In other words, the report card communicates *with intent*. Obviously, the best use of that information depends on the primary audience. The report card may, for example, provide families and other adults with information about their children's academic strengths and difficulties so successes can be celebrated and specific steps taken to remedy any problems. For students, the report card might recognize their accomplishments and identify areas where they need additional study. The key point is that rather than offering a culminating, final evaluation, the report card should be seen as part of a continuous and ongoing reporting process. Above all, the report card communicates information to facilitate improvements in student learning.

> *"The secret of success is constancy to purpose."*
>
> —Benjamin Disraeli

Communicating the Report Card's Purpose

To ensure that everyone understands the report card's purpose, it should be printed directly on the report card (Guskey & Bailey, 2010). The purpose statement should be spelled out in bold print and appear in a special box either on the front of the card or above the first section. This helps identify the report card's intent, the information it includes, and the targeted audience. It also helps minimize miscommunication and misinterpretation.

Even though they include the common elements described earlier, purpose statements can vary widely. An example from an elementary-level report card is as follows:

> The purpose of this report card is to describe students' learning progress to families and others, based on our school's learning goals for each grade level. It is intended to inform parents and families about learning successes and to guide improvements when needed.

Note that this statement tells the specific aim of the report card, for whom the information is intended, and how to use that information. An example for the middle school or high school level is as follows:

> The purpose of this report card is to communicate with families and students about the achievement of specific learning goals. It identifies students' current levels of progress with regard to those goals, students' areas of strength, and areas where additional time and effort are needed.

This statement identifies both families *and* students as recipients of the report card's information. It also makes clear the information describes students' *current level*—not where they started or their average of scores over the grading period. It further adds how to use that information. The next example comes from a college-level report card:

> The purpose of this report card is to inform students of instructors' evaluations of their academic performance in each of their classes. Grades reflect how well students met the established learning goals of each class, areas of outstanding performance, and areas where additional study and effort are required.

Note in this example that the audience is students alone, which is generally the case only at the postsecondary level. A fourth example comes from the American School of Paris, an international school where the school leaders and faculty have been especially thoughtful in their approach to grading and reporting reform.

> The primary purpose of grading is to effectively communicate student achievement toward specific standards at a certain point in time. A grade should reflect what a student knows and is able to do. Students will receive separate feedback and evaluation on their learning habits, which will not be included in the academic achievement grades.

This statement clarifies the focus on students' *current level* of performance and the use of *multiple grades*, the topic of the next chapter (page 83).

The purpose statement that works best varies depending on the context. Differences across education levels also are common. The purpose of an elementary report card, for example, may be slightly different from that of a middle school or high school report card. At all levels, however, it's essential that the purpose be clearly stated to everyone involved in the grading and reporting process—teachers, parents and guardians, students, and administrators—so everyone understands its intent and can use it appropriately.

Benefits of a Clear Purpose

As emphasized in chapter 1 (page 17), *you cannot initiate reforms in grading and reporting with the report card.* A multitude of decisions must be made about which learning goals are most important and how to gather valid evidence on students' achievement of those goals before you consider how to evaluate and report that evidence. But simply clarifying the purpose of grading brings important benefits.

A well-designed study by Jessica Gogerty (2016) showed that when the purpose of grading is clearly articulated, teachers approach student learning more deliberately. They prioritize curriculum standards and adjust their instructional procedures to more closely align the content, format, and difficulty of classroom assessments. Teachers also express less tolerance of colleagues who fail to align their teaching and learning practices to the grading purpose. They see this failure as negligence that causes unnecessary confusion for students and families (Gogerty, 2016). Apparently, when the grading purpose is set, more coordinated efforts to uphold that purpose are expected.

Permanent Record or Transcript

The third and most general element in any grading system is the permanent record or transcript. This summary of students' performance in school is generally referred to as a *permanent record* for students through the elementary and middle grades, and as a *transcript* for students in high school. It goes with students when they transfer from one school to another. This record is also used for college and university admission, examined upon entry to military service, and viewed by potential employers.

We will refer to the data recorded in permanent records or transcripts as *summary grades.* Like report card grades, summary grades may be letters, numbers, words, symbols, or any set of descriptors that designate different levels of student performance. Teachers implementing standards-based grading typically use the permanent record or transcript to summarize students' summative achievement of grade-level or course standards. But like with the report card, teachers usually report on strands or domains of standards within a subject area or course, rather than on individual standards, in order to simplify the report and make it more efficient.

Two important characteristics distinguish the permanent record or transcript from the gradebook and report card: (1) the summative nature of the data included, and (2) its availability to third parties.

1. **The summative nature of the data included:** The gradebook and report card portray evidence of work in progress that is generally interpreted as more formative. The permanent record or transcript, however, describes culminating evidence of students' overall performance at a grade level or in a course. Although this record or transcript is sometimes subject to change in continuous progress systems or through doing remedial work and retaking courses, it is typically considered a summative evaluation of students' performance at a specific point in time, usually at the completion of a school year or course.

2. **Its availability to third parties:** Because individuals other than parents, families, and students can view these records, certain legal restrictions apply to the information that can be included, especially with regard to students with special needs (Jung & Guskey, 2012). These restrictions must be kept in mind when designing permanent records or transcripts, and especially when determining what information to include.

Purpose of the Permanent Record or Transcript

Among the three elements in a grading system, the permanent record or transcript has the most obvious purpose. It provides a culminating summary of students' performance in school. Schools make these records or transcripts available to parents and families, students, and, in some cases, third parties, such as other schools to which the student might transfer, college or university admissions offices, and potential employers. Just as with the report card, however, the purpose should be stated directly on the permanent record or transcript to clarify its intent for all readers.

To ensure more thorough understanding, the purpose statement should address two additional questions: (1) What student performance data do the permanent record or transcript summarize? and (2) How do teachers determine the summary grades in the permanent record or transcript?

1. **What student performance data do the permanent record or transcript summarize?** This question refers to the depth and breadth of the information included on the permanent record or transcript. Most educators agree, for example, that the permanent record or transcript should contain summary data on students' academic achievement. But will the report offer a single summary grade for each subject area or course, or will it include a breakdown by strands or domains of standards within each subject area or course? For example, will it include a single summary grade for language arts or provide separate grades for reading, writing, listening, speaking, and language skills? Will it also offer information on nonacademic skills such as collaboration, initiative, self-regulation, and other work habits? If these noncognitive skills are reported, by what criteria will they be judged? Here, again, in answering these questions, educators must find a critical balance in providing information that is detailed enough to be accurate and meaningful but not so detailed that it overwhelms readers or obscures what is most important.

2. **How do teachers determine the summary grades in the permanent record or transcript?** This question requires clarification as to whether summary grades reflect purely students' mastery of important academic content and skills, or whether they are also based on students' compliance with classroom rules regarding completing homework or turning in assignments on time. If they reflect mastery of academic learning goals, then summary grades should closely align with other indicators of achievement, such as scores on required end-of-course exams, Advanced Placement (AP) exams, or International Baccalaureate (IB) exams. If the grades

and assessment scores do not align, then factors other than students' academic achievement might explain the disparity (Bowers, 2019; Welsh, 2019). Reporting on academic as well as nonacademic learning outcomes, as shown in figure 4.3, might help clarify such inconsistencies if they exist. Chapter 5 (page 117) and chapter 6 (page 143) will also discuss this.

Format of the Permanent Record or Transcript

Permanent records and transcripts vary widely in their format depending on the prescribed purpose and, in many cases, on the computerized grading program the district or school uses. For elementary students, most permanent records report a single summary grade for each subject area at each grade level, and this often extends into the middle grades. At the end of fifth grade, for example, teachers might give students a single grade to represent their performance in language arts, mathematics, science, and other subjects during the fifth-grade academic year. At the middle school and high school levels, this typically transitions to a single summary grade per course, so students receive a summary grade for English, algebra, or biology.

> *"If you have a common purpose and an environment in which people want to help others succeed, the problems will be fixed quickly."*
>
> —Alan Mulally

Most high school transcripts also include information about students' cumulative GPA and their scores on external examinations, especially state or provincial assessments, AP exams, IB exams, and college admissions exams like the SAT or ACT. In addition, many transcripts, like the one in figure 4.3, have sections that explain differences in course levels and the grading scale the school uses.

Standards-Based Transcripts

Districts and schools implementing standards-based approaches to grading and reporting frequently work to align permanent records and transcripts with the format they use in their gradebooks and report cards. Almost all begin by distinguishing academic achievement grades from indicators of nonacademic factors, like the example shown in figure 4.3 does. Although this alone doesn't make a transcript standards based, it is an essential first step.

Seashores High School
Official Transcript

Student Personal Information

Date of Enrollment:
Date of Graduation:
Date of Birth:

Parent/Guardian:
Address:
Phone: Email:

Courses	Proficiency Level	Year/ Semester	Type
2015–2016			
Algebra 1	3.0	Year	Course
World History	3.5	Year	Course
English 3	3.75	Year	Course
Spanish 1	3.0	Year	Course
Economics	3.5	Year	Course
Art History 1	3.5	Year	Course
2016–2017			
Algebra 2	3.0	Year	Course
Physics	3.5	Year	Course
English 4	4.0	Year	Course
U.S. History	4.0	Year	Course
Spanish 2	3.5	Year	Course
Physical Education	4.0	Year	Course
2017–2018			
Geometry	3.5	Year	Course
Spanish 3	3.0	Year	Course
Art History 2	4.0	Year	Course
English 5 (AP)	4.0	Year	Honors
Drama	3.75	Semester	Course
Biology	3.5	Semester	Course
2018–2019			
English 6 (AP)	3.75	Year	Honors
Physical Education	4.0	Year	Course
Statistics	3.0	Semester	Course
Calculus 1	4.0	Year	Course
Software Development	4.0	Semester	Course
Psychology (AP)	3.5	Year	Honors

Academic Summary

GPA: 3.5
SAT/ACT Scores:
Academic Achievements/
    Awards:

Grading System

3.6–4.0: Exceeds Proficiency
3.0–3.5: Proficient
2.0–2.9: Developing Proficiency
1.0–1.9: Insufficient Evidence

Graduation Requirements

Mathematics
Science/Technology
English Language Arts
World Languages
Career Education
Social Studies
Humanities/The Arts

Graduation Standards/Skills

Graduation standards
achievement is validated
over time as students develop
and demonstrate proficiency
through various assessments
and projects.

Proficiency Level

Creative problem solver and thinker	3.5
Effective communicator	3.0
Responsible citizen	4.0
Disciplined, self-directed learner	3.5

Figure 4.3: Example high school transcript.

The next step is to establish strands or domains of learning goals for each subject area or course and provide separate grades for each. Instead of offering only a single grade for mathematics, for example, separate summary grades could be provided for operations and algebraic thinking, numbers and operations for base ten, numbers and operations for fractions, measurement and data, geometry, and mathematical practices. This gives readers of the permanent record or transcript a broader and more detailed understanding of each student's academic strengths and accomplishments. Figure 4.4 shows an example of an elementary learning record.

Concerns About Standards-Based Transcripts

The transition to standards-based models of grading in report cards and transcripts sometimes raises concerns about how college and university admissions officers will receive these new forms. Parents and families, as well as students, often worry that admissions personnel might find a more detailed standards-based transcript more difficult to review and interpret, and as a result, it will disadvantage students in the admissions process. This becomes especially important in applications to highly selective universities like the Massachusetts Institute of Technology, where the admissions office typically receives more than twenty thousand applicants for a freshman class of about one thousand students (Riede, 2018).

Surveys of admissions officers indicate, however, that applying under a standards-based grading system does *not* disadvantage students in any way in the admissions process (Riede, 2008). Admissions directors report their offices are accustomed to considering a wide variety of transcripts, including those of students from other countries, students from international schools, and homeschooled students. Others indicate that they may find a well-constructed standards-based transcript more informative than a traditional one. In particular, reporting nonacademic factors separately from academic achievement grades provides a more comprehensive picture of students' attainment and may enable admissions officers to evaluate students at a deeper level. Jerome Lucido of the Center for Enrollment Research, Policy and Practice at the University of Southern California, an organization that studies enrollment policies and practices at colleges and universities to improve student access and success, comments:

Sunrise Elementary School Report Card: 2018–2019: Third Grade

Student:

Teacher:

Mathematics: Common Core Standards	1	2	3	4
Operations and Algebraic Thinking				
Number and Operations in Base Ten				
Number and Operations: Fractions				
Measurement and Data				
Geometry				
Mathematical Practices				

English Language Arts: Common Core Standards	1	2	3	4
Reading: Literature				
Reading: Informational Text				
Reading: Foundational Skills				
Writing				
Speaking and Listening				
Language				
Range, Quality, and Complexity				

Special Courses	1	2	3	4
Music				
Art				
Physical Education				
Drama				

Attendance	1	2	3	4
Absences				
Tardies				

Social and Classroom Citizenship Skills	1	2	3	4
Completes homework in timely manner				
Follows classroom and school rules				
Follows instructions (written and verbal)				
Demonstrates the following traits: polite, cooperative, respectful, helpful				
Uses time efficiently for activities and assignments				
Is organized and accountable				
Works well with others in groups or pairs				

Science	1	2	3	4
Demonstrates knowledge and understanding of grade 3 science through class activities, assignments, assessments, and discussions				

Social Studies	1	2	3	4
Demonstrates knowledge and understanding of grade 3 science through class activities, assignments, assessments, and discussions				

Comments:

Figure 4.4: Example elementary learning record.

> [Standards-based applications] might be even a more efficient way than we currently have to assess elements of a student's character, whether it's moral character or performance character. . . . Is the student conscientious? Is the student someone who commits to civic responsibility? Is it someone who engages in school activities and leadership roles? Is it someone who brings different kinds of students together in conversation and in learning? Is it someone who's not just comfortable with but learns from different cultures? If there are ways to get that in a really readable form, wow, we want to know about this. (as quoted in Riede, 2018, p. 28)

Another advantage of standards-based transcripts noted in these reports is the closer correspondence between course grades and external examination results, particularly end-of-course exams and AP exams. Traditional transcripts sometimes report inflated course grades due to extra-credit options and good behavior, or deflated grades because of missing homework assignments or late class projects (Gershenson, 2018). When teachers remove these factors from course achievement grades, those grades typically align more closely with the scores students attain on external examinations in those subjects. Reports describing the results of these and other surveys of college and university admissions officers are listed in the box on page 113.

Mastery Transcripts

Another development gaining notoriety in many education circles is the *mastery transcript* developed by the Mastery Transcript Consortium™ (MTC), a group of elite public and private high schools mostly from around the United States. Unlike traditional high school transcripts, the mastery transcript includes not courses or grades but levels of proficiency in various areas. Instead of stating that a student earned a certain grade in French II, for example, the mastery transcript might say the student can *understand and express ideas in two or more languages*, and perhaps provide a link to a video of the student speaking French.

The mastery transcript indicates different levels of mastery as well. So instead of providing a grade in algebra or geometry, for instance, the mastery transcript might indicate a student understands and can use various kinds of mathematical concepts. It would also include a list of character traits the student has mastered, such *foster integrity, honesty,*

Reports of College Admissions Offices' Perspectives on Standards-Based Transcripts

Buckmiller, T. M., & Peters, R. E. (2018). Getting a fair shot? *School Administrator, 75*(2), 22–25.

Clinedinst, M. (2019). *2019 State of college admissions.* Arlington, VA: National Association for College Admission Counseling. Accessed at www.nacacnet.org/globalassets/documents/publications/research/2018_soca/soca2019_all.pdf on January 23, 2020.

Great Schools Partnership. (2018). *College admissions: 79 New England institutions of higher education state that proficiency-based diplomas do not disadvantage applicants.* Portland, ME: Author. Accessed at www.greatschoolspartnership.org/proficiency-based-learning/college-admissions on June 6, 2019.

Hanover Research. (2011). *Effective grading practices in the middle school and high school environments.* Washington, DC: Author. Accessed at https://njctl-media.s3.amazonaws.com/uploads/Effective%20grading%20practices%20in%20the%20middle%20school%20and%20high%20school%20environments.pdf on June 6, 2019.

National Association for College Admission Counseling. (2017). *The state of college admission report.* Arlington, VA: Author. Accessed at www.nacacnet.org/news--publications/publications/state-of-college-admission on November 10, 2019.

Riede, P. (2018). Making the call inside admissions offices. *School Administrator, 75*(2), 26–29.

Segerstrom, D., & Hansen, A. M. (2014, June 18). *Grading the future: The Illinois State Board of Education's 2014 Student Advisory Council.* Springfield, IL: Author. Accessed at www.isbe.net/Documents/2014-board-presentation.pdf on July 2, 2019.

fairness, and respect; *lead through influence*; and *build trust, resolve conflicts, and provide support to others* (Martin, 2020).

Figure 4.5 (page 114) shows an example of what the mastery transcript document might look like, but this could change considerably as the work of the Consortium evolves.

Earned Credits:

1 Analytical and Creative Thinking

b. Detect bias, and distinguish between reliable and unsound information.
e. Analyze and create ideas and knowledge.

2 Complex Communication—Oral and Written

a. Understand and express ideas in two or more languages.
c. Listen attentively.
d. Speak effectively.

3 Leadership and Teamwork

a. Initiate new ideas.
b. Lead through influence.
c. Build trust, resolve conflicts, and provide support for others.
d. Facilitate group discussions, forge consensus, and negotiate outcomes.
f. Enlist help.
g. Coordinate tasks, manage groups, and delegate responsibilities.
h. Implement decisions and meet goals.
i. Share the credit.

4 Digital and Quantitative Literacy

a. Understand, use, and apply digital technologies.
c. Use multimedia resources to communicate ideas effectively in a variety of forms.
d. Master and use higher-level mathematics.
e. Understand traditional and emerging topics in mathematics, science, technology, environmental sciences, robotics, fractals, cellular automata, nanotechnology, and biotechnology.

5 Global Perspective

b. Understand non-Western history, politics, religion, and culture.
e. Develop social and intellectual skills to navigate effectively across cultures.
h. Leverage social and cultural differences to create new ideas and achieve success.

6 Adaptability, Initiative, and Risk Taking

a. Develop flexibility, agility, and adaptability.
b. Bring a sense of courage to unfamiliar situations.
d. Work effectively in a climate of ambiguity and changing priorities.
g. Develop entrepreneurial literacy.

7 Integrity and Ethical Decision Making

a. Sustain an empathetic and compassionate outlook.
b. Foster integrity, honesty, fairness, and respect.
c. Exhibit moral courage in confronting unjust situations.
d. Act responsibly, with the interests and well-being of the larger community in mind.
e. Develop a fundamental understanding of emerging ethical issues and dilemmas regarding new media and technologies.

8 Habits of Mind

b. Exhibit creativity.
e. Have persistence.

Note: MTC member schools have the flexibility to define the mastery credits that their students can earn. This listing is representative of some of the mastery credits that schools could use as they design a credit architecture that is appropriate for their school community. Visit mastery.org for more information.

Source: © 2017 by Mastery Transcript Consortium™ (MTC). Used with permission.

Figure 4.5: Mastery transcript example.

Perspectives on the mastery transcript and its prospects of success are mixed. Scott Looney, head of Cleveland's Hawken School and founder and board chair of the Mastery Transcript Consortium, believes that "once the new mastery transcript takes hold, colleges will value it over traditional materials they currently receive" (Jaschik, 2017). He argues it will help send high school students a different message about what is important—something radically different from an oppressive, exhausting, and single-minded focus on grades and test scores (Mastery Transcript Consortium, 2017).

Others offer a more cautious perspective. Lucido warns that schools may experience "a bit of irony" when they make this drastic transcript transformation (as quoted in Riede, 2018, p. 4). If applications and their accompanying transcripts are not as clear and accessible as college admissions officers would like them to be, there may be a tendency to fall back into the safety net of standardized test scores (Riede, 2018).

Michael Reilly, executive director of the American Association of Collegiate Registrars and Admissions Officers, notes both potential and challenges in the mastery transcript idea:

> My initial read is that this would be a good set of information to augment a traditional transcript but, by itself, could harm students seeking to attend institutions that are mandated to evaluate admissions, at least in part, on completion of a core set of courses and the performance (grades) in those courses. . . . Until these [transcripts] are common currency, students would be negatively impacted when they seek to transfer to more traditional institutions if that is the only document they present. Promising, but I'd like to hear how it would be transitioned into the existing processes. (as quoted in Jaschik, 2017)

Catherine Rampell (2017), writing for the *Washington Post*, offers a more ominous perspective, suggesting that use of the mastery transcript could have detrimental effects on economically disadvantaged students:

> However well-intended, this brave new grade-free world would have at least one very pernicious effect: It would probably help mediocre (generally rich) prep school kids and hurt high-achieving (generally less well-off) public school students.
>
> Grades are imprecise and imperfect measures of achievement. But they do provide *some* useful information about relative achievement among students. Obfuscating distinctions—whether through grade inflation or grade elimination—helps students in schools where average achievement is high and hurts those where that average is low.

Changing the way we grade will most certainly bring changes in permanent records and transcripts. Whether these changes take the form of the mastery transcript, adapted versions of a standards-based transcript, or some other modification remains uncertain. What seems clear, however, is that older forms of transcripts that only list courses and grades no longer suffice. They simply don't capture all that is important about students' performance, academically or otherwise. Instead, educators need forms that offer information about students' academic achievement *as well as* their performance in other important areas of affective, emotional, social, and character development. The challenge for educators rests in creating forms that communicate this information efficiently, succinctly, reliably, and effectively.

> "Great minds have purpose, others have wishes. Little minds are tamed and subdued by misfortunes; but great minds rise above them."
>
> —Washington Irving

Summary

All grading systems consist of three elements: (1) the gradebook, (2) the report card, and (3) the permanent record or transcript. Reform initiatives that set out to improve grading and reporting procedures *must* begin with inclusive, broad-based discussions that involve various stakeholders and focus on each element's purpose. These discussions should center on the information the teacher should communicate through grading and reporting, the audience or audiences for that information, and the intended goal of the communication. Once educators decide on the purpose of grades and grading, they will much more easily resolve crucial issues about the form and structure of each element, as well as issues related to broader grading and reporting policies and practices.

CHAPTER 5

Report Multiple Grades: Cognitive Outcomes

Pick battles big enough to matter, small enough to win.

—Jonathan Kozol

Imagine going to your physician for a health examination. During the exam, the physician records data on your height, weight, blood pressure, and heart rate, and asks you a series of questions about your lifestyle and how you feel. After gathering all this information, the physician enters the data into a computer and uses a mathematical algorithm to calculate a single number that describes your physical condition. The physician reports the number to you, offers a few suggestions on how you might improve that number, and then sends you on your way.

Would you be satisfied with such an examination? Would you have faith in a physician who analyzed information about you in this way? Would you trust a computer algorithm to tally the information and accurately assess your health? Would you find a single computer-generated number to be informative or helpful?

Few people would answer *yes* to any of these questions. Many would find such a process insulting. We need and expect more. In particular,

Portions of this chapter appear in "Making High School Grades Meaningful" (Guskey, 2006b), "Why the Label 'Exceeds Standard' Doesn't Work" (Guskey, 2014b), "New Direction in the Development of Rubrics" (Guskey, 2017b), and "Multiple Grades: The First Step to Improving Grading and Reporting" (Guskey, 2018c).

we want our physician to be a thoughtful and knowledgeable professional who carefully looks at different aspects of the data in assessing our health. We expect that individual to evaluate the information thoroughly and understand its nuances. And we certainly want more than a single, computer-tallied number from the diverse information the physician gathers (Guskey, 2018c).

Even though most of us find such a process unacceptable in a health examination, few object to teachers' using a nearly identical process when determining students' report card grades. But combining all that diverse evidence is just as inadequate and inappropriate when describing students' school performance as when describing a person's physical condition. Instead, we must find ways to provide a more descriptive profile or "dashboard" of information that meaningfully summarizes the different aspects of student performance. At a minimum, we must provide *multiple grades*. Not only is this a necessary element of standards-based or competency-based approaches to education, but it is also an essential first step in implementing any grading reform and a necessary prerequisite to success.

Three major types of grading criteria must be distinguished in reporting on students' performance: (1) *product criteria* and (2) *progress criteria*, which relate to academic achievement and cognitive outcomes; and (3) *process criteria*, which describe noncognitive behaviors, attitudes, dispositions, and social and emotional skills that are important for students' success in school and in life (Guskey, 1994b, 1996).

This chapter focuses on product and progress criteria related to cognitive outcomes. In chapter 6 (page 143), we turn our attention to process criteria associated with noncognitive outcomes. Here, we describe critical issues involved in reporting these criteria and outcomes clearly and efficiently, and offer evidence-based suggestions on how to successfully communicate the criteria and outcomes to students, parents, and families. We explore recently discovered aspects of reporting on these criteria and outcomes that enhance effectiveness and present examples to guide both development and implementation.

This chapter also considers the specific inadequacies of a single grade, the advantages of multiple grades, the challenge that reporting multiple grades poses for secondary educators, and the necessary role that reporting multiple grades has in successful grading reform. Finally, we consider how teachers can provide multiple grades without adding to their reporting workload in ways that enhance the meaning of grades, improve communication with parents and families, and direct efforts to improve students' performance.

The Inadequacy of a Single Grade

Every marking period, teachers gather evidence on students' performance from many different sources in determining students' grades. Studies show that teachers use different procedures to combine or summarize that evidence to calculate students' grades (Cizek, Fitzgerald, & Rachor, 1996; McMillan, 2005, 2019; McMillan, Myran, & Workman, 2002). Some of the major sources of evidence teachers use include the following (Guskey & Bailey, 2010; Guskey & Link, 2017).

- Major exams
- Oral presentations
- Compositions
- Homework completion
- Formative assessments
- Homework quality
- Class quizzes
- Cooperative group projects
- Projects or reports
- Class participation
- Student portfolios
- Work habits and neatness
- Exhibits of student work
- Effort
- Laboratory projects
- Attendance
- Student notebooks or journals
- Punctuality of assignments
- Classroom observations
- Class behavior or attitude
- Daily classwork
- Progress made

As described in *On Your Mark* (Guskey, 2015), if asked *which* of these evidence sources they consider in determining student grades, some portion of teachers typically report using each one. If teachers are asked *how many* they include, however, their responses vary widely. Some teachers base grades on as few as two or three indicators, while others incorporate evidence from as many as eleven or twelve—and this is true even among teachers who teach at the same grade level in the same school. They enter scores from these various sources of evidence into a computerized grading program that calculates a single number or grade, which is then recorded on a report card.

Two reasons generally account for this tremendous variation among teachers. First is a lack of clarity about the purpose of grading. As chapter 4 (page 83) described, it is extremely difficult to make consistent decisions about what evidence to use in determining students' report card grades when we don't agree on the purpose of grading. Different sources of evidence vary in their appropriateness and validity depending on the identified purpose (Guskey & Link, 2019a).

A second reason for the variation is simply the format teachers use to report grades. Most computerized grading programs produce forms based on traditional grading models that only allow teachers to assign a single grade for each subject area or course. This forces teachers to distill all these diverse evidence sources into a single number or symbol, which results in what researchers refer to as a *hodgepodge grade* (Brookhart, 1991) that mixes achievement and other factors related to effort, behavior, attitude, and improvement. Even when teachers clarify the weighting strategies they use to combine these elements and they employ a common mathematical algorithm in tallying the scores, the final grade remains a confusing amalgamation that is impossible to interpret with any accuracy or clear meaning (Cross & Frary, 1999).

The simple truth is that a single number describing a student's performance in school is just as ineffectual and difficult to interpret as a single number describing someone's health or physical condition. That number or grade combines highly diverse data, gathered through different means, and measures a variety of different attributes. As such, it's not informative, meaningful, or helpful.

> "Mystification is simple; clarity is the hardest thing of all."
> —Julian Barnes

Types of Grading Criteria

Educators at all levels generally agree that grades should describe how well students have achieved the learning goals established for a grade level or course. In other words, they believe grades should reflect students' performance based on specific learning criteria. Both teachers and students favor this approach because they consider it both fair and equitable (Guskey, 2002a, 2002b, 2006a).

The varying sources of evidence that teachers use in determining students' grades, however, reflect different types of learning criteria. In most cases, we can classify these evidence sources into three broad categories: (1) product criteria, (2) progress criteria, and (3) process criteria.

Product Criteria

Product criteria reflect how well students have achieved specific cognitive learning goals, standards, or competencies. Teachers might determine product criteria through students' performance on major examinations, compositions, projects, reports, exhibits, or other culminating learning demonstrations. Product criteria describe students' academic achievements—that is, what they have learned and are able to do at a particular point in time as a result of their experiences in school. Advocates of standards-based or competency-based approaches to teaching and learning emphasize the importance of clear product criteria for grading purposes.

Progress Criteria

Progress criteria show how much students have gained or improved in their learning. Sometimes these are referred to as *growth*, *development*, or *value-added criteria*. Although related to product criteria, progress criteria are distinct. It would be possible, for example, for students to make outstanding progress but still not be achieving at grade level or meeting specific course academic goals. It also would be possible for highly skilled and talented students to show they have achieved the product criteria without making notable progress or improvement.

As noted in *On Your Mark* (Guskey, 2015), some educators draw distinctions between *progress*, which they measure backward from a final performance standard or goal, and *growth*, which they measure forward from the place a student begins on a learning continuum (Wiggins, 1996). When teachers clearly specify the criteria for student learning along that continuum, however, such distinctions do little to clarify what a student has accomplished and are unnecessary.

Process Criteria

Process criteria describe student behaviors that facilitate, broaden, or extend learning. These may be things that enable learning, such as formative assessments, homework, and class participation. They also may reflect extended learning goals related to noncognitive social and emotional learning skills such as collaboration, responsibility, goal setting, perseverance, habits of mind, or social skills. In some cases, process criteria relate to students' compliance with class procedures, like turning in assignments on time or not interrupting during class discussions.

Educators who emphasize process criteria believe that product criteria alone do not provide a sufficiently complete picture of students' performance. They believe that grades should reflect not only final achievement results but also *how* students got there. Others stress that certain noncognitive skills may be just as important to student success in school and in life as their academic achievement will be. Teachers need to consider these skills in grading, therefore, so students and families recognize these skills' value and worth. Reporting on noncognitive skills is addressed in chapter 6 (page 143).

Advantages of Multiple Grades

Because of concerns about student motivation, student self-esteem, and the social consequences of grades, few teachers use only product criteria in determining grades. Instead, most routinely base their grading procedures on some combination of all three types of evidence (Gullickson, 1985; Liu, 2008; Sun & Cheng, 2013). Many also vary their grading criteria from student to student, taking into account individual circumstances (Duncan & Noonan, 2007). Although teachers defend this practice on the basis of fairness, it seriously blurs the meaning of any grade. A grade of A, for example, might mean that the student knew all the material before instruction began (product), did not achieve the grade-level or course learning goals but made significant improvement (progress), or simply tried very hard and put forth extraordinary effort (process).

Recognizing these interpretation problems, most researchers and measurement specialists recommend the exclusive use of product criteria in determining students' grades. They point out that the more progress and process criteria come into play, the more subjective and biased grades become (Randall & Engelhard, 2010). How can a teacher know, for example, how difficult a task was for students or how hard they worked to complete it?

Many teachers point out, however, that if they use only product criteria in determining grades, some high-ability students will receive high grades with little effort, while the hard work of less-talented students will go unacknowledged. Consider, for example, two students enrolled in the same physical education class. The first is a well-coordinated athlete who can easily perform any task the teacher asks (Guskey, 2006b). However, this student puts forth little effort and displays unsportsmanlike conduct. The second student is currently struggling with a weight problem but consistently tries hard, exerts exceptional effort, and also displays outstanding sportsmanship and cooperation. Nevertheless, this student cannot perform tasks at the same level as the athlete. Few teachers would consider it fair to use only product criteria in determining the grades of these two students.

Teachers also emphasize that if they only consider product criteria, low-ability and disadvantaged students—the students who must work hardest—have the least incentive to do so. These students find the relationship between high effort and low grades frustrating and often express their frustration with indifference, deception, or disruption (Guskey, 2006b). For this reason, the use of nonacademic factors in determining students' grades appears prevalent in every subject area and at all grade levels. A survey of secondary music teachers, for example, revealed that their grades contained an average of 60 percent given to nonacademic factors like attendance, attitude, and students' self-reported practice time (Russell & Austin, 2010).

Although these types of learning criteria vary in their importance depending on the subject area and grade level, all three are essential to school success. Meaningful communication about students' school performance, however, requires that teachers *report these criteria separately*. In other words, students must receive different grades for whatever product, progress, and process criteria teachers consider most important in their learning.

The Challenge for Secondary Educators

Advocates of standards-based or competency-based approaches to teaching and learning often find that secondary teachers are more reluctant than elementary teachers to implement major changes in grading policies and practices. Some attribute this to general differences in teacher dispositions or experience (Snyder, 2017; Zimmerman, 2006). But as discussed in chapter 2 (page 35), a more likely explanation lies in the challenges involved in implementation due to context, especially with regard to curriculum differentiation.

Basically all students in second grade are learning the same things. The curriculum and learning goals for students at the second-grade level all tend to be quite similar. This means that second-grade teachers can collaborate on most tasks involved in implementing standards-based or competency-based reforms and then share resources, materials, and strategies.

But the same is not true of high school sophomores or their teachers. Middle school and high school standards are developed and clarified not by grade level but by individual classes or courses. This can compound the work of secondary teachers in curriculum development, instructional planning, assessment design, and grading and reporting. The unique responsibilities of secondary teachers simply make collaborative planning and development more difficult.

Ironically, reporting multiple grades for product and process criteria in particular does not require a lot of extra work for teachers at any level. In fact, in many instances, it requires less work. All teachers gather evidence on these different criteria and record the data separately in their gradebooks. They keep detailed records of students' scores on various achievement measures, as well as students' formative assessment results, homework completion, class participation, collaboration in teamwork, and so on. When teachers report separate grades for these different aspects of learning, they avoid the dilemmas involved in determining how much weight to give each in calculating a single grade.

Reporting multiple grades on the report card *and* on the transcript further emphasizes to students that these different aspects of their performance are *all* important. Teachers indicate that students actually take process elements like homework more seriously when they receive a separate grade for homework (Guskey, Swan, & Jung, 2011b).

Parents and families benefit from the reporting of multiple grades because the report card now provides a more detailed and comprehensive picture of their child's performance in school. In addition, because product grades are no longer tainted by evidence of student behavior or compliance, they more closely align with content mastery and external achievement measures, such as Advanced Placement (AP) or International Baccalaureate (IB) exam results and SAT or ACT scores—a quality that college and university admissions officers have been shown to favor (Buckmiller & Peters, 2018; Welsh, 2019).

A Necessary Prerequisite

Reporting multiple grades doesn't just improve the value and meaningfulness of report cards; experience indicates it may also be a necessary first step to the successful implementation of standards-based or competency-based reforms, especially at the secondary level. Simply providing separate grades for product and process criteria can yield significant advantages without requiring a great deal of extra work from teachers.

During the initial implementation stages, teachers in many middle and high schools continue to record only a single grade for academic achievement (product) in each subject area or course on the report card (Yaffe, 2017). This grade may be a letter, a number, or another label used to designate different levels of student performance. In other words, at the outset, teachers *don't* provide separate grades for different academic learning standards or goals within a subject area or course. They simply pull out the nonachievement or noncognitive elements from that achievement grade and report those separately.

Teachers must take steps to ensure the evidence they use to determine achievement grades comes from defensible measures of what students have learned and are able to do, of course. But evidence on other important noncognitive aspects of students' performance is tallied and reported separately. Figure 5.1 (page 126) shows an example of a high school report card that does this, adapted from a reporting form used in a school district in Canada.

Ms. Angelou—Language Arts					
	Achievement	Participation	Homework	Punctuality	Effort
	A	4	2	3	3
Teacher Photograph	This quarter we focused on poetry and different poetic forms. Students read both well-known and lesser-known poets and constructed their own poems. Chris actively participated in class discussions and wrote several excellent poems but needs to be more conscientious about completing homework assignments on time.				

Mr. Mori—Algebra II					
	Achievement	Participation	Homework	Punctuality	Effort
	B	3	1	3	3
Teacher Photograph	Our class worked on solving complex problems using higher-order equations. We also explored problem applications in physics. Chris did fairly well on class quizzes and assessments, and I am sure Chris would have done better if he had completed homework exercises.				

Ms. Roosevelt—Western Civilization					
	Achievement	Participation	Homework	Punctuality	Effort
	A	4	3	4	4
Teacher Photograph	We explored the influence of the Roman Empire on modern society, especially in language and government. Students also worked in teams to develop cooperative projects related to various aspects of Roman society. Chris was an active participant in all class activities, demonstrated a deep understanding of all issues, and was a valued contributor on the project.				

Mr. Einstein—Physics					
	Achievement	Participation	Homework	Punctuality	Effort
	B	2	2	3	3
Teacher Photograph	This quarter we concentrated on the physics of atomic and subatomic particles. Students solved problems related to relativity. Chris did well on most classroom quizzes and large assessments but needs to become a more active participant in class discussions.				

Source: Guskey & Bailey, 2010, p. 152. Used with permission.

Figure 5.1: Example high school report card with multiple grades.

Note that this report card would *not* be considered a true standards-based or competency-based report card. The teachers report no grades for individual learning standards within each course. In addition, in this district's case, no policies direct teachers on how to determine the achievement (product) grade. Teachers may use whatever evidence sources they believe best reflect students' academic achievement and align with the stated purpose of the grade. The teachers just pull evidence on the selected noncognitive (process) elements of participation, homework, punctuality, and effort out of the achievement grade and report those separately on the report card. The same multiple grades are then summarized and reported on the transcript.

After teachers become accustomed to reporting multiple grades, they generally find it much easier to transition to standards-based or competency-based reporting formats. They recognize how they can break down the overall achievement grade to report separately the strands or domains of standards that it summarizes. This transition is seen as a natural progression in their efforts to provide a more accurate and meaningful summary of students' performance.

The biggest challenge for teachers and school leaders in reporting multiple grades rests in determining which particular product, progress, and process criteria to report. This requires deep thinking about the learning criteria most important to students' success in school and beyond. From a practical perspective, it also involves finding an acceptable balance in providing enough detail to be meaningful but not so exhaustive that it creates a bookkeeping burden for teachers.

> *"Clarity precedes success."*
>
> —Robin Sharma

In the remainder of this chapter, we will explore aspects of reporting the cognitive outcomes related to product and progress criteria. In the next chapter (page 143), we turn our attention to important noncognitive outcomes and process criteria. For each type of criteria, we will consider the challenges involved in developing clear rubrics that describe the criteria in ways that make expectations for students' performance clear and unambiguous. We will also describe what has been learned about this process from the mistakes made in some districts and schools and how we can proceed in ways that make sense to different stakeholders in order to ensure success.

Product Criteria

Educators can easily find numerous examples of standards-based or competency-based report cards. The book *Developing Standards-Based Report Cards* (Guskey & Bailey, 2010) includes more than a dozen excellent examples. A quick internet search will yield many more. Because of the ready availability of these forms, there seems no reason to include additional examples here. Instead, we will focus on what we've learned through their implementation.

The school leaders and teachers who have used these forms have uncovered a great deal about what works—and, in some cases, what doesn't. As described in chapter 1 (page 17), many have discovered that the logic and intuition that guided their initial implementation efforts turned out to be wrong, despite assurances from consultants. Nevertheless, their struggles, mistakes, and occasional failures provide important insights, especially about how to proceed and the missteps to avoid.

Four aspects of implementation related to product criteria, especially in the context of standards-based or competency-based reforms, appear particularly significant and, in many cases, vital to success. These include the following.

1. Limit the number of reporting standards on the report card.

2. Move from end-of-year standards to grading-period benchmarks.

3. Recognize that labels matter.

4. Begin with a model of excellence.

Limit the Number of Reporting Standards on the Report Card

In their initial implementation efforts, many districts and schools try to replicate the gradebook on the report card. In other words, they record grades on the report card for *every* standard. At the elementary level, for example, standards-based report cards often require teachers to record grades for as many as twenty standards in language arts and a comparable number in mathematics. The educators who developed these report cards believed they were offering important and necessary detail. But more often than not, these incredibly detailed report cards prove far too complicated. They overwhelm parents and families with information they don't understand and don't know how to use. After looking over the report card, parents inevitably turn to the teacher and ask, "This is great, but how's my kid doing?" (Guskey, 2002a). In addition, these minutely detailed report cards create bookkeeping nightmares for teachers.

Taking a different approach to implementation, several school districts in Kentucky and Indiana began their grading reform efforts by surveying parents and families about the nature of reporting (Guskey, Swan, & Jung, 2011a, 2011b; Link, 2018b). One survey question specifically asked parents about the number of components or skill areas within each subject area or course that they would find useful to see reported. In other words, in how many ways would it be helpful to break down language arts? Mathematics? Social studies? Biology? Music? Parents' and family members' answers were strikingly consistent; most indicated no more than *four to six*.

This means report cards should *not* list twenty or more learning standards in a subject area or course. Parents and families already have this information in the gradebook, and there is no need to repeat it on the report card. Instead, report cards should *summarize* the gradebook data by reporting on students' learning in *strands* or *domains* of standards within a subject area or course. And in each subject area or course, teachers must report no more than four to six strands or domains for product learning criteria.

As described in chapter 4 (page 83), teachers can, for example, break down students' performance in language arts into separate strands for reading, writing, listening, speaking, and language skills (specifically, grammar, punctuation, spelling, and so on). Parents and family members who want additional information about the specific standards within each strand that the teacher emphasized during the marking period need simply consult the gradebook.

A particular advantage of using strands or domains for reporting at the elementary level is that teachers can use the same report card for all grade levels. Although individual standards in each subject area change with every grade level, the strands or domains remain the same. Therefore, the same report card can be used in kindergarten and first, second, third, fourth, and fifth grades (Guskey et al., 2011a).

Another advantage of reporting on strands or domains is that, in most instances, teachers don't have to create these strands or domains. The professional organizations of teachers in every subject area have created standards for student performance and grouped these standards into strands or domains. These organizations include, for example, the National Council of Teachers of Mathematics (www.nctm.org/ccssm), the National Council for the Social Studies (www.socialstudies.org /standards/introduction), the Next Generation Science Standards (www.nextgenscience.org), and the National Coalition for Core Arts Standards (www.nationalartsstandards.org). The structure these organizations use for grouping standards typically provides an excellent framework for reporting.

> "A lack of clarity could put the brakes on any journey to success."
>
> —Steve Maraboli

To guarantee effective communication, it is best to express these strands or domains in parent-friendly language. In some cases, however, this can prove challenging. Algebra teachers, for example, find it difficult to come up with a parent-friendly synonym for a word like *polynomial*. Still, whenever possible, it's preferable to adapt the language so parents and family members can easily understand it. The key is to limit the number of reporting strands or domains for product learning criteria to no more than four to six in each subject area or course.

Move From End-of-Year Standards to Grading-Period Benchmarks

When the standards movement began in the early 2000s, standards for students' performance were established for grade levels in elementary school and for courses in secondary school. These standards articulated what students should know and be able to do at the completion of a particular grade level or course. Standards-based reporting forms similarly described students' achievement of these end-of-grade-level or end-of-course learning goals. If things went well, all students would demonstrate mastery of the grade-level or course standards, and report cards distributed to parents and families at the end of the year would include all high grades.

The problem was that report cards weren't distributed just at the end of the year. Instead, they were distributed at the end of each marking period or quarter. At the end of the first quarter, students are just starting on their learning trajectory toward mastery of the standards, and their grades reflect that—typically 1s or 2s on a four-level scale. Although this made sense to the teachers who assigned the grades, it did not make sense to parents and families. To them, those 1s and 2s reflected low grades and were cause for concern. They saw the grades as a sign that their child was struggling and in need of extra assistance.

Although teachers tried to explain that they expected 1s and 2s at that time of the year, parents and families remained unconvinced that these marks did not indicate learning problems. If their child was behind or having difficulty, how would the teacher communicate that other than by assigning a low grade?

To resolve this problem, many districts and schools set *grading-period benchmarks*. In other words, they establish specific student performance expectations for each grading period, documenting progress toward the end-of-grade-level or end-of-course standards. Therefore, grades on the report card for the first grading period reflect how well students have performed based on expectations for their performance *at this time* in the school year. Thus, students receive high grades at the end of the first grading period if they have performed well based on expectations set for that grading period. If their performance falters based on expectations for the second grading period, their grades may go down.

Because this is similar to the way teachers determined grades when most parents and family members were in school, where learning expectations changed with each grading period, this eases the transition to a strictly standards-based or competency-based approach. It also greatly diminishes parents' and families' concerns about wanting to quickly know when their child is struggling or experiencing learning difficulties.

Recognize That Labels Matter

Educators implementing standards-based or competency-based approaches to grading and reporting often struggle with how to label the different levels of student performance. Although the number of performance levels varies, four levels seems most common. Educators in the United States and Canada generally consider three levels insufficient in discriminating important differences in student performance. When the number of levels climbs to five or six, however, the consistency of teachers' rating rapidly diminishes.

In choosing labels for these levels, many educators begin by describing level 3 as *proficient.* This performance level means the student has achieved the learning target and mastered the standard. Level 2 is typically considered *progressing* or *approaching mastery* of the standard, and level 1 is deemed *struggling* or *needs improvement.* The challenge comes in labeling the highest level, level 4.

Some educators believe that level 4 should designate a truly exceptional level of achievement—performance that knocks the teacher's socks off or prompts a "Wow!" reaction from the teacher. They use this level to recognize students who do something special related to the standard or demonstrate genuinely outstanding performance regarding the standard.

Others believe level 4 should describe performance at a more complex or more advanced level with regard to the standard (Marzano, 2017). They use the label *exceeds standard* to indicate the student has gone beyond or above what teachers expected. In other words, these students have achieved at a higher and more sophisticated level. But, while this label seems reasonable, serious communication problems often arise when educators try to clarify the meaning of *exceeds standard* to students, parents, families, or fellow educators.

Unfortunately, many parents and families find the label *exceeds standard* vague and difficult to interpret. The message it implies to them from educators is, "It's more than we expect, but we cannot tell you precisely what that is until we see it!" Such imprecision troubles parents and families, especially those who encourage their children to strive for the highest grade possible in every subject (Guskey, 2014b). In situations in which teachers rarely assign this highest-level grade, parents refer to it as the *unicorn grade*—something you believe exists but you've never really seen (St. George, 2017).

From a practical perspective, *exceeds standard* presents additional difficulties. In most standards-based environments, mastering a standard means hitting the target. It signifies achieving the goal and learning at the expected level. Olympic archers who place their arrows in the center of the bull's-eye from a distance of seventy meters, for example, have hit the target. They have achieved the goal and accomplished precisely what was expected. How, then, could an Olympic archer ever *exceed* the standard? How would the archer achieve at a higher or more advanced level?

"More important than the quest for certainty is the quest for clarity."

—François Gautier

Maybe we could make the bull's-eye smaller or move the target farther away from the archer, making it more difficult to hit the bull's-eye.

The problem with that, however, is it *changes the standard*. As soon as you make the task more difficult or move the learning expectation to a higher and more advanced level, you have changed the standard and altered the goal. Students who achieve at that level have not really exceeded the standard. More accurately, they have mastered a different standard. If you want archers to hit smaller bull's-eyes from a greater distance, then that becomes the new standard for archers.

Some argue that *proficient* can imply placing arrows near the bull's-eye while *exceeds standard* means hitting the bull's-eye directly. But does *proficient* then mean *almost* hitting the target? Does getting close suffice? And if it does, then how close is good enough? Who makes that decision?

This interpretation problem also affects educators who want to equate these distinctions to percentages correct on assessments. For example, on an assessment designed to measure students' ability to solve single-digit addition problems, teachers might designate students who get 80 percent correct as *proficient*, while they rate students who answer 90 percent or more correct as *exceeds standard*. But do students who get 90 percent correct truly exceed the standard if all the problems they answer correctly involve single-digit addition?

Some counter that the assessment for this standard should include double-digit addition problems as well. Students who answer the double-digit problems correctly can then accurately be rated as *exceeds standard*. But again, this miscommunicates what is measured. With the inclusion of double-digit addition problems, the assessment now clearly measures a different standard. The same holds true if *proficient* requires students to apply or transfer what they have learned, while *exceeds standard* involves the higher-level skills of analyzing or synthesizing. The point is that you are now measuring a different standard.

The nature of specific standards makes things even more complicated. If a standard related to students' ability to safely cross a busy street, for example, would anyone consider 80 percent—or even 90 percent—to be proficient? What about a standard for being honest or telling the truth? If a student tells the truth 80 percent of the time, is the student proficient at truth telling? And in these examples, how could students ever *exceed* the standard?

This does not imply that exceptional performance should go unrecognized. A grade that denotes truly distinguished performance can be useful in many instances. But if such a grade is included in the grading system, then it must be associated with clear criteria that identify precisely how students can attain that grade. Those criteria must be clearly communicated to students and parents alike, accompanied by illustrative examples of student performance or samples of student work and agreed upon by fellow teachers.

With these criteria articulated and openly communicated to all stakeholders, labels such as *distinguished*, *exceptional*, or *exemplary* generally serve intended communication purposes far better than *exceeds standard* (Guskey, 2014b).

Begin With a Model of Excellence

For decades, educators have used rubrics to describe different levels of student performance. Although we don't know the exact origin of rubrics, their theoretical roots could be traced to the seminal work of Benjamin Bloom and his colleagues in developing the *Taxonomy of Educational Objectives* (Bloom, 1956; Krathwohl, Bloom, & Masia, 1964).

Interest in rubrics surged during the 1990s as educators turned their focus to documenting student achievement of specific learning standards. Today, rubrics for describing and assessing student performance can be found at every level of education from preschool and kindergarten to graduate and professional school. They are especially important in distinguishing different categories of students' performance when determining grades.

Rubrics give direction to instructional activities and bring precision to assessments of student learning. They identify the criteria by which teachers judge student performance and describe graduated levels of quality associated with those criteria to recognize student progress. In recent years, however, educators have come under fire for the way they develop rubrics and especially how they translate rubric scores to grades. Although many believe the problem lies with grades, closer analysis reveals the real problem lies in the way educators have traditionally developed rubrics.

As the previous section described, most educators begin developing rubrics by articulating what students must do to meet a particular learning standard or goal, or to be proficient. From there, they identify two or three levels below proficient to describe students' progress and a level above to recognize exceptional performance or higher or more complex learning. This approach generally works well in elementary grades, where higher or more complex learning usually means *above grade level* or *at the next higher grade level*.

Problems arise, however, when application extends to the secondary level, where students and parents have concerns about grades, GPAs, transcripts, and college admissions (Field, 2019). The question many high school students and their parents ask is not, "How do I meet the standard?" or "What makes my work proficient?" Instead, they want to know, "What must I do to reach the highest level possible?" Because in most secondary schools that highest level translates to a letter grade, the real question becomes, "What do I need to do to get an A?"

Some educators believe they can solve this problem by getting rid of letter grades. But letter grades are simply one of a variety of ways to label different categories of student performance. As long as those categories are ordered, whether the labels are letters, numerals, words, or symbols makes little difference.

Other educators try to change students' and parents' attitudes about grades, exhorting them to focus more on learning and less on the grades. But such efforts rarely succeed (Rado, 2016). As described in chapter 3 (page 61), attitudes are shaped by experience, and most students' and parents' experiences tell them that grades are important. In addition, students and parents look ahead to the college application process, where, despite recent trends to consider a broader range of student data in granting admission and scholarships, grades still count (National Association for College Admission Counseling, 2019).

Furthermore, as discussed earlier, many parents urge their children to strive for the highest level of achievement possible. They may accept the teacher's explanation that the highest level is reserved for truly exceptional performance—that is, work that goes above and beyond the standard. Nevertheless, they want their child to achieve that level, especially if teachers tie levels to grades. For these parents, being *proficient* is not sufficient. They want their child to make every effort to reach whatever level the teacher defines as highest.

> "When the meaning is unclear, there is no meaning."
> —Marty Rubin

To solve this problem, educators are changing the way they develop rubrics. Specifically, they are returning to the approach Benjamin Bloom (1968, 1971) recommended when he outlined the process of *mastery learning* (Guskey, 2007b).

Nearly all teachers evaluate student performance and assign grades or marks on the basis of those evaluations. Bloom recognized that if the grades or marks are criterion based—that is, based on what students have learned and are able to do, rather than on students' relative standing among classmates—then teachers have already identified *mastery*. Mastery is the level of performance established for the highest grade possible, typically a grade of A. So rather than press teachers to define *mastery* anew, Bloom simply asked them, "What do you expect from students who receive a grade of A?" That performance level then becomes the learning expectation for all.

As Bloom (1968) described in his classic article, "Learning for Mastery":

> We are expressing the view that, given sufficient time and appropriate types of help, 95% of students . . . can learn a subject up to a high level of mastery. We are convinced that the grade of "A" as an index of mastery of a subject can, under appropriate conditions, be achieved by up to 95% of the students in a class. (p. 4)

So instead of developing rubrics by starting in the middle and working up and down, educators today are beginning at the top by describing excellent performance. In other words, *they start by clearly articulating the top performance level and then work down*. If the highest level represents learning at a higher and more complex level than the standard, then they clearly identify what that is. They begin by addressing questions such as, What does the highest performance level look like? What kind of evidence demonstrates it? and How will the teacher recognize it? If some students and parents want to make that level their standard, that's fine. And if *proficient* is below that highest level, that's fine too.

Debates about what level of student performance represents excellence and true mastery are useful and necessary. But it's important to recognize these decisions are matters of choice and involve value judgments on the part of educators when it comes to developing rubrics. Students' and parents' frustrations rarely come from the rigor of educators' expectations for student performance. Instead, they come from a lack of clarity regarding those expectations and a lack of appropriate support to help students meet those expectations.

At all levels of education, we must be specific about what it means to achieve at the highest level. We must clearly define the criteria we use to describe that level of learning and share those criteria with students, parents, colleagues, and school leaders. We must explicitly identify what types of evidence reflect that level of achievement and how we will evaluate that evidence. Most important, we need to determine what we can do to help *all* students achieve that level (Guskey, 2017b).

Progress Criteria

Like product criteria, progress criteria describe students' cognitive or academic achievement. But instead of depicting academic *status*—that is, what students have learned and are able to do at this point in time—progress criteria describe academic *improvement*. They explain how much students have gained, grown, or developed over a particular period of time. Simply put, student progress shows how much academic improvement or growth students have made between two points in time. This could occur, for example, during an instructional unit, over a grading period or term, from the start of the year to the end of the year, or even from one school year to the next. As mentioned earlier, progress criteria are sometimes referred to as *value-added criteria*, indicating what has been added to students' knowledge or skill development during a specified period of time.

Progress Monitoring

Some of the most significant work and most relevant research on progress criteria come from efforts to document students' academic development and growth through *progress monitoring* (Fuchs & Fuchs, 2001; Jung, 2015). Educational researchers Lynn Fuchs and Douglas Fuchs (2001) define *progress monitoring* as:

> When teachers assess students' academic performance on a regular basis (weekly or monthly) for two purposes: to determine whether children are profiting appropriately from the typical instructional program and to build more effective programs for the children who benefit inadequately from typical instruction.

Because what is determined to be adequate or appropriate progress can vary from student to student depending on entry-level skills, learning history, and academic needs, progress monitoring is typically highly individualized. To accurately monitor students' academic progress, three specific elements must be in place.

1. **A clearly articulated curriculum or learning pathway for documenting progress:** Such a curriculum sets forth a well-defined, developmentally appropriate learning continuum of content and skills along which students' performance can be tracked. In some contexts, this continuum is labeled a *learning progression* (Shepard, 2018). The continuum purposefully sequences teaching and learning expectations or standards across multiple developmental stages, ages, or grade levels.

2. **Accurate and reliable assessments:** Quite simply, this means teachers must have accurate and reliable measures of students' level of achievement or cognitive development in relation to the curriculum or progression. These standardized formative assessments—referred to as *curriculum-based measurement* (Stecker, Fuchs, & Fuchs, 2005)—allow teachers to analyze students' skill level, provide students with accurate and timely feedback, identify students in need of additional or different forms of instruction, and then form appropriate instructional modifications when needed. *Standardized* simply means the procedures for creating the

assessments, administering and scoring the assessments, and summarizing and interpreting results are prescribed. By standardizing these methods and relating results to an established sequence of learning goals, curriculum-based measures produce a broad range of scores across students of the same age or at the same grade level.

In addition, educators must design curriculum-based measures to tap a sufficiently wide range of knowledge and skills so they ensure accurate measures of student progress and improvement. Because all assessments measure a finite set of concepts and abilities, some have *ceiling effects*—high scores that students can't exceed due to the restricted range of the knowledge and skills measured. Students who score at this level demonstrate they have mastered the curriculum goals but may, in fact, have learned even more. This would be especially true of those talented, fast learners who regularly engage in enrichment or extension activities as part of a mastery learning approach (Guskey & Jung, 2011).

If the curriculum-based measures do not tap more advanced skills, these students may consistently score at the top level and appear not to have made any progress. When documenting the progress of such highly talented students, educators must extend curriculum-based measures to include these more advanced skills.

3. **Thoughtful judgments about the adequacy or sufficiency of particular students' progress:** Often, this element entails comparing students' progress with that of their peers in the classroom, school, district, or country. Because students build knowledge and develop skills at different rates, sometimes experiencing bursts of development as well as areas of extended academic challenge, such comparisons help teachers ensure that students receive the equitable and comprehensive preparation they need to succeed in school and beyond (Moran, 2014).

Growth and Development

Effectively monitoring, assessing, and reporting on student learning progress can be challenging. Developing the curriculum or learning progression, finding or creating valid assessments, and then judging the adequacy of students' learning progress requires time and precise work from teachers. Simply helping parents and families understand the difference between reporting on *status* and reporting on *improvement* can be difficult. Making this distinction is especially important for those with children who may have identified learning disabilities and qualify for special education services.

The parents and families of children with special needs must know the specific learning standards or goals on which their children are working and the progress they are making (Gersten, Vaughn, & Brengelman, 1996; Jung & Guskey, 2007). And they also need to know how those learning standards or goals align with grade-level or course expectations. For this reason, reporting both progress *and* product criteria to these parents and families can be especially helpful.

However, teachers must do this in sensitive and meaningful ways. It does little good, for example, to say to these parents and families, "Your child is making progress but isn't working at grade level." Such information isn't helpful or informative. In addition, it simply confirms what they already know. Instead, teachers must be prepared to explain, "These are the things your child is working on, this is the progress she's made, and here is our plan to help her get to grade-level work on this standard."

Applications

Teachers report on progress criteria related to academic or cognitive learning goals primarily at the elementary level. This is because most elementary curriculums, especially in language arts and mathematics, are developmentally structured to describe expectations for student learning in kindergarten through fifth or sixth grade.

Beginning in middle school and extending through high school, curriculum learning goals or standards become less developmentally oriented and more course based. In other words, all students enrolled in the course have the same learning goals or standards, regardless of students' entry-level skills. Therefore, reporting on students' academic or cognitive achievement at this level tends to focus exclusively on product criteria. Although documenting middle school and high school students' progress can still be informative and have important meaning (Esty & Teppo, 1992), in most cases, this occurs only for students who qualify for special services and have individualized education programs (IEPs).

Summary

Grading and reporting are much more of a challenge in effective communication than simply a task of quantifying data on students' performance. Providing multiple grades that reflect product, progress, and process criteria enhances the meaning and accuracy of that communication. Without significantly adding to teachers' workload, this simple strategy of giving multiple grades can do much to improve the effectiveness of grading and reporting. It provides more meaningful information, facilitates communication between school and home, and offers specific direction in efforts to improve student learning.

Teachers typically use product and progress criteria to describe student achievement of cognitive or academic learning goals. They use product criteria to depict students' current academic status—that is, what students have learned and are able to do at this point in time. Progress criteria, on the other hand, describe how much students have gained, grown, or developed academically over a particular period. While product and progress criteria are both important, they reflect different learning outcomes. The next chapter turns to process criteria and how teachers can use progress criteria to report students' achievement of noncognitive or behavioral learning goals.

CHAPTER 6

Report Multiple Grades: Noncognitive Outcomes

Educating the mind without educating the heart is no education at all.

—Aristotle

The major purpose of schools has always been to help students gain essential knowledge and develop important cognitive skills such as problem solving and critical thinking. School curriculums describe these academic competencies and set forth the specific knowledge and abilities we, as educators, want students to acquire. Students who learn these academic things well and succeed in school are referred to as *book smart*.

But there are other things we hope students will gain as a result of their experiences in school in addition to being *book smart*. These other competencies relate to the attitudes, dispositions, traits, and behaviors that are vital for students' success in school and in their lives beyond school. Students who develop such traits are referred to as *life smart*. Some researchers group these life-smart traits into *intra*personal skills, like persisting in achieving goals and being self-reflective, and *inter*personal skills, like communicating, showing empathy, and collaborating with others (Goodwin, 2018). As this chapter explores, however, there are several views on how best to classify these competencies.

The importance of these noncognitive, life-smart skills was reflected in a study of seven hundred American millionaires, which found their average college GPA was just 2.9 on a four-point scale (Stanley, 2001). In fact, this study showed there was no significant statistical correlation between economic productivity factors, such as net worth and income, and SAT scores, class rank, or grades in college. Obviously, something other than academic prowess accounted for their success.

A comprehensive study by Karen Arnold (1995) also exemplified the importance of noncognitive skills. Arnold followed the lives of eighty-one high school valedictorians for fourteen years after graduation to determine what "doing well in school" actually means. She found that most of the valedictorians achieved many traditional markers of success. Nearly all of them graduated from college, where their average GPA was 3.6. The majority went on to earn graduate degrees, and nearly half achieved top-tier professional jobs. But how many of these number-one high school performers went on to change the world, lead organizations, or become truly outstanding in their chosen field? The answer was clear: none.

Part of the reason for this, according to Arnold (1995), is that high schools typically reward conformity and willingness to go along with the system. In other words, these valedictorians found out exactly what their teachers wanted and consistently delivered it. The world's most influential thinkers and leaders, however, typically come up with unique solutions to social, political, or scientific issues. They go against the flow and challenge traditional thinking. Going along with what is already working moderately well never made anyone famous (Barker, 2017).

Historically, development of noncognitive, life-smart competencies has pretty much been left to chance. Although teachers have long considered noncognitive skills important in students' development and they sometimes address basic elements in preschool and the earliest elementary grades (Fulghum, 2003), these skills are rarely included in school curriculums, addressed directly in instructional activities, or measured in classroom assessments. The only place we find these skills frequently considered is among the factors teachers use in determining students' grades (Galla et al., 2019). Teachers at all grade levels generally believe that students should receive some "credit" in their grades for trying hard, showing persistence, or demonstrating responsibility (Bonner & Chen, 2019; Bowers, 2019; McMillan, 2019).

And herein lies the problem. Even though these noncognitive competencies are typically absent from school curriculums, not explicitly taught, and seldom reliably measured, they often play an important role in the grades teachers assign to students and record on report cards (Guskey & Link, 2019a; Randall & Engelhard, 2010).

This chapter explores these noncognitive outcomes as they relate to the process criteria teachers use in determining students' grades. We will describe the relationship between noncognitive and cognitive outcomes and how the focus on life skills, 21st century skills, college and career readiness, and social and emotional learning has brought new attention to these outcomes and their important role in students' success in school and beyond. We discuss the mixed and contradictory research results on noncognitive competencies, consider an approach to noncognitive skill development that focuses on corrective consequences rather than punishments, and offer guidance for selecting noncognitive outcomes. Finally, we explore the specific skills advocated, the characteristics of rubrics that guide students' development of these skills, and procedures for reporting that development to students, parents, and families.

> "We must remember that intelligence is not enough. Intelligence plus character—that is the goal of true education."
> —Martin Luther King Jr.

The Relationship Between Noncognitive and Cognitive Outcomes

Educators often want to turn immediately to the challenges of reporting on the noncognitive outcomes associated with process criteria. But a series of crucial decisions needs to be made *before* considering how to report on these noncognitive learning goals. Specifically, educators must acknowledge the important relationship between noncognitive and cognitive outcomes but also recognize their conceptual distinctions.

Most educators—as well as most students, parents, school leaders, board members, and others—understand that cognitive and noncognitive learning goals are related. They know, for example, that students who put forth appropriate effort and persist in learning tasks generally attain higher classroom assessment scores and receive higher grades. Likewise, students who don't work hard or who give up easily tend to get lower assessment scores and lower grades. But although these things are related, traits such as effort and persistence are plainly different from academic achievement. And because they are conceptually different, teachers need to report them separately. Combining effort, persistence, and achievement into a single grade makes little sense and leads to misinterpretation.

Another way to think of this would be to consider the relationship between height and weight. Persons who are taller tend to weigh more, and shorter persons generally weigh less. Measures of height and weight are clearly related. But combining measures of height and weight into a single score or grade would distort any meaningful interpretation. It would result in a tall, thin person receiving the same score or grade as a short, stocky person. Because they received the same combined score, we might think these two persons are the same, but separate measures of their height and weight would reveal they are quite different.

Determining students' grades by combining measures of noncognitive goals with measures of cognitive goals is similarly misleading. It doesn't make sense to give the same grade to a persevering low achiever and a procrastinating high achiever. Doing so disregards the primary communication purpose of grades. As chapter 5 (page 117) stressed, to clearly communicate students' performance in school and report on these various criteria, we must provide multiple indicators and different grades in a dashboard of information. A combined hodgepodge grade clearly muddles any interpretation.

In addition, we must always keep in mind that being related does not imply causation. Although height and weight are related, gaining weight does not necessarily make you taller, nor does losing weight make you shorter. Similarly, persistence in learning tasks and higher levels of academic achievement are generally related. But does greater persistence lead to higher achievement, or is it improved achievement that prompts increased persistence? Perhaps the relationship is cyclical and actually both are true. Simply knowing that these two aspects of school performance are related gives us no clue about causation. All we do know for certain is that combining measures of persistence and academic achievement in a single grade misconstrues both.

Before worrying about how best to report on these process criteria, however, educators must decide what particular noncognitive outcomes or competencies are most important for students to learn. With these competencies identified, they then must determine what evidence best reflects students' attainment of the competencies and how to evaluate that evidence. After deciding on the most valid evidence, attention can turn to planning classroom learning experiences that help students develop these competencies, practice them, and gain prescriptive feedback on their performance to guide improvement when needed. Only after addressing these important *why* and *what* questions is it appropriate to consider *how* best to report students' attainment of the noncognitive learning outcomes to students, parents, and families. Reporting always comes last.

> *"It takes something more than intelligence to act intelligently."*
> —Fyodor Dostoyevsky

To determine how best to report on process criteria, we must complete several steps.

1. Decide on the specific noncognitive outcomes or competencies that are most important for students to learn.

2. Determine what evidence best reflects students' attainment of these competencies.

3. Plan classroom learning experiences that help students develop the competencies.

4. Provide students with prescriptive feedback on their performance of the competencies.

5. Report on students' attainment to students, parents, and families.

Process Criteria

Throughout the world, education reform initiatives have begun to emphasize noncognitive student learning outcomes related to process criteria. Although considerable overlap exists in the competencies and skills that different groups and organizations advocate, each framework contains unique elements. Among the better known of these frameworks are those associated with 21st century skills, college and career readiness skills, and social and emotional learning skills.

21st Century Skills Framework

A major effort to identify vital noncognitive skills was the *Partnership for 21st Century Skills*, now called the *Partnership for 21st Century Learning*, or simply *P21* (www.p21.org/our-work/p21-framework). Founded as a nonprofit organization in 2002 by a coalition of members of the business community, education leaders, and policymakers, the group identified 21st century skills that they stressed are important to their organizations now and will be even more important in the future. The learning and innovation skills they identified as most crucial are today known as the Four Cs. They include:

1. Creativity and innovation

2. Critical thinking and problem solving

3. Communication

4. Collaboration

In addition to the Four Cs, the partnership added what it considers essential Life and Career Skills, including:

1. Flexibility and adaptability

2. Initiative and self-direction

3. Social and cross-cultural skills

4. Productivity and accountability

5. Leadership and responsibility

P21 has released several reports describing how to integrate the Four Cs and the Life and Career Skills into K–12 learning environments.

College and Career Readiness Skills Framework

Although states, provinces, districts, and schools have long made preparing students for postsecondary education opportunities and productive careers a priority, the growing global economy and shifts in the labor market compel educators to look beyond academic preparation alone. They must also consider the attitudes, dispositions, and behaviors most needed for success in the middle- and high-skills jobs of the future.

A report by the College and Career Readiness and Success Center of the American Institutes for Research (AIR; Mishkind, 2014) provides a review of thirty-six states' and the District of Columbia's definitions of *college and career readiness*. This summary groups the knowledge, skills, and dispositions students will need into the following six actionable categories.

1. Academic knowledge

2. Critical thinking and/or problem solving

3. Social and emotional learning, collaboration, and/or communication

4. Grit/resilience/perseverance

5. Citizenship and/or community involvement

6. Other additional activities (for example, knowledge of technology, lifelong learning, and responsibility to environment and family)

The AIR report concludes that research on the noncognitive skills included in definitions of *readiness* "is still emerging and, in some instances, is controversial as we have yet to conclusively determine the impact that instruction and educational supports can have on the development of these lifelong learning skills" (Mishkind, 2014, p. 6). Nevertheless, it's clear that the world economy has changed and educational shifts are necessary if students are to compete in this new environment.

> *"As the world we live in is so unpredictable, the ability to learn and to adapt to change is imperative, alongside creativity, problem-solving, and communication skills."*
>
> —Alain Dehaze

Social and Emotional Learning Framework

In their book *Building Academic Success on Social and Emotional Learning: What Does the Research Say?* editors Joseph Zins, Roger Weissberg, Margaret Wang, and Herbert Walberg (2004) posit that social and emotional learning (SEL) plays an important role not only in influencing nonacademic outcomes but also in improving students' academic performance and lifelong learning. They define *SEL* as "the process through which children enhance their ability to integrate thinking, feeling, and behaving to achieve important life tasks" (Zins et al., 2004, p. 6). The framework of key SEL competencies that they present includes five major categories, each with specific subcategories:

1. Self-awareness

    i. Identifying and recognizing emotions

    ii. Accurate self-perception

    iii. Recognizing strengths, needs, and values

    iv. Self-efficacy

    v. Spiritualty

2. Social awareness

    i. Perspective taking

    ii. Empathy

    iii. Appreciating diversity

    iv. Respect for others

3. Responsible decision making

    i. Problem identification and situation analysis

    ii. Problem solving

    iii. Evaluation and reflection

    iv. Personal, moral, and ethical responsibility

4. Self-management

    i. Impulse control and stress management

    ii. Self-motivation and discipline

    iii. Goal setting and organizational skills

5. Relationship management

    i. Communication, social engagement, and building relationships

    ii. Working cooperatively

    iii. Negotiation, refusal, and conflict management

    iv. Help seeking and providing
    (Zins et al., 2004, p. 7)

According to Zins and his colleagues (2004), students competent in these skills have awareness of themselves and others, make responsible decisions, are ethical and respectful of others, consider situations and relevant norms, manage their emotions and behaviors, and possess behavioral social skills that enable them to effectively carry out solutions with others. This early research-based framework has become the basis of social and emotional learning programs throughout the world (Belfield et al., 2015).

More recent work has extended the definition of *SEL*. The Collaborative for Academic, Social, and Emotional Learning (CASEL, 2017), for example, defines it as "the process through which children and adults acquire and effectively apply the knowledge, attitudes, and skills necessary to understand and manage emotions, set and achieve positive goals, feel and show empathy for others, establish and maintain positive relationships, and make responsible decisions."

> *"A good head and good heart are always a formidable combination. But when you add to that a literate tongue or pen, then you have something very special."*
> —Nelson Mandela

In addition, strong research evidence shows that SEL can positively contribute to students' academic success, their ability to navigate challenges, and their skill in developing supportive networks that lead to improved school culture and relationships (Durlak, Weissberg, Dymnicki, Taylor, & Schellinger, 2011). Such evidence has led school systems and education organizations to integrate SEL into curriculums and instructional programs so they can help students develop life skills that will lead to their future success not only in school but also throughout their lives (Foster, 2017).

Other Organizational Frameworks

Two other frameworks that describe noncognitive student learning outcomes related to process criteria are particularly noteworthy: (1) the University of Chicago Consortium on School Research's framework and (2) an Integrated Framework. Both these frameworks focus on noncognitive competencies that influence students' performance in school and teachers frequently consider in determining students' grades.

University of Chicago Consortium on School Research Framework

A group of researchers at the University of Chicago's Consortium on School Research (Farrington et al., 2012; Nagaoka et al., 2013) examined evidence on noncognitive factors that are strongly linked to students' academic performance in school and that predict positive life outcomes. Based on a critical literature review, they identify specific factors that appear crucial in students' development at *all* ages and at *all* education levels. Their review also revealed that these factors are not fixed traits that students either do or do not have. Rather, they are shaped by the environment in which students learn. The noncognitive factors that the researchers identify as crucial to students' academic performance fall into five categories:

1. Academic behaviors
    i. Going to class
    ii. Doing homework
    iii. Organizing materials
    iv. Participating
    v. Studying
2. Perseverance
    i. Grit
    ii. Tenacity
    iii. Delayed gratification
    iv. Self-discipline
    v. Self-control
3. Mindsets
    i. A sense of belonging
    ii. Belief in one's ability to grow and succeed with effort
    iii. Belief in the value of academic work
4. Learning strategies
    i. Study skills
    ii. Metacognitive strategies

    iii. Self-regulated learning

    iv. Goal setting

5. Social skills

    i. Interpersonal skills

    ii. Empathy

    iii. Cooperation (Farrington et al., 2012)

Consortium researchers also analyzed evidence on the relationship between these noncognitive factors and students' academic performance as reflected in their grades. They found academic behaviors to have the strongest evidence of a direct relationship with grades, while social skills have the weakest. Evidence in the other categories was generally mixed, with effects varying depending on the quality of studies and the fidelity of implementation. The review also suggests some promising levers for classroom-level change and challenges the notion that hard work and effort are character traits of individual students. Instead, the researchers stress that the amount of effort a student puts into academic work can depend, in large part, on instructional and contextual factors in the classroom (Farrington et al., 2012).

> "Through my education, I didn't just develop skills, I didn't just develop the ability to learn, but I developed confidence."
>
> —Michelle Obama

Integrated Framework

Our work in synthesizing the extensive grading and reporting research conducted since the early 1900s (Brookhart et al., 2016; Guskey & Brookhart, 2019), combined with experiences in helping districts and schools implement grading reforms, led to development of an Integrated Framework for categorizing the noncognitive student learning outcomes related to process criteria. This framework is especially influenced by the work of Sarah Bonner and Peggy Chen (2019) and James McMillan (2019). It divides the process criteria into one academic/cognitive category and three noncognitive categories. The noncognitive skill categories include (1) learning enablers, (2) social and emotional learning, and (3) compliance behaviors.

Academic Skills (Cognitive)

The academic skills category consists of often-neglected cognitive learning goals that relate to higher-level academic competencies (Bloom, 1956). Although these academic skills would more accurately appear under product or progress criteria, they are included here to align with the previously described organizational frameworks. These skills include:

- Application/transference
- Communication
- Creativity/innovation
- Critical thinking/problem solving

Learning Enablers

The first of the three noncognitive categories, *learning enablers*, includes skills, dispositions, behaviors, or procedures that facilitate and enhance learning. Factors in this category include the following.

- Attitude in class
- Class attendance and participation
- Class quizzes or spot checks
- Daily classwork
- Effort
- Engagement
- Formative assessments
- Goal setting
- Homework (completion and quality)
- Notebook or journal completion
- Planning and organization
- Study skills
- Time management
- Work habits

These factors can take many forms and vary in their effectiveness depending on context and grade level. Evidence on these factors is not measures of learning per se, but rather the processes students use in order to learn. In some instances, these factors reflect students' actions (for example, class attendance and participation, effort, study skills, time management, and work habits). In other cases, they are the processes teachers use to offer feedback to students and guide them in their learning (for example, class quizzes, daily classwork, formative assessments, and homework).

Social and Emotional Learning

The second and most extensive noncognitive skill category includes noncognitive competencies related to aspects of *social and emotional learning*. These particular factors were derived from two sources. First is AIR's research on SEL described earlier (Mishkind, 2014). AIR researchers (Berg et al., 2017) have identified 136 frameworks and models that define such competencies. The competencies included here represent those that these frameworks and models most frequently note (Berg et al., 2017).

The second source of the skills in this noncognitive category involved an analysis of report cards. These noncognitive competencies related to SEL come from the attributes, behaviors, dispositions, and skills that report cards most commonly list where they report noncognitive outcomes separately from students' academic achievement grades. Examples of these report cards can be found in Guskey and Bailey (2010) and through internet sources that include images of standards-based or competency-based report cards. These noncognitive competencies related to social and emotional learning include the following.

- Citizenship and community involvement
- Collaboration and teamwork
- Compassion
- Cooperation with classmates
- Empathy and perspective taking
- Ethics
- Flexibility and adaptability
- Grit
- Growth mindset
- Habits of mind
- Help seeking and providing
- Initiative and self-direction
- Integrity
- Leadership
- Motivation
- Persistence and perseverance
- Reflection
- Resilience
- Respect
- Responsibility and accountability
- Self-advocacy

- Self-awareness
- Self-efficacy
- Self-discipline and motivation

- Self-regulation
- Social skills
- Tenacity
- Tolerance

Compliance Behaviors

The third noncognitive category consists of *compliance behaviors*. These actions or behaviors generally relate to how well students follow classroom rules or conduct themselves during class sessions. Teachers seldom use evidence related to these aspects of performance as a major factor in determining students' grades. More often, teachers consider these factors when students are on the cusp of two different grades to raise the grades of students who display compliance or to lower the grades of students who are ill behaved, irresponsible, or noncompliant (Randall & Engelhard, 2010). This category includes the following aspects of performance.

- Behavior in class
- Conduct
- Neatness of work
- Punctuality in turning in assignments
- Punctuality in arriving to class

> *"Some people think only intellect counts: knowing how to solve problems, knowing how to get by, knowing how to identify an advantage and seize it. But the functions of intellect are insufficient without courage, love, friendship, compassion, and empathy."*
>
> —Dean Koontz

Although these lists of learning enablers, SEL, and compliance behaviors are not totally comprehensive, they include the most frequently mentioned noncognitive student learning outcomes related to process criteria. Please keep in mind, however, that other equally important learning outcomes may be identified (for example, courage, courtesy, generosity, honor, kindness, and sympathy) and added to these lists.

Table 6.1 outlines these three frameworks and their associated skills.

Table 6.1: Four Noncognitive Learning Outcomes Frameworks and Associated Skills

Frameworks	Associated Skills
21st Century Skills	**Four Critical Learning and Innovation Skills (Four Cs)** 1. Creativity and innovation 2. Critical thinking and problem solving 3. Communication 4. Collaboration **Five Essential Life and Career Skills** 1. Flexibility and adaptability 2. Initiative and self-direction 3. Social and cross-cultural skills 4. Productivity and accountability 5. Leadership and responsibility *Source: Partnership for 21st Century Learning, n.d.*
College and Career Readiness	**Knowledge, Skills, and Dispositions** 1. Academic knowledge 2. Critical thinking and problem solving 3. Social and emotional learning, collaboration, and communication 4. Grit, resilience, and perseverance 5. Citizenship and community involvement 6. Other additional activities (for example, knowledge of technology, lifelong learning, and responsibility to environment and family) *Source: Mishkind, 2014.*
Social and Emotional Learning	**Five Competencies** 1. **Self-awareness:** Identifying and recognizing emotions; accurate self-perception; recognizing strengths, needs, and values; self-efficacy; spirituality 2. **Social awareness:** Perspective taking, empathy, appreciating diversity; respect for others 3. **Responsible decision making:** Problem identification and situation analysis; problem solving; evaluation and reflection; personal, moral, and ethical responsibility

continued →

Frameworks	Associated Skills
Social and Emotional Learning	4. **Self-management:** Impulse control and stress management, self-motivation and discipline, goal setting and organizational skills
	5. **Relationship management:** Communication, social engagement, and building relationships; working cooperatively; negotiation, refusal, and conflict management; help seeking and providing
	Source: Zins, Weissberg, Wang, & Walberg, 2004, p. 7.
Other Organizational Frameworks (University of Chicago Consortium on School Research)	1. **Academic behaviors:** Going to class, doing homework, organizing materials, participating, and studying
	2. **Perseverance:** Grit, tenacity, delayed gratification, self-discipline, and self-control
	3. **Mindsets:** Sense of belonging, belief in one's ability to grow and succeed with effort, belief in the value of academic work
	4. **Learning strategies:** Study skills, metacognitive strategies, self-regulated learning, goal setting
	5. **Social skills:** Interpersonal skills, empathy, cooperation
	Source: Farrington et al., 2012.
Other Organizational Frameworks (Integrated Model)	**Cognitive Skills (Academic):** Application and transference, communication, creativity or innovation, critical thinking or problem solving
	Noncognitive Skills: Learning enablers, social and emotional learning, compliance behaviors

Mixed and Contradictory Research Results

A few cautions should be noted before moving on to ways teachers can report students' performance on noncognitive outcomes related to process criteria. In a review of the research evidence on social and emotional learning, Bryan Goodwin (2018) refers to such cautions as "pesky caveats" (p. 78) that complicate our understanding of these important skills.

The noncognitive student outcomes associated with process criteria clearly have great intuitive appeal for educators at all levels. Every teacher has seen students struggle academically due to a lack of perseverance, dedication, or sufficient effort. Most have also experienced students who surpassed expectations because of their determination, persistence, and grit. Nevertheless, the results of studies on the precise nature of these noncognitive competencies and their importance to school success vary widely.

A RAND Corporation study of sixty SEL programs, for example, found that many programs yielded positive effects but mostly on non-cognitive outcomes such as self-esteem, self-concept, and growth mind-set. Relatively few studies (about 10 percent) showed a positive impact on academic outcomes (Grant et al., 2017). An earlier meta-analysis of 213 school-based SEL programs involving over 270,000 K–12 students found similarly modest effects on student achievement, equivalent to a gain of about 11 percentile points (Durlak et al., 2011). Programs that yielded the most positive results engaged students in intensive learning reflecting the acronym SAFE: the programs were *sequenced* with step-by-step approaches, included *active* learning, *focused* time and attention on skills development, and had clear, *explicit* learning objectives (Goodwin, 2018; Mahoney & Weissberg, 2018).

Reviews of instruments used to measure SEL skills reveal additional complications. Joshua Cox, Brandon Foster, and David Bamat (2019) reviewed the reliability and validity of sixteen instruments designed to measure three SEL skills among secondary school students: collaboration, perseverance, and self-regulated learning. They concluded that while these instruments offer teachers valuable formative information that can be useful in guiding students in the development of these skills, none should be used for summative purposes.

Other research reviews raise serious questions about the accuracy and usefulness of measures of some of the most popular noncognitive competencies. A review by Marcus Credé, Michael Tynan, and Peter Harms (2017), for example, suggests that many core claims about *grit* (Duckworth, 2017; Duckworth, Peterson, Matthews, & Kelly, 2007) either have been unexamined or are directly contradicted by the accumulated empirical evidence. Credé (2018) contends:

> Specifically, there appears to be no reason to accept the combination of perseverance and passion for long-term goals into a single grit construct, nor is there any support for the claim that grit is a particularly good predictor of success and performance in an educational setting or that grit is likely to be responsive to interventions. (p. 606)

> "Nothing in the world can take the place of persistence. Talent will not; nothing is more common than unsuccessful persons with talent. Genius will not; the world is full of educated derelicts. Persistence and determination alone are omnipotent."
>
> —Calvin Coolidge

The crucial point of these mixed results for the purpose of grading and reporting is that *grit* and other noncognitive competencies associated with process criteria are *different* from academic, cognitive competencies. Because noncognitive competencies describe attitudes, dispositions, traits, and behaviors that may relate to but are clearly *distinct* from evidence of students' academic achievement, clarity of meaning requires that teachers report these competencies separately on students' report cards, permanent records, and transcripts.

Consequences Rather Than Punishment

In their efforts to reform grading policies and practices, some teachers find students occasionally take the perspective, "If it's not part of the grade, then it doesn't count." This problem seems especially prevalent among teachers implementing standards-based or competency-based approaches to grading and reporting in the upper grades. It usually occurs when teachers identify the purpose of grading as "to describe what students have learned and are able to do at this time" and then no longer include results from formative assessments or homework assignments in determining students' academic achievement grades.

Students who believe their primary job in school is to earn high grades sometimes choose to ignore those things that don't count in determining their grades. Parents and families may struggle with this purpose as well because it differs so drastically from what they experienced in school, where *everything* they did in school counted as part of their grades.

Resolving this problem requires that teachers incorporate three essential procedures into grading policies at all grade levels. They should discuss these procedures with all stakeholders prior to implementation, again emphasizing *why* before *what*. In addition, *all* teachers need to consistently implement these procedures throughout the school. Uneven or inconsistent implementation will make the procedures seem capricious and potentially unfair. These three essential procedures are to:

1. Include evidence on noncognitive outcomes in the gradebook

2. Report noncognitive outcomes separately on report cards and transcripts

3. Attach specific corrective consequences to guide improvement

Include Evidence on Noncognitive Outcomes in the Gradebook

The gradebook should include evidence on *all* aspects of students' performance in school. Parents and families should know, for example, the purpose of formative assessments and how their children performed on these important feedback tools. They should know the purpose of every homework assignment and whether their children completed those assignments correctly and on time. Students, too, should have access to teachers' records of this crucial evidence on these learning enablers.

But as we described in chapter 4 (page 83), just because teachers record this evidence in the gradebook and give parents, families, and students access to this information, it doesn't mean it will used to determine students' academic achievement or product grades. Academic achievement grades reflect that grades' defined purpose, and teachers typically base those on evidence related to product criteria only. Those grades designate what students have learned and are able to do at a particular point in time. So while formative assessment results and homework may not count as part of an achievement grade, they still count in the sense that teachers record the results in the gradebook and report them to parents and families as vital aspects of the learning process.

Report Noncognitive Outcomes Separately on Report Cards and Transcripts

Students, parents, and families need to know that what *counts* regarding students' performance in school is both recorded and reported. By reporting noncognitive aspects of students' performance separately on report cards and transcripts, educators make them *count* even more than they did in more traditional forms of reporting. Instead of disguising it as an unknown component of an overall, amalgamated hodgepodge grade, teachers identify, report separately, and may even highlight student performance of these noncognitive competencies. This provides a more complete and comprehensive picture of students' school performance.

Reporting noncognitive outcomes separately not only brings clarity to the meaning of academic achievement grades but also offers guidance and direction for improvement. For example, a student's low achievement grade might be partially explained by a lack of class participation, carelessness on formative assessments, or neglect of critical homework assignments. As such, evidence on these noncognitive aspects of performance can help parents and families assist in students' improvement efforts.

Attach Specific Corrective Consequences to Guide Improvement

Teachers at all grade levels need to understand that their influence on students' performance and behavior in school extends far beyond the control of grades. Likewise, students need to know that what they do and do not do in school has consequences—and those consequences need not be tied to grades. Instead, those consequences should require students to take purposeful, corrective actions that will help amend behaviors that are unproductive, inappropriate, or detrimental to students' learning or the learning of their classmates.

The consequence for not completing a homework assignment, for instance, could be required attendance at a teacher-directed study session held during lunch or after school that day—and no excuses are accepted. This communicates to students that completing homework assignments is important, and it counts. Furthermore, it doesn't allow students to get away with not completing assignments and simply accepting a lower grade.

Similarly, doing poorly on formative assessments may mean students are required to participate in teacher-directed corrective sessions held during class, rather than joining their classmates in exciting and rewarding enrichment activities. Again, this lets students know that doing well is important and putting forth the effort has tangible benefits.

Most important, the consequences in both of these cases are purposefully directed. Rather than punishing students, teachers provide students with a structured environment that supports students in developing the initiative and self-direction they need to complete assignments and adequately prepare for formative assessments on their own. When students show they can complete assignments independently and appropriately prepare for formative assessments, teachers simply withdraw the support.

To implement corrective consequences such as these, teachers may need support from the school board for essential resources. Study sessions held outside the regular school schedule, for example, typically require staffing and facilities. After-school sessions may require student transportation. School staffs that implement such policies, however, generally find that once teachers get serious about them, students do as well. Students quickly realize that the way to avoid having to attend required study sessions simply lies in completing their homework assignments and appropriately preparing for regular formative assessments. So in a relatively short time, the number of students involved in the study sessions drastically diminishes, and fewer resources are needed.

It is imperative, however, that teachers consistently implement these consequences, both individually and as a school faculty. This means that they must prescribe consequences based on the infraction, not the individual student. For example, each teacher should require all students who didn't complete an assignment or who did poorly

> "We are free to choose our paths, but we can't choose the consequences that come with them."
>
> —Sean Covey

on a formative assessment to attend the study session, regardless of their background or history in the class. Furthermore, making the policy schoolwide means consequences are the same in every teacher's class. This avoids the inevitable difficulties encountered when consequences for the same infraction vary from one teacher to the next.

Teachers certainly must be allowed professional discretion in making adaptations based on students' individual situations. For example, it is one thing for a student to miss an assignment or perform poorly on a formative assessment because he or she was ill or had to care for a sick parent. It is quite another to do so because of involvement in video games. Nevertheless, consistency among teachers in implementing these consequences is critical to students', parents', and families' perceptions regarding the fairness of all grading policies and practices.

Noncognitive Outcomes Selection

Chapter 5 (page 117) discussed the importance of finding an appropriate balance in reporting students' performance on cognitive learning goals or standards. We described the need to provide enough detail to be helpful, but not so much that it overwhelms students, parents, and families with information they don't understand or don't know how to use. We also cautioned against making reporting tasks too burdensome for teachers.

The same balance is critical in reporting on noncognitive competencies related to process criteria. But because of the nature of these outcomes, we achieve this balance in a different way. Instead of finding ways to summarize or synthesize on the report card, we must concentrate on *focus* and *consistency*.

Focus

The simple truth is that we cannot report on all the important noncognitive outcomes. There are simply far too many outcomes to consider, and the process would be much too complicated. Our Integrated Framework, for example, lists twenty-seven competencies in the SEL category alone. Add to those the factors describing learning enablers, and they would total more than forty! And remember, this is *in addition* to what we report for cognitive outcomes.

Finding a more reasonable number of noncognitive outcomes to accurately assess and meaningfully record on a report card requires a different approach. In Chapter 5 (page 117), we suggested that students' performance on product and progress learning goals be synthesized and summarized using strands or domains of standards within each subject area or course. We discussed how professional teacher organizations in every academic discipline have grouped standards for student learning into specific strands or domains, and how this provides an excellent framework for summarizing students' performance on a report card. But unfortunately, this approach does not apply to noncognitive learning goals.

Finding a more reasonable number of noncognitive outcomes to accurately assess and meaningfully record on a report card requires a different approach. Several of the organizational frameworks described earlier group noncognitive competencies into broader categories, although the specific competencies within each category vary widely among frameworks. In addition, overlap certainly exists among the outcomes within each category. For example, *collaboration* and *cooperation* are generally considered synonymous. Similarly, *perseverance, persistence*, and *grit* may be difficult to distinguish.

Because of the diversity of outcomes in each category, however, summarizing or synthesizing by category would not be particularly helpful. Instead, we must *prioritize* noncognitive outcomes by considering what we believe to be most important for students' development and success, both in school and in life.

Ideally, we would turn to the research to determine which among these many noncognitive learning goals are vitally important and most contribute to students' success in school and afterward. But as noted earlier, results of the research in this area are mixed and far from definitive (Goodwin, 2018). As an alternative, we must take specific steps to identify the noncognitive competencies that essential stakeholders believe are most crucial to students' development and most influential in their success. These outcomes then become the focus of instructional activities, assessment practices, and reporting procedures.

Consistency

Although cognitive learning goals vary considerably depending on the subject area or course, the noncognitive learning goals teachers identify as most important for students to achieve should not. In other words, the attitudes, dispositions, traits, and behaviors considered most important for student success in school and beyond should be the same in language arts as they are in mathematics, science, social studies, or any other subject. This means that the same noncognitive competencies should be emphasized by all teachers at a grade level and in the school. They should also have consistency in the way they assess those competencies (for example, consistent rubrics), the way they provide feedback to students on their development (that is, consistent forms of evidence), and the procedures they use in reporting on those competencies (that is, consistent report cards and transcripts).

In some cases, differences may exist between school levels. For example, the noncognitive outcomes deemed vital in early elementary grades may be different from those considered most important in later elementary grades, in middle school, or in high school. In addition, students might evidence a particular noncognitive competency in different ways depending on the subject area, course, or level. For instance, students might display collaboration differently in language arts than in science. Students in kindergarten might exhibit collaboration differently than high school students. Still, all teachers at a particular level should be consistent in their emphasis, implementation, and reporting procedures.

"Talent wins games, but teamwork and intelligence win championships."

—Michael Jordan

Selection Process

In most settings, the Coalition for Change selects and prioritizes the noncognitive outcomes, often with broader-based involvement by critical stakeholder groups, especially teachers. In smaller districts or schools, the entire faculty and staff might actually take part. This selection process involves first reviewing a list of possible noncognitive competencies, such as those presented in the Integrated Framework described earlier in this chapter (page 153). Each person then individually identifies the six or seven competencies he or she believes to be most important for students. Certain competencies should probably be given priority, particularly communication and collaboration or cooperation, because they are consistently emphasized by education leaders, the business community, and policymakers.

When stakeholders have completed their selections, they form groups to discuss similarities and differences in their chosen competencies. One of the most productive ways to structure these groups is by grade level or school level. In some cases, this results in only two groups: one composed of elementary educators and a second of secondary educators. However, three groups may be used if elementary educators split up into groups of lower and upper elementary grades, or even four groups if secondary educators divide themselves by middle school and high school. If the high school is large and many teachers are involved, discussions may begin within departments and then transition to all the school staff.

With the groups assembled, members begin by sharing their personal competency lists while one member tallies the results. Most groups discover they have a general agreement on the importance of the top two or three competencies, but opinions vary about the other three or four.

Next, each group must reach consensus through the *disagree-and-commit* principle described in chapter 2 (page 54). However, during the selection process, two guidelines must be kept in mind: (1) the number of noncognitive competencies included on the report card and recorded on transcripts should be limited to no more than four to six, and (2) clear and concise rubrics must be developed for each competency.

Limit the Number of Noncognitive Competencies to No More Than Four to Six

First, similar to cognitive outcomes, groups must limit the number of noncognitive competencies included on report cards and recorded on transcripts to no more than four to six. This helps keep the extra evidence gathering and record keeping required of teachers to a reasonable amount. For the sake of efficiency, most groups actually limit the number to four or five.

Keep in mind, too, that prioritizing noncognitive outcomes can be a particularly thorny process. Finding an appropriate balance between the outcomes most crucial for students' development and success, and the behavioral and compliance outcomes believed essential for classroom management, can be particularly challenging for teachers. For example, should homework completion be included? If not, will students think completing homework is no longer important? What about punctuality in turning in assignments? Can we trust that the consequences we've attached to these behaviors will provide sufficient motivation for students? Can we be sure the positive corrective actions we've planned will remedy neglect or irresponsible actions on the part of students?

These questions don't have definitive answers at this time. Questions such as these simply illustrate the many value choices that stakeholders must make when considering what is most vital for students to learn and most important for teachers to report. Procedures must be tried, evidence gathered on the effects, and adaptations made if needed.

Develop Clear and Concise Rubrics for Each Competency

The second guideline in the selection process is to remind group members that they must develop clear and meaningful rubrics for each competency they select. In other words, teachers need to decide what evidence best represents students' mastery of each competency and then distinguish varying degrees of quality for that evidence. Although at first this may appear to be a simple task to accomplish, the following story reveals that teachers often find it exceedingly nuanced and challenging.

The Challenge of Rubric Development

Several years ago, teams of teachers and school leaders from three school districts came together in a summer institute at the University of Kentucky to develop plans for implementing standards-based grading reforms in their schools (Guskey et al., 2011b). Working collaboratively, the elementary teachers identified four noncognitive outcomes that they wanted to include on the report card, one of them being *effort*. For several years prior to taking part in the institute, these teachers had assigned effort grades to their students and believed effort was an important competency to report.

When they turned to developing a rubric for effort, however, unexpected difficulties arose. While identifying defining behaviors, they found it difficult to distinguish between students who were sincerely trying but may not have appeared to be and those who were simply good at faking it. In examining students' assignments, they also found it hard to distinguish students' work from what they suspected in some instances was parents' work.

For an entire day, these dedicated teachers struggled to reach consensus on a suitable rubric for effort but were unable to do so. Concluding that spending more time on it would unlikely yield a different result, they abandoned effort and chose other important but more easily verifiable noncognitive outcomes to report. They stopped giving effort grades. Although initially perceived as a failure, the teachers involved all reported it was an extremely valuable learning experience.

The next section provides guidance on how the stakeholder groups can develop clear and concise rubrics for each noncognitive competency they select.

Development of Noncognitive Outcome Rubrics

After coming to consensus on the top four to six noncognitive learning goals to be reported, the next step involves developing level-appropriate rubrics for each goal. Just as was the case with cognitive outcomes, however, teachers don't need to do this work from scratch. Instead, they can begin this process with online resources.

Because of increased recognition of the importance of noncognitive student learning goals, numerous professional organizations have taken on the task of designing rubrics to evaluate and then report students' performance on these goals. Examples include the International Reading Association (www.readwritethink.org/files/resources/30860 _rubric.pdf), Buck Institute for Education (https://my.pblworks.org /resource/document/6_12_collaboration_rubric_ccss_aligned), and WE Impact (www.rit.edu/affiliate/weimpact/documents/FinalWEIMPACT _Teamwork%20%20Rubric%202%201%20(2).pdf).

The quality and appropriateness of these models, however, varies greatly. In addition, few schools have broadly implemented them or thoroughly evaluated the implementation results. Therefore, one must review these various models with caution to ensure they align with the interpretations and goals of a district or school. Nevertheless, these online resources offer a good starting point from which adaptations and improvement can be made.

Two important issues must be kept in mind when developing or adapting rubrics for the selected noncognitive outcomes related to process criteria.

- **Base rubrics on models of excellence:** As with cognitive outcomes, rubrics for noncognitive outcomes should be based on *models of excellence.* Instead of beginning with some moderate proficiency level and adding a higher, more advanced, or more complex achievement level, teachers should base the rubric on what they consider to be truly excellent performance. As described in chapter 5 (page 117), that means beginning with the question, What level of performance would you consider worthy of an A or the highest grade possible? With the criteria for excellent or exemplary performance clearly articulated, identifying the steps leading to that level becomes much easier.

- **Design rubrics to *describe* performance rather than *evaluate or judge* performance:** The rubrics teachers develop need to offer students a clear picture of what excellent performance looks like and precisely what makes it excellent so they know specifically what they are striving to attain. In this sense, *rubrics are teaching and learning tools* more than evaluation tools (Brookhart, 2013). They provide students with clarity on the expectations for their performance, along with guidance and direction in their learning progress.

The following sections present the essential characteristics of effective rubrics, questions teachers should consider when evaluating rubrics, example rubrics, and guidance on including descriptors of quantity and quality in rubrics.

Essential Characteristics of Effective Rubrics

Rubrics that effectively describe the performance or work that students are expected to do have three essential characteristics.

1. **They identify the primary criteria for describing the performance or work:** These criteria define the most important attributes, characteristics, or dimensions of a performance or piece of work that make it truly excellent.

2. **They define graduated levels of quality for each criterion:** These quality levels describe distinguishable steps from poor to excellent for each criterion identified. The steps not only allow students to see their progress but also help students identify more precisely where they are in their journey to reaching excellence and what their next steps in that process should be (Brookhart, 2013).

3. **They include a limited number of both criteria and levels of quality:** As teaching and learning tools, rubrics must bring focus to what is most essential in order to direct both teachers' and students' efforts. Quite simply, this requires emphasizing a reasonable number of things that individuals can meaningfully attend to and readily recall. Early research on cognitive functioning indicated that with organization or "clustering," this number was about seven (Miller, 1956).

More recent studies suggest, however, that this number is closer to four (Cowan, 2001, 2010).

Therefore, in developing effective rubrics, teachers must keep the number of criteria to no more than four or five. Likewise, they should limit the levels of quality to no more than three or four. Restricting the number of criteria and levels of quality and then clearly articulating each helps both teachers and students focus on what is most important and direct their efforts in making meaningful improvements.

Rubric Evaluation

As discussed earlier, examples of rubrics for noncognitive student outcomes are plentiful. Because these rubrics vary in their quality and appropriateness, however, it is imperative that teachers analyze them carefully—and in some cases skeptically—before considering their use. In reviewing and evaluating rubrics, teachers should consider the following questions.

- Does the rubric make sense?
- Does the rubric align with our understanding of the attitude, disposition, trait, or behavior we want to emphasize?
- Does the rubric capture the criteria we believe are important for this attitude, disposition, trait, or behavior?
- Will students, parents, and families understand the rubric?
- Will the rubric provide a framework for gathering defensible evidence that reflects student performance?
- Will the rubric serve to guide improvements?

If teachers can answer each question with an unqualified *yes*, then it's likely they can use the rubric. An answer of *no* to any question identifies an area where revision is probably necessary.

Rubric Examples

Figure 6.1 (pages 172–175) shows an example rubric for student collaboration in grades 6–12 developed by the nonprofit Buck Institute for Education (2013). This rubric aligns with the Common Core State Standards Initiative (www.corestandards.org). This particular rubric is

Individual Performance	Below Standard (–)	Approaching Standard (+)	At Standard (++)
Takes Responsibility for Oneself	• Is not prepared, informed, and ready to work with the team • Does not use technology tools as agreed on by the team to communicate and manage project tasks • Does not do project tasks • Does not complete tasks on time • Does not use feedback from others to improve work	• Is usually prepared, informed, and ready to work with the team • Uses technology tools as agreed on by the team to communicate and manage project tasks, but not consistently • Does some project tasks, but needs to be reminded • Completes most tasks on time • Sometimes uses feedback from others to improve work	• Is prepared and ready to work; is well informed on the project topic and cites evidence to probe and reflect on ideas with the team • Consistently uses technology tools as agreed on by the team to communicate and manage project tasks • Does tasks without having to be reminded • Completes tasks on time • Uses feedback from others to improve work

| Helps the Team | • Does not help the team solve problems; may cause problems
• Does not ask probing questions, express ideas, or elaborate in response to questions in discussions
• Does not give useful feedback to others
• Does not offer to help others if they need it | • Cooperates with the team but may not actively help it solve problems
• Sometimes expresses ideas clearly, asks probing questions, and elaborates in response to questions in discussions
• Gives feedback to others, but it may not always be useful
• Sometimes offers to help others if they need it | • Helps the team solve problems and manage conflicts
• Makes discussions effective by clearly expressing ideas, asking probing questions, and making sure everyone is heard, responding thoughtfully to new information and perspectives
• Gives useful feedback (specific, feasible, supportive) to others so they can improve their work
• Offers to help others do their work if needed |

Source: Adapted from Buck Institute for Education, 2013.

Figure 6.1: Collaboration rubric.

continued →

Individual Performance	Below Standard (−)	Approaching Standard (+)	At Standard (++)
Respects Others	• Is impolite or unkind to teammates (may interrupt, ignore ideas, or hurt feelings) • Does not acknowledge or respect other perspectives	• Is usually polite and kind to teammates • Usually acknowledges and respects other perspectives and disagrees diplomatically	• Is polite and kind to teammates • Acknowledges and respects other perspectives; disagrees diplomatically
Makes and Follows Agreements	• Does not discuss how the team will work together • Does not follow rules for collegial discussions, decision making, and conflict resolution • Does not discuss how well agreements are being followed • Allows breakdowns in teamwork to happen; needs the teacher to intervene	• Discusses how the team will work together, but not in detail; may just "go through the motions" when creating an agreement • Usually follows rules for collegial discussions, decision making, and conflict resolution • Discusses how well agreements are being followed, but not in depth; may ignore subtle issues • Notices when norms are not being followed but asks the teacher for help to resolve issues	• Makes detailed agreements about how the team will work together, including the use of technology tools • Follows rules for collegial discussions, decision making, and conflict resolution • Honestly and accurately discusses how well agreements are being followed • Takes appropriate action when norms are not being followed; attempts to resolve issues without asking the teacher for help

Organizes Work	• Does project work without creating a task list • Does not set a schedule and track progress toward goals and deadlines • Does not assign roles or share leadership; one person may do too much, or all members may do random tasks • Wastes time and does not run meetings well; materials, drafts, and notes are not organized (may be misplaced or inaccessible)	• Creates a task list that divides project work among the team, but it may not be detailed or followed closely • Sets a schedule for doing tasks but does not follow it closely • Assigns roles but does not follow them, or selects only one "leader" who makes most decisions • Usually uses time and runs meetings well but may occasionally waste time; keeps materials, drafts, and notes but is not always organized	• Creates a detailed task list that divides project work reasonably among the team • Sets a schedule and tracks progress toward goals and deadlines • Assigns roles if and as needed, based on team members' strengths • Uses time and runs meetings efficiently; keeps materials, drafts, and notes organized
Works as a Whole Team	• Does not recognize or use special talents of team members • Does project tasks separately and does not put them together; it is a collection of individual work	• Makes some attempt to use special talents of team members • Does most project tasks separately and puts them together at the end	• Recognizes and uses special talents of each team member • Develops ideas and creates products with involvement of all team members; tasks done separately are brought to the team for critique and revision

rather complex because it divides collaboration into the components of individual and team performance, identifies specific criteria under each (three for individual and three for team), and then lists two to five defining statements for each quality level under each criterion. The symbols -, +, and ++ designate three levels of performance. Despite these complications, however, the rubric provides a useful framework for discussions about how teachers might judge collaboration and offer feedback to improve students' collaboration skills.

Figure 6.2 features an example rubric for homework that has been adapted from a rubric developed by iRubric (Rcampus, 2019). This rubric identifies three criteria for homework: (1) completion, (2) accuracy, and (3) legibility—and four quality levels for each criterion. As such, it's simpler than the rubric for collaboration, which is typical for learning-enabling outcomes compared with SEL outcomes.

This rubric illustrates an important complication that is common in rubrics describing behavioral learning goals—that is, how to provide an adequate and meaningful summary of both *quantity* and *quality*. In this case, for example, how would we distinguish between the student who neatly completed the homework assignment but did so incorrectly and the student who neatly completed only half the assignment but did so correctly? Teachers could resolve this quantity-versus-quality distinction by reporting on separate criteria within the rubric, but that would further complicate the reporting process. Still, if accurate and meaningful communication is our goal, then such distinctions may be necessary.

Quantity and Quality

Mixing quantity and quality is a common error in rubrics describing student performance. Rubric developers usually begin with descriptors of performance quality related to specific learning goals. Some may use descriptors such as *beginning, progressing, meets,* and *exemplary.* Others may use *unsatisfactory, needs improvement, satisfactory,* and *outstanding* or even *poor, mediocre, good,* and *excellent.* But then, in the same rubric, they sometimes add indicators of how many essential parts of the performance, project, or product students included, using adjectives such as *few, some, most,* and *all.* Brookhart (2013) refers to this as combining a *learning* rubric with a *compliance* rubric.

Homework Completion				
	1 Struggling	2 Progressing	3 Proficient	4 Exemplary
Performance Level	You must do better than this. Don't give up hope. If you need assistance, please see me.	You've made minimal improvement. But more effort is required.	Now we're talking. Let's continue to do better.	You've done very well. Keep up the excellent work.
Completion	Less than one-half of the assignment was completed.	At least one-half of the assignment was completed.	Three-fourths of the assignment was completed.	The entire assignment was completed.
Accuracy	Less than one-half of the assignment was done correctly.	At least one-half of the assignment was done correctly.	Three-fourths of the assignment was done correctly.	The entire assignment was done correctly.
Legibility	Not legible. Hard to read. Ideas expressed are difficult to understand.	Slightly legible. Writing illustrates little thought or preparation.	Mostly neat and legible. Writing illustrates some thought and preparation.	Very neat. Writing illustrates a lot of thought and preparation.

Source: Adapted from Rcampus, 2019.

Figure 6.2: Homework completion rubric.

In other cases, rubric developers make matters even more confusing by combining descriptors of quality with indicators of frequency, such as *rarely, occasionally, frequently,* and *consistently* or *never, seldom, usually,* and *always.* As described earlier, this thoroughly confounds interpretation. How would you distinguish between a student who consistently completes work at a mediocre level and a student who only occasionally completes work but at an excellent level? Although we certainly want all our students to consistently perform at an excellent level, consistency and quality are clearly two different performance dimensions.

Unfortunately, this problem has no simple solution. An important axiom in education measurement is that with every step we take to summarize information, we lose some precision and accuracy. When we compute the average of a group of scores, for example, we lose the precision that individual scores reveal. Summarizing, therefore, always requires balance and compromise between the clarity gained through creating the abbreviated summary and the precision lost by reducing the information. Chapter 4 (page 83) stressed the importance of keeping this in mind as we move from the gradebook to the report card and permanent record or transcript. Summaries are important and necessary, but they always involve a reduction in precision and detail.

The process of developing rubrics requires similar balance and compromise. If both quality and compliance or consistency are important, then each must be assessed and reported separately. Doing so plainly gives students, parents, and families better information and clearer direction in making improvements. To combine ratings of both quality and compliance or consistency in a single rubric grade or score masks their meaning.

But if teachers decide that an overall rubric score that combines these diverse dimensions suffices for their purposes, then they might use a single amalgamated grade or score, recognizing its shortcomings. As with so many aspects of grading and reporting, it all comes down to purpose—and we must decide that purpose first.

Student Involvement in Developing Rubrics

Faced with the challenge of developing accurate and meaningful rubrics that describe students' acquisition of important noncognitive competencies, some teachers and schools have taken the creative approach of turning the task over to students. At Issaquah Middle School in Issaquah, Washington, teacher Holly Stipe made the process a class project.

A coalition of school leaders and teachers in Issaquah chose *initiative* as an important noncognitive competency for students to develop. In their discussions, they decided there were three aspects to initiative: (1) self-advocacy, (2) reflection, and (3) persistence. Holly then assigned her students the task of explaining how they would demonstrate these traits during class sessions. Students began by describing what they believed each aspect of initiative means, what initiative looks like, and what initiative sounds like. Figure 6.3 shows a chart of their initial work.

Source: © 2018 by Holly Stipe, Isaaquah Middle School. Used with permission.

Figure 6.3: Student-developed chart describing initiative.

From this beginning exploration, students developed criteria for initiative and defined graduated levels of performance for each criterion. Holly then guided her students through a series of reflective activities in which they considered how they would show initiative and recognize it in their classmates. As a result, students considered the rubric to be theirs, engaged in regular self-assessment, understood the rubric scores, and were able to explain those scores to their parents.

Summary

The noncognitive outcomes related to process criteria play an important role in students' success in school and beyond. They also are becoming increasingly important as education goals and, in turn, as explicit factors in determining students' grades. The focus on 21st century skills, college and career readiness, and social and emotional learning has brought new attention to these outcomes and compels educators to consider how they will teach, assess, and report them in gradebooks, report cards, and permanent records or transcripts.

Effective grading and reporting systems give special attention to these important noncognitive learning goals. By explicitly including these goals and competencies in the school curriculum, constructing clear rubrics that guide students in age-appropriate development of noncognitive competencies, and creating procedures to meaningfully report on acquisition of these competencies, educators can build grading and reporting systems that are truly honest, accurate, meaningful, fair, and ultimately much more successful.

CHAPTER 7

Get Assessment Policies and Practices Right

If I have seen a little further, it is by standing on the shoulders of giants.

—Isaac Newton

Thus far, this book has focused exclusively on reforms in grading and reporting student learning. We have explored why so many reform initiatives fail and how to establish Coalitions for Change to guide reform efforts. We've discussed the change process, the purpose of grading, and the importance of reporting both cognitive and noncognitive learning outcomes. Therefore, it may seem odd that before moving on to integrating these elements in a systematic plan for implementation, we turn to the topic of assessment. After all, grading and reporting are about what you do with assessment information—not about how you gather it.

What makes this change in direction even odder is the fact that as a philosophy of education, standards-based learning actually says little about assessments. Chapter 1 (page 17) emphasized that the basic idea of standards-based learning is to ensure *transparency* in all elements of the teaching and learning process: curriculum, instruction, assessment, and grading and reporting. We stressed that each of these elements must

Portions of this chapter appear in "How Classroom Assessments Improve Learning" (Guskey, 2003), "The Rest of the Story" (Guskey, 2008), and "Grades Versus Comments: Research on Student Feedback" (Guskey, 2019a).

be carefully articulated, completely transparent, and clearly understood by all stakeholders—teachers, students, parents, families, school leaders, board members, and community members.

Aside from its requirements to ensure transparency and align assessments with these other elements, however, standards-based learning is basically neutral with regard to assessment practices. Although most standards-based learning advocates offer numerous suggestions regarding assessments, these suggestions are actually *embellishments* rather than defining characteristics. Unfortunately, when these embellishments are opinion-based rather than evidence-based or research-based, they can become entanglements or entrapments that seriously hamper implementation efforts.

In this chapter, we turn our attention to assessments for two important reasons. First, for grades to be honest, accurate, meaningful, and fair, they must be based on reliable and valid assessment evidence. You can't have a quality grading and reporting system without high-quality assessments. To ensure that grades accurately describe how well students have achieved established cognitive and noncognitive learning goals, we must first ensure the evidence we gather on student achievement is accurate and trustworthy.

A second and more important reason to consider assessments is that in addition to using them as a primary source of evidence on student learning, teachers can purposefully use assessments to enhance and improve learning. This formative purpose of assessments has a long history in education based on the work of truly brilliant education scholars. Everyone who works in the area of assessment or grading owes a great debt to these remarkable scholars and the significant, extensive research base they helped establish. We all stand on the shoulders of these giants in our field, and it's important to recognize their contributions.

Far too often, however, we overlook that important history, ignore the contributions of those brilliant scholars, and disregard or misinterpret the research they helped establish. These misinterpretations have resulted in modern educators' getting bad advice about which assessment practices are effective and how those practices can be successfully implemented in modern classrooms. The intent of this chapter is to set the record straight by tracing that distinguished history, honoring the contributions of the talented individuals who developed the ideas involved, and reviewing specific research-based implications for effective practice.

The following sections describe the use of assessments to improve learning, teachers' lack of assessment training, Benjamin Bloom's guidance regarding formative assessments, effective assessment's similarities to tutoring and coaching, practices to avoid with second assessments, the differences between formative and summative assessments, and the complexities of grades and comments on assessments.

The Use of Assessments to Improve Learning

All assessments in education are designed for a specific purpose. The large-scale assessments used in most states and provinces are designed to rank-order schools and students for the purposes of accountability—and some do that fairly well. But assessments designed for ranking generally do not help teachers enhance their instruction or guide students in improving their learning.

There are three reasons for this. First, students take these assessments at the end of the school year when most instructional activities are near completion. Second, teachers don't receive the results of accountability assessments until two or three months after students take them, by which time their students have usually moved on to other teachers. And third, the results that teachers and students receive typically lack the level of detail needed to target specific improvements (Barton, 2002; Kifer, 2001).

The assessments best suited to guide improvements in student learning are the quizzes, writing assignments, projects, demonstrations, and performances that teachers administer on a regular basis in their classrooms. Teachers trust the results from these assessments because of their direct relationship to classroom instructional goals. Plus, the results are immediate and easy to analyze at the individual student level.

To use classroom assessments to make improvements, however, teachers must change both their view of assessments and the way they interpret assessment results. Specifically, they need to see their assessments as *integral to the instruction process* and crucial for helping students learn (Guskey, 2003).

Lack of Assessment Training

Despite the importance of assessments in education, few teachers receive much formal training in assessment design or analysis. Preservice programs for teachers rarely include coursework or practicum experiences that specifically address assessment or grading issues (Stiggins, 1999). Only with education's growing emphasis on accountability have aspects of assessment literacy appeared in both undergraduate and graduate education programs (Popham, 2018).

Lacking specific training, teachers heavily rely on the assessments that the publishers of their instructional materials provide. When they have no suitable assessments available, teachers haphazardly construct their own assessments with questions and essay prompts similar to the ones that their teachers used. They treat assessments as evaluation devices to administer at the completion of instructional activities and primarily for assigning students' grades.

> *"We definitely need to move beyond the misguided notion that a single test, taken on a single day, defines the success of a school, a teacher, or a kid."*
> —Patrick Riccards

Unfortunately, this not only restricts what positive benefits the assessments might have but also perpetuates poor assessment practices.

Benjamin Bloom and Formative Assessments

In order to use assessments formatively—to improve instruction and student learning—teachers must change their approach to assessments in three important ways.

1. They must make assessments sources of information.

2. They must follow assessments with high-quality corrective instruction.

3. They must allow students a second chance to succeed on assessments.

Each of these changes was initially described by Benjamin Bloom in the late 1960s (1968, 1971) when he outlined the process of *mastery learning*. Each requires teachers to think about assessment differently and to do things differently than they experienced when they were students.

Assessments Must Be Sources of Information

At all levels of education, assessments must be seen as *sources of information for both students and teachers.* Nearly every student has suffered the experience of spending hours preparing for a major assessment only to discover that the material he or she studied was different from what the teacher chose to emphasize on the assessment. This experience teaches students two unfortunate lessons. First, students realize that hard work and effort don't pay off in school because the time and effort they spent studying had little or no influence on results. And second, they learn that they cannot trust their teachers. These are hardly the lessons that responsible teachers want their students to learn (Guskey, 2000b).

Nonetheless, this experience is common because many teachers still mistakenly believe that they must keep their assessments secret. As a result, students come to regard assessments as guessing games, especially from the middle grades on. They view success as dependent on how well they can guess what their teachers will ask on quizzes, tests, and other assessments administered at the end of each instructional unit (Guskey, 2003).

Some teachers even take pride in their ability to outguess their students. They ask questions about isolated concepts or obscure understandings just to see whether students are reading carefully. Generally, these teachers include such *gotcha* questions not maliciously but unconsciously, because they were asked such questions when they were students (Guskey, 2008).

The following sections discuss how teachers can ensure classroom assessments serve as meaningful sources of information for their students and for themselves.

For Students

Classroom assessments that serve as meaningful sources of information don't surprise students. Instead, these assessments reflect the concepts and skills that the teacher emphasized in class, along with the teacher's clear criteria for judging students' performance. These concepts, skills, and criteria align with the teacher's instructional activities and, ideally, with state, provincial, or district standards. Students see such assessments as fair measures of important learning goals. Teachers facilitate learning by providing students with important feedback on their learning progress and by helping students identify learning problems (Guskey, 2003, 2008; Hattie & Timperley, 2007). This is what it means for assessments to be *formative* (Bloom, 1968; Bloom, Madaus, & Hastings, 1981; Scriven, 1967; Stiggins, 2002).

In his original description of this formative assessment process, Bloom (1968, 1971) distinguished formative assessments from the regular checks that teachers use *during* lessons to ensure student understanding. Asking students, "Show me thumbs-up if it's clear to you" or "Turn to your partner and explain your understanding," is a useful teaching technique. But Bloom did *not* regard these intermittent checks as formative assessments.

Bloom (1968, 1971) defined *formative assessments* as more formal checks that occur during natural breaks in an instructional process when teachers want to stop to ensure that students have mastered important concepts or skills. He stressed that if the segments of learning that a formative assessment addresses are too short, then learning becomes fragmented, and it is more difficult to build higher-level cognitive skills. But if they are too long, students who experience difficulties early will have greater difficulty catching up. Bloom (1968, 1971) estimated that the appropriate learning segment before a formative assessment might be perhaps a week of class time at the elementary level and possibly two weeks at the secondary level.

Bloom (1968, 1971) also stressed that formative assessments can take any form depending on the content and skills that are most important for students to learn. They may be short pencil-and-paper quizzes that ask students to describe important issues or solve problems. But they may also be written essays or compositions, skill demonstrations, or performances. In essence, formative assessments can involve any means that teachers use to gather accurate and authentic evidence on student learning.

Rather than serving as evaluation devices that mark the end of a learning segment, however, formative assessments serve two important purposes for students. First, they are considered part of the instructional process to recognize learning successes and to diagnose individual learning difficulties. Second, they provide the framework for prescribing remediation procedures for students who experience difficulties.

For Teachers

The best classroom assessments also serve as meaningful sources of information for teachers, helping them identify what they taught well and which aspects of their instruction they may need to adjust or modify. Gathering this vital information doesn't require a sophisticated statistical analysis of assessment results. Teachers need only make a simple tally of how many students missed each assessment item or failed to meet a specific criterion. State and provincial assessments sometimes provide similar item-by-item information, but concerns about item security and the cost of developing new items each year usually make assessment developers reluctant to offer such detailed information. Once teachers have made these specific tallies based on their classroom assessments, they can pay special attention to any identified trouble spots, especially those items or criteria that many students in the class missed (Guskey, 2008).

In reviewing these trouble spots, teachers must first consider the quality of the item or criterion. Perhaps the question is ambiguously worded or the criterion is unclear. Perhaps students misinterpreted the question. Whatever the case, teachers must determine whether these items or criteria adequately address the knowledge, understanding, or skill they were intended to measure (Guskey, 2003).

If teachers find no obvious problems with the item or criterion, then their attention must turn to their teaching. When as many as half the students in a class answer a clear question incorrectly or fail to meet a particular criterion, it's not a student learning problem—*it's a teaching problem.* Whatever teaching strategy was used, whatever examples were employed, or whatever explanation was offered, it simply didn't work.

> "A person who never made a mistake never tried anything new."
> —Albert Einstein

Analyzing assessment results in this way means setting aside some powerful ego issues. Sometimes, when teachers look at disappointing results, they say, "How can this be? I taught them; they just didn't learn it!" On reflection, however, most recognize that their effectiveness as a teacher depends not on what *they* do but rather on what *students* can do. Could we say our teaching was effective if students didn't learn? Can effective teaching take place in the absence of learning? Certainly not.

Some might argue that this perspective puts too much onus on teachers and not enough on students. Teachers might ask, "Don't students have responsibilities in this process? Shouldn't students display initiative and personal accountability for their own learning?"

Indeed, teachers and students both share responsibility for learning. Even with valiant teaching efforts, we cannot guarantee that *all* students will learn everything excellently. Only rarely do teachers find items or assessment criteria that every student answers correctly. In addition, a few students may not be willing to put forth the necessary effort. But these students tend to be the exception, not the rule. If a teacher is reaching fewer than half the students in the class, the teacher's method of instruction needs to improve. And this kind of evidence is precisely the information teachers need to target in their instructional improvement efforts (Guskey, 2003).

Critics sometimes contend that this approach to analyzing assessment results promotes "teaching to the test." But the crucial issue is, really, What determines the content taught and methods of teaching? If a test or assessment is the primary determinant of what teachers teach and how they teach it, then, indeed, teachers are "teaching to the test." But if teachers use desired learning goals as the foundation for determining their students' instructional experiences and assessments, then they will ensure that assessments of student learning are simply extensions of those same goals. Instead of "teaching to the test," teachers are more accurately "testing what they teach." If a concept or skill is important enough to assess, then it should be important enough to teach. And if it is not important enough to teach, then there's little justification for assessing it.

Assessments Must Be Followed With High-Quality Corrective Instruction

Formative assessments alone do little to improve student learning or teaching quality. What really counts is what happens *after* the assessments. Just as regularly checking your weight or blood pressure does little to improve your health if you do nothing with the information, what matters most with formative assessments is how students and teachers use the results. Unfortunately, many educators overlook this vital aspect of formative assessment. As a result, they fail to realize the most valuable benefits of the formative assessment process.

If assessments provide information for both students and teachers, then they cannot mark the end of learning. Instead, teachers must follow assessments with high-quality corrective instruction designed to remedy whatever learning errors the assessment identified (Bloom, 1968, 1971; Guskey, 1997, 2008, 2010). To charge ahead knowing that students have not learned well important concepts or skills would be foolish.

Simply going over the assessment, however, is not sufficient. Even if students are shown which of their initial responses are incorrect, they may have no clear understanding of the nature of their errors. To correct their learning errors and misunderstandings, students need specific guidance and direction from their teachers that is different from the initial instruction. Without it, little improvement can be expected. Therefore, teachers must follow their assessments with instructional alternatives that present those concepts in new ways and engage students in different and more appropriate learning experiences.

> "If a child can't learn the way we teach, maybe we should teach the way they learn."
>
> —Ignacio Estrada

Perhaps most important, *this corrective work initially must be done in class and under the teacher's direction.* Because this process is new and unfamiliar to most students, teachers must initially guide students through it. They *cannot* make this work an optional activity that students complete on their own time as homework or in a special study session before or after school. Experience shows that if teachers make this activity optional, those students who need it the most and would most benefit from engaging in corrective work are the least likely to take part (Guskey, 1997). Expecting students to remedy learning problems from the past while keeping up with new learning as the teacher moves ahead also puts these most vulnerable students in double jeopardy. Only after seeing how the corrective process benefits them and the improvements they can make are students likely to engage in corrective activities on their own. As described in chapter 3 (page 61), *experience shapes attitudes and beliefs.* Teachers must actively and purposefully change students' learning experience and show them they can succeed.

The following sections describe how teachers can plan, make time for, and choose effective corrective activities, as well as how they can provide enrichment activities for those students who learned well during the teachers' initial instruction and don't need corrective work.

How to Plan Corrective Activities

Effective corrective activities possess three essential characteristics that teachers must keep in mind as they plan corrective activities (Guskey, 1997).

1. **Effective corrective activities present concepts or skills differently:** For example, if a language arts teacher initially taught the use of metaphors in poetry with a deductive approach (presenting the general concept and then giving specific examples), the corrective activity might use an inductive approach (presenting a variety of specific examples and building students' understanding of the general concept from these examples). If the initial instruction was based on an advanced organizer approach to solving complex problems in mathematics, corrective work might begin by explaining important facts and procedures and then turning to their application in problem-solving tasks. The best corrective activities involve a change in *format, organization,* or *method of presentation.*

2. **Effective corrective activities engage students in learning differently:** These activities consider different learning preferences or modalities (Sternberg, 1994) or different forms of intelligence (Armstrong, 2000; Gardner, 2006; Silver, Strong, & Perini, 2000). If students in a science class initially learned about cell structure through a group activity, for example, a good corrective activity might involve an individual activity, such as reviewing an informative website and then writing or illustrating a report. If students originally learned the events of the American Revolutionary War in a social studies class by reading textbook passages and studying wall maps and charts, a useful corrective activity might employ a group discussion of the events (Guskey, 2008). In other words, effective corrective strategies engage

students in ways that are *qualitatively different* from what took place during the initial instruction.

3. **Effective corrective activities provide students with successful learning experiences:** If an activity does not help students overcome their learning difficulties and see tangible improvement, teachers should abandon it for another option. Corrective activities should help students experience learning success so they feel better prepared, more confident in themselves as learners, and more motivated for future learning tasks.

Although ideas for effective corrective activities can come from many sources, the best ideas generally come from fellow teachers. Even if they don't teach the same subject or grade level, teaching colleagues often can recommend new insights or offer different examples, alternative materials, and new ways of presenting concepts. Professional development sessions that provide teachers with structured opportunities for this type of sharing reduce individual teachers' workload and typically yield higher-quality corrective activities (Guskey, 1998, 2000b). Faculty meetings devoted to examining classroom assessment results and developing corrective strategies also work well. These meetings might involve district-level personnel or content experts from local colleges and universities to provide additional guidance.

The emphasis on being different from the initial instruction in both presentation and student engagement shows the corrective process is *not simply reteaching*. Too often, reteaching consists of restating original explanations louder and more slowly, admonishing students to "Pay attention!" or "Try harder this time!" Repeating an approach that hasn't worked for these students will unlikely yield better results the second time around. Instead, teachers must provide students with alternative pathways to learning success, adapted to meet their individual learning needs and interests (Duffy & Kear, 2007).

In essence, when teachers provide students with alternative learning pathways, they are saying these students can learn—it's just that they may learn *differently*. Although teachers usually try to incorporate different teaching approaches when they plan their lessons, corrective instruction involves extending and strengthening those lessons. It is in correctives that differentiation becomes most apparent and most effective (Guskey, 2007a; Tomlinson, 2003).

How to Make Time for Corrective Activities

Occasionally, teachers express concern that taking class time to offer corrective instruction will require them to sacrifice curriculum coverage. They believe that while providing corrective activities may help some students learn better, using class time for corrective work will leave less time for presenting new content and, hence, all students will learn less.

Because corrective work must initially occur *in class and under the teacher's direct guidance and supervision*, early instructional units do take more time. But this is typically an extra class period or two, when teachers first introduce corrective work. Involvement in corrective activities *is not optional for students* in these early units. It is a required, teacher-directed activity conducted in class.

As students become accustomed to the corrective process and realize the personal benefits it offers, however, teachers find they can significantly reduce the class time allocated to corrective work and accomplish much of it through homework assignments or in special study sessions before or after school. Furthermore, because the corrective process does not allow minor errors to become major learning problems, teachers can ensure students are better prepared for subsequent learning tasks and need less time for corrective work (Whiting, Van Burgh, & Render, 1995). This means teaching can proceed at a more rapid pace in later learning units, with less time spent on review (Guskey, 2003).

Most teachers find they don't have to sacrifice curriculum coverage to offer students the benefits of high-quality corrective instruction when they pace their instructional units more flexibly, allowing more time in early units but less time in later units. The key is to be mindful of where students need to be at the end of a course of study, and to have flexibility in terms of pathways to that end.

How to Choose Among Different Types of Corrective Activities

Many teachers find it useful to organize corrective activities into three groups: (1) those that students do with the teacher, (2) those that students do with a classmate, and (3) those that students do by themselves. Although any particular activity may fall into more than one category, teachers should design every activity to provide students with a different presentation and a different mode of engagement. Most teachers plan several types of corrective activities for each instructional unit to give students some choice and to accommodate a wider variety of learning preferences and modalities. Further, if a particular activity falls flat, having several activities planned makes it easier to immediately turn to another without wasting valuable time.

Reteaching

The simplest and most frequently used corrective activity, especially in the primary and early elementary grades, involves thoughtful reteaching. The teacher, or another teacher in team-teaching situations, explains difficult concepts again using a different approach or different examples. Most teachers reteach while reviewing formative assessment results with students, re-explaining concepts that many students misunderstood or found difficult, before they turn to other types of corrective activities (Guskey, 2008).

The greatest challenge with reteaching, of course, is ensuring that it involves a truly different presentation and type of engagement. Having students repeat exactly the same experience that didn't work for them the first time rarely yields better results the second time around.

Individual Tutoring

One of the most effective corrective activities is individual tutoring. In most cases, the tutor goes through the formative assessment with the student, explaining concepts that he or she missed in a new way or from a different perspective, continually checking for understanding as they move along. Even teachers who employ other forms of correctives usually monitor students' understanding with some individual tutoring, especially for those students with more serious learning difficulties. Many teachers have obtained excellent results using older students, teacher's aides, and classroom volunteers as tutors (Topping & Bryce, 2004; Wright & Cleary, 2006). Regardless of who serves as the tutor, individual tutoring consistently ranks among the most efficient and most effective types of corrective activities.

Peer Tutoring

Students who have already mastered the unit's important concepts and skills often make excellent tutors for their classmates. Like other tutors, peers typically explain concepts from a different perspective or in a different way (Kourea, Cartledge, & Musti-Rao, 2007). In addition, research indicates that students who serve as peer tutors generally benefit as much as the students they assist (Eskreis-Winkler, Milkman, Gromet, & Duckworth, 2019; Medcalf, Glynn, & Moore, 2004). Helping classmates understand new concepts or master new skills often deepens their own understanding. Most teachers find, however, that peer tutoring is best presented as one of several corrective options from which students can choose. Requiring two mismatched students to work together can be counterproductive.

Cooperative Teams

Cooperative teams include three to five students assigned by the teacher in order to ensure the teams have heterogeneous members. Team members get together during the corrective session to review the formative assessment item by item, discuss their learning errors, and help one another. When one or more students find they missed a question or crucial element, another team member can explain it. If all the team members are having difficulty, they can work collaboratively to find a solution or call on the teacher for assistance. Cooperative teams usually stay intact for several learning units. With modest direction and supervision, cooperative teams can be highly effective at any level of education (Johnson & Johnson, 1995; Slavin, 1991).

Course Texts or Materials

Another simple but highly effective corrective is to have students reread relevant sections in the course text or related course materials. Rereading is especially effective when combined with other activities, such as having students write a short paragraph explaining the concept in their own words. Teachers who use texts as a corrective resource typically list page-number references beside each item or problem on the formative assessment so students can turn directly to the relevant sections or examples. Although referring students to the text may seem to be simply repetition of the same thing, focusing their attention on specific passages often helps students recognize or clarify important concepts and information they may have missed in their initial reading.

Alternative Texts or Materials

When available, alternative texts or materials often provide a different presentation or explanation of crucial ideas or concepts. Many teachers save several copies of their older texts whenever they adopt a new one so that they can offer students an additional source of information. Other teachers draw alternative materials from other instructional resources to provide additional practice exercises, examples, or problems (Guskey, 2008).

Alternative materials might also include videos, audio recordings, hands-on materials, manipulative models, or various online resources. Workbooks and study guides usually present ideas and concepts in a different way than related texts do, and they often include examples or practical applications. In addition, the variety of presentation formats offered by these alternative resources allows students to choose materials that best suit their preferred learning modality.

Academic Games

Most academic games consist of group activities in which students work together to solve a particular problem or accomplish tasks that relate to specific learning goals (Harnadek, 1992; Larson, 2002). Teachers can adapt or modify many academic games to fit a variety of learning situations. Like cooperative teams, academic games typically promote cooperation and collaboration among students and can be highly effective corrective activities.

Learning Kits

Learning kits usually present ideas and concepts visually and often involve the manipulation of materials. In addition, most kits can be used with the teacher, among small groups of students, or by students working alone. Learning kits might include puzzles, learning tools, or other instructional materials. Many involve the use of models; others are based on interactive multimedia content (Learning Kit Project, 2007). Although learning kits are widely available from commercial publishers and web-based sources, many teachers assemble their own from materials they gather.

Learning Centers

Directing students to learning centers or learning laboratories in the classroom or in another part of the school often serves as a highly effective corrective activity. In these centers, students get help on their specific learning difficulties, often under the guidance of a learning supervisor or center aide. Center activities typically engage students in more hands-on and manipulative tasks than might have been possible during the initial instruction. Centers are most effective as a corrective activity when students are involved in a structured activity and receive specific assignments to complete.

Online Resources

Many teachers use computers and other forms of technology as a primary source of corrective activities. The highly versatile, user-friendly nature of technology makes it appropriate for almost any subject area and grade level. Online resources enable students to work alone or in collaboration with classmates. Many tutorial programs, such as those offered by Khan Academy (www.khanacademy.org), also enable students to control the kind and amount of assistance they receive. Such individualized interaction makes assistance better tailored to students' needs and potentially less embarrassing. When students become familiar with a program's operation, and when the software closely matches the learning goals, online resources can be highly effective as a corrective (Dillon & Gabbard, 1998; Guskey, 2008; Kumar, Greer, & McCalla, 2005; Nguyen, 2015; Perry, Thauberger, MacAllister, & Winne, 2005).

Table 7.1 shows an overview of the corrective activities that many teachers find effective.

Table 7.1: Examples of Corrective Activities

Corrective Activities	With the Teacher	With a Classmate	By Oneself
Reteaching	X		
Individual tutoring	X	X	
Peer tutoring		X	
Cooperative teams		X	
Course texts or materials	X	X	X
Alternative texts or materials	X	X	X
Academic games	X	X	X
Learning kits	X	X	X
Learning centers		X	X
Online resources		X	X

How to Provide Enrichment Activities

On any given formative assessment, some students will demonstrate mastery of unit concepts and skills on the first try and have no need for corrective activities. Rather than sitting around, biding their time while other students are working to remedy learning difficulties, these students need opportunities to extend their learning through enrichment or extension activities.

> "Successful persons never lose. They either win or learn."
> —John Calipari

Effective enrichment activities must provide valuable, challenging, and rewarding learning experiences. Students who master the learning goals the first time and perform well on the formative assessment should view enrichment activities as exciting opportunities—not simply as harder tasks or busywork. Rather than narrowly restricting enrichment activities to the content of specific learning units, teachers should broadly interpret enrichment activities to cover a wide range of related topics. Because teachers typically take charge of guiding students involved in corrective work, students engaged in enrichment activities usually work in small groups or independently.

In addition, students should have some degree of choice in selecting enrichments. For example, if a student takes a special interest in some aspect of the subject area, he or she might use enrichment time to prepare a special report on that topic. Such an activity not only provides a unique learning opportunity for students; it also enhances students' motivation to do well in subsequent learning units so they can return to working on their report. Other examples of enrichment activities include challenging academic games and exercises, various multimedia projects, and peer tutoring (Guskey, 2008). Table 7.2 includes more examples of enrichment activities.

Table 7.2: Examples of Enrichment Activities

Enrichment Activities	With a Classmate	By Oneself
Peer tutoring	X	
Cooperative teams	X	
Practice exercises	X	X
Special projects or reports	X	X
Games, problems, or contests	X	X
Advanced online resources	X	X
Activities for gifted students	X	X

Managing Corrective and Enrichment Activities

Ms. Tanabe's high school algebra class studied a five-day unit on polynomial equations. She administered a twenty- to twenty-five-minute formative classroom assessment and corrected it with her students in class, reviewing each item and stopping occasionally to re-explain ideas or concepts that appeared troublesome to many students. After completing the review, she reminded students that the mastery or proficiency standard was seventeen of the twenty problems correct.

She then divided the class into two groups: students who attained the mastery standard and those who did not. Mastery students chose various enrichment activities, including working with partners to write original word problems, doing a guided internet search to learn about famous but quirky mathematicians, or serving as peer tutors. Students not reaching mastery began their corrective work with Ms. Tanabe. The cooperative teams that Ms. Tanabe put into place for peer tutoring moved their desks together and began working with teammates.

Ms. Tanabe did three important things when dividing the class into corrective and enrichment groups. First, she recognized students who attained the mastery standard for their achievement. A quick show of hands helps sustain these students' persistence in future learning units. Next, she reminded students that group membership is temporary and can change with every unit and every formative assessment. As students' performance changes, so will the members of both corrective and enrichment groups.

Finally, she emphasized her confidence in the skills of those students who had not yet attained mastery. She assured these students that with a little more time and effort, they too would reach the mastery standard and be well prepared to tackle upcoming units.

After starting the enrichment group on its activities, Ms. Tanabe turned her attention to the corrective group. She began with reteaching, using some supplemental materials to present difficult ideas and concepts in new and different ways. She then moved to guided practice activities, leading students through structured problems or exercises. She included practice time when some students worked independently to demonstrate their understanding, and others worked with peer tutors. As students worked, she moved from student to student, asking questions and offering individualized assistance. At the same time, she checked on students engaged in enrichment activities, making sure they remained on task.

When first implementing the corrective and enrichment process, most teachers find they must keep it fairly structured. They direct students involved in enrichments to move quickly to independent activities while they guide students engaged in correctives. However, after students become familiar with the process and related classroom routines, teachers typically allow more options and offer students greater choice.

As the example on page 198 shows, correctives rarely involve a single activity. In this case, Ms. Tanabe combined reteaching with alternative materials, guided practice, independent practice, and individual tutoring. When students work on their own or with a friend, most teachers require completion of a written assignment that summarizes their work. Enrichment activities may be similarly diversified, and many teachers require a tangible product from these students as well. After students become accustomed to the corrective and enrichment process, however, teachers often relax or eliminate this requirement.

Students Must Be Given a Second Chance to Succeed

Teachers need to give students a second chance to demonstrate success. To become an integral part of the instructional process, assessments cannot be a one-shot, do-or-die experience for students. Instead, teachers must make assessments part of an ongoing effort to help students learn. And if teachers follow assessment with helpful corrective instruction, then students should have a second chance to demonstrate their new level of competence and understanding. This second chance not only helps determine the corrective instruction's effectiveness but also offers students another opportunity to experience success in their learning.

Writing teachers have long recognized the many benefits of a second chance. They know that students rarely write well on an initial attempt. Teachers build into the writing process several opportunities for students to gain feedback on early drafts and then use that feedback to revise and improve their writing. Teachers of other subjects frequently balk at the idea, however, mostly because it differs from their personal learning experiences.

Some teachers express concern that giving students a second chance might be unfair, warning that "life isn't like that." They point out that a surgeon doesn't get a second chance to successfully perform an operation and a pilot doesn't get a second chance to safely land a jumbo jet. Because of the very high stakes involved, each must get it right the first time.

But how did these highly skilled professionals learn their craft? The first operation performed by the surgeon was on a cadaver—a situation that allows a lot of latitude for mistakes. Similarly, the pilot spent many hours in a flight simulator before ever attempting a landing from the cockpit of a real jumbo jet. Such experiences allowed these professionals to learn from their mistakes and improve their performance. Similar instructional techniques are used in nearly every professional endeavor. Only in schools do students face the prospect of one-shot, do-or-die assessments, with no chance to demonstrate what they learned from previous mistakes.

All educators strive to have their students become lifelong learners and develop learning-to-learn skills. What better learning-to-learn skill is there than learning from one's mistakes? A mistake often becomes the beginning of true learning. Some assessment experts argue, in fact, that students learn nothing from a successful performance. Rather, students learn best when their initial performance is less than successful, because then they can gain guidance and direction on how to improve (Wiggins, 1998).

> *"I didn't fail the test; I just found 100 ways to do it wrong."*
>
> *—Benjamin Franklin*

Other teachers suggest that it's unfair to offer the same privileges and high grades to students who required a second chance that were given to students who demonstrated a high level of learning on the initial assessment. After all, these students may simply have failed to prepare appropriately or put forth the necessary effort.

Certainly, we should recognize students who do well on the initial assessment and provide opportunities for them to extend their learning through exciting and challenging enrichment activities. But those students who do well on a second assessment have also learned well. More important, their poor performance on the first assessment may not have been their fault. Maybe the teacher's initial instructional strategies were inappropriate for these students, and the corrective activities proved more effective (Guskey, 2008). If the purpose of a grade is to describe what students have learned and are able to do, and these students have performed at the same high level, then they certainly deserve the same grades as those who scored well on their first try.

A comparable example is the driver's license examination. Many individuals do not pass their driver's test on the first attempt. On the second or third try, however, they ultimately reach the same high level of performance that others did on their first. Should these drivers have restricted driving privileges? For instance, should they be allowed to drive only in fair weather? In inclement weather, should they be required to pull their cars over and park until the weather clears? Of course not! They demonstrated their driving skill at an established proficiency level. And because they eventually met the same high standards of performance, they are granted the same privileges. The same should hold true for students who show that they, too, have learned well (Guskey, 2003).

Similarities to Tutoring, Coaching, and Successful Students

When tutoring individual students, teachers naturally use assessments as sources of information, follow assessments with corrective instruction, and give students second chances at success. If the student they are tutoring makes a mistake, they stop and point out the error (feedback), re-explain the idea or concept in a different way (corrective), and then ask a follow-up question or pose a similar problem to ensure the student's understanding before going on (another chance at success). The challenge for teachers is to use their classroom assessments in similar ways to provide *all* students with this type of individualized assistance in group-based classroom settings (Bloom, 1981).

Successful coaches use the same process in training athletes. For example, immediately following a gymnast's performance on the balance beam, the coach explains to her what she did correctly and what she could improve. The coach then offers specific strategies for improvement and encourages her to try again. As the athlete repeats her performance, the coach watches carefully to ensure that she has corrected the problem and improved her performance.

Successful students use similar strategies on their own to improve their performance in school. They save their assessments and review the items or criteria that they missed. They rework problems, look up answers in online sources or other resource materials, and ask the teacher about ideas or concepts that they don't understand. Less-successful students, however, rarely take such initiative. After looking at their grades and the teachers' comments, they typically crumple up their assessment and deposit it in the trash can as they leave the classroom. Teachers who use classroom assessments as part of the instructional process help *all* of their students do what the most successful students have learned to do for themselves.

Practices to Avoid With Second Assessments

This chapter emphasized that using classroom assessments to improve student learning is not a new idea. As previously noted, Bloom (1968, 1971) proposed this process in his description of mastery learning in the late 1960s. Bloom was the first to apply the term *formative* to assessments in education and coauthored the first book on the topic, *Handbook on Formative and Summative Evaluation of Student Learning* (Bloom, Hastings, & Madaus, 1971). Since then, Bloom's ideas have been implemented in widely varied education contexts and consistently found to yield significant improvements in student learning (Anderson, 1994; Guskey & Pigott, 1988; Klecker & Chapman, 2008; Kulik, Kulik, & Bangert-Drowns, 1990; Miles, 2010).

The current emphasis on using assessments to inform instruction and "assessments for learning" (Chappuis & Stiggins, 2017) has led to a resurgence of interest in Bloom's ideas. Unfortunately, many advocates of these ideas fail to mention Bloom's originating contribution. Among the many books available to educators today on formative assessment, relatively few mention the foundational work of Bloom and his colleagues.

Even more disconcerting is that many writers and consultants recommend practices related to Bloom's work on formative assessment that have no basis in the established theory of mastery learning or any supporting research evidence. When these untested practices fail to yield the promised results, doubts arise about the effects of the formative assessment process and the potential of teachers to use formative assessments to improve student learning.

This section describes some of those recommended practices, explains why they are misaligned with Bloom's ideas, and presents specific, tested practices that teachers can use to ensure more positive results.

Expecting Students to Do Correctives on Their Own

Some teachers believe it's sufficient simply to go over formative assessments and offer students a redo or retake opportunity without engaging students in teacher-directed corrective activities that offer a new and different approach to learning. This strategy seldom yields significant improvement in students' performance. Even if students recall which of their initial responses were incorrect, they may have no clear understanding of the nature of their errors. Students need specific guidance and direction *from their teachers* that is different from the initial instruction to correct their learning errors and misunderstandings. Without it, little improvement can be expected.

> "Some people drink from the fountain of knowledge; others just gargle."
>
> —Robert Anthony

Making Correctives Voluntary

Teachers sometimes take the step of recommending corrective strategies to students that involve different presentations and different forms of engagement in learning, but then allow participation in these activities to be voluntary. Without experiencing the personal benefits of corrective work, however, students often doubt that it will make any difference. Recall the discussion in chapter 3 (page 61) regarding how *experience shapes attitudes and beliefs*. Students must personally experience how their involvement in well-designed corrective activities helps them achieve learning success. Teachers who initially *require* students to take part in the corrective process and conduct corrective activities in class ensure that students gain this direct experience.

Having Correctives Completed Initially as Homework or in a Special Study Session

To avoid the perceived loss of instructional time, many teachers require students to complete their corrective work outside of class, either as a homework assignment or in a special study session held before or after regular school hours. But as discussed earlier, students who could benefit most from this corrective work are typically the least likely to engage in these out-of-class options. Only after students become accustomed to the corrective process, experience success, and realize the personal benefits it brings can most of the corrective work be completed outside of regular class time.

Proceeding to More Advanced Units Before Corrective Work Is Completed

Fearing that the use of class time for corrective activities will diminish the curriculum content they can cover, some teachers begin instruction on subsequent units before students complete their corrective work and take the second formative assessment. However, this doubles the learning challenge for students engaged in correctives. They must keep up with the new unit's concepts and skills while working to remedy learning difficulties experienced in the previous unit.

Teachers who allow class time for students to complete corrective work before proceeding to the next unit not only ensure that all students have the necessary prerequisites for success with the new material, but they also eliminate the double burden for those students involved in correctives. As explained earlier, completing corrective work typically doesn't require a lot of time. Most teachers use only a class period or two for students to complete their corrective work and take the second assessment. In addition, as students become accustomed to the process, teachers gradually reduce that time. Furthermore, most teachers find that completing corrective activities and guaranteeing greater student success in early units allow them to cover later units more rapidly so that no curriculum content is lost.

Having No Positive Corollary for Success on the First Assessment

Occasionally teachers get so involved in developing and implementing corrective activities that they neglect enrichment options for the students who learn well. These students then simply bide their time while class-mates complete correctives and have little motivation to do well on the first assessments in subsequent learning units. Teachers must remember that planning exciting and rewarding enrichment activities for students who have demonstrated their mastery of the important learning goals is an essential aspect of this process. These enrichment activities should be enticing to students, offer valuable learning experiences, and motivate students to do well on subsequent classroom assessments. They represent a tangible benefit for doing well on the first assessment.

Limiting Scores on the Second Assessment

To motivate students to put forth their best effort and do well on the first assessment, some teachers limit the score students can achieve on the second assessment. With this policy, even if students take the corrective process seriously, remedy all their learning difficulties, and perform excellently on the second assessment, they cannot achieve the highest score. However, such a policy contradicts the purposes of both instruction and assessment. If assessment results accurately depict students' performance, and if students show they've mastered the identified learning goals, a lower score is inaccurate, unjustified, and unfair. In addition, no evidence confirms that such a policy has any positive impact on students' motivation to put forth their best effort. If students perform well and demonstrate their mastery of learning goals on the second assessment, then their score should reflect that.

Making the Second Assessment More Difficult

Teachers are sometimes advised that making the second assessment more difficult will motivate students to put forth their best effort on the first assessment. But again, no evidence supports this practice, and it contradicts Bloom's (1968, 1971) ideas regarding the purpose of the formative assessment process. It is also inherently unfair and unjust.

In his original descriptions of using assessments to enhance learning, Bloom (1968, 1971) stressed that the second formative assessment must be *parallel* to the first. This means it must assess the same concepts and skills at the same level of cognitive complexity and with the same level of difficulty. Making the second assessment more difficult alters the expectations for student performance. It also changes the rules for students in the middle of the game.

Making the second assessment harder is like saying to students, "Your task is to jump over a three-foot hurdle. If you can't do it, we are going to offer you some additional training to improve your skill. But to be fair to those students who didn't need the extra training and to ensure you try harder in upcoming tasks, we're next going to insist you jump over a four-foot hurdle." Not only does this change the learning goal, but it also makes the goal more difficult for students to achieve. At all levels and in all subject areas, the second assessment should *always* be truly parallel to the first—*not more difficult.*

Formative Versus Summative Assessments

In his earliest writings on using assessments as an integral part of the instructional process, Bloom (1968, 1971) drew clear distinctions between *formative* and *summative* assessments. He stressed, however, that this difference does not lie in an assessment's appearance, content, or structure. One cannot look at an instrument, composition, performance task, or demonstration and determine whether it's a formative or summative assessment. The difference lies instead in the assessment's purpose and how teachers use the results.

As previous noted, Bloom (1968, 1971) defined *formative assessment* as any instrument or diagnostic process a teacher uses to determine how well students have learned. Formative assessments further serve as a principal aid in preparing corrective measures to remedy students' learning errors and to improve instructional procedures. The primary purpose of formative assessments, therefore, is to offer diagnostic feedback and prescribe steps for improvement.

Bloom further stressed that a formative assessment can take many forms. Some are short, objective quizzes made up of matching, multiple-choice, or completion items. Others are essays, compositions, skill demonstrations, projects or reports, performance tasks, or oral presentations. Any one or combination of these assessment forms is appropriate, so long as specific performance expectations are clearly defined and communicated to students.

Summative assessments, on the other hand, are culminating demonstrations of what students have learned and are able to do (Bloom, 1968, 1971). They are typically broader in scope than individual formative assessments and usually administered after several units of instruction. While formative assessments are similar to classroom quizzes, summative assessments more closely resemble full class-period examinations. They measure students' mastery of criterion goals or standards for a subject area or course. Teachers generally use summative assessments as a primary source of evidence for certifying competence and assigning grades.

Therefore, Bloom (1968, 1971; Bloom et al., 1971) saw summative assessments as a synthesis of the concepts and skills measured on formative assessments across several instructional units. As such, summative assessments contain nothing new or unfamiliar to students. They typically focus on the most essential understandings in a subject area or course, but teachers have asked students to demonstrate mastery of these important concepts and skills before this time. Summative assessments give students a concluding opportunity to show how well they have learned and what they have accomplished—a true culminating demonstration of learning.

Figure 7.1 shows the relationship between the concepts and skills taught, formative assessments, and summative assessments. Note that nothing included on the formative assessments rests outside what is taught. If it's important enough to assess, then it's surely important enough to teach. Similarly, nothing included on the summative assessments lies outside what teachers have addressed on the formative assessments. If it's important that students show how well they've achieved these learning goals at the end, then it's essential they have opportunities to practice and receive feedback along the way.

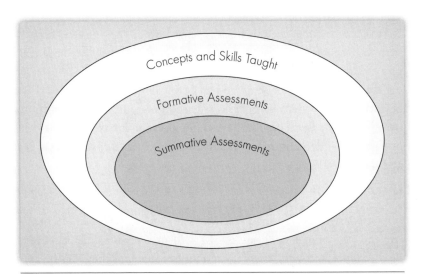

Figure 7.1: The relationship between formative and summative assessments.

Second Chances on Summative Assessments

Clarifying the relationship between formative and summative assessments also sheds light on the debate about second chances on summative assessments. Just as athletes do not run plays for the first time in a championship game and musicians do not play compositions for the first time at a major recital, students are not demonstrating what they have learned for the first time on summative assessments. *Everything* included on a summative assessment students should have seen previously on formative assessments. If they experienced difficulties on the formative assessments, students should have received guidance and direction on correcting those difficulties, and had another chance to demonstrate their learning on a second formative assessment. If their teacher included spiraling items or prompts on formative assessments (for example, items or prompts that refer to concepts addressed in previous instructional units), they may have had a third and fourth chance, or even more. The point is that when formative assessments are used well, summative assessments are *never* the first opportunity.

For this reason, second chances on summative assessments are usually unnecessary. Just as athletes don't get second chances in championship games or musicians don't get second chances in major recitals, summative assessments may be considered a similar sort of crowning performance.

At the same time, there is nothing that forbids the practice. If time permits, teachers certainly may offer students a second chance opportunity on summative assessments. In addition, if the teacher has reason to believe that factors outside of students' control may have affected their performance on that one occasion, a second opportunity is not only permissible but advisable. In the end, the decision is based on teachers' professional judgment, often in consultation with teaching colleagues and school leaders.

How to Find Time

As discussed earlier, some teachers fear that taking time for corrective and enrichment activities following formative assessments in every instructional unit will lessen the amount of material they will be able to cover. They believe that using class time to help students remedy learning errors will mean that critical curriculum elements will need to be omitted. As a result, some students may reach a higher level of learning, but all students will learn less.

Corrective and enrichment activities do add time to early instructional units. But after students become accustomed to the process and realize its advantages, most teachers reduce the class time they allocate to these activities. They use more student-initiated activities and ask students to complete more of their corrective work outside class. As students remedy their learning problems in early units, they also perform better on formative assessments in subsequent units. These improvements lead to more students becoming involved in enrichment activities and fewer students engaged in correctives. The amount of corrective work each student needs to reach the mastery standard also diminishes (Whiting et al., 1995).

Modest changes in instruction further lessen the extra time needed. For example, many teachers eliminate review sessions prior to formative assessments and shift that time to corrective and enrichment activities. With the results from formative assessments, teachers become more efficient in their review, concentrating on only those concepts and skills that pose problems for students. In addition, by allowing fast learners to demonstrate their proficiency and move on to independent enrichment activities, teachers can spend their time with the students who most need their assistance.

> "Yesterday is history, tomorrow is a mystery, today is a gift; that is why they call it the present."
> —Kung Fu Panda

In general, teachers do not need to sacrifice content coverage to implement corrective and enrichment activities, but they need to be flexible in pacing their instruction. The time used for correctives and enrichments in early units yields powerful benefits that will allow the pace of instruction to be faster later on. Teachers need to keep in mind what students need to accomplish by the end of any learning sequence, but they also must see students' pathways to that end in more flexible and accommodating terms.

Grades Versus Comments on Assessments

Across the decades, battles have raged over whether teachers should put grades, comments, or both on assessments of student learning. Opinions on this issue vary widely among teachers, school leaders, and even grading and assessment consultants. Some are adamant that assessments, especially formative ones, must *never* be graded and should include comments only. Others point out that, in some schools, the results of formative assessments are included as part of the reporting process, and thus grades are needed. A number of schools, for example, have implemented 80/20 grading policies where 80 percent of a student's grade is based on the results from summative assessments and 20 percent from formative assessments (Brumage-Kilcourse, 2017; Stoskopf, 2016; Trembath, 2017).

The debate on grades versus comments extends to summative assessments as well. Most educators believe that summative assessments are specifically designed for assigning grades to certify student competence and report on their learning progress (Brookhart & Nitko, 2008). Others contend, however, that grades have such negative consequences that they should be eliminated from summative assessments, leaving comments as the sole form of feedback students receive on their learning (Barnes, 2018; Kohn, 1994, 1999; Spencer, 2017).

Like many issues in education, the truth is not as clear-cut as some suggest. The research on this issue is far more complicated and more highly nuanced than most writers acknowledge. By considering the complexities identified in this research, educators can develop feedback policies and practices that are far more effective and much more likely to benefit students.

Early Research on Grades and Comments

One of the earliest studies on how grades and teacher comments affect students' achievement was conducted by psychologist Ellis Page in 1958. In this classic study, seventy-four secondary school teachers administered an assessment to the students in their classes and scored it in their usual way. A numerical score was assigned to each student's paper and, on the basis of that score, a letter grade of A, B, C, D, or F. Teachers then randomly divided students' papers into three groups.

Papers in the first group received only the numerical score and letter grade. The second group, in addition to the score and grade, received the following standard comments with the associated grade.

- **A:** *"Excellent! Keep it up."*
- **B:** *"Good work. Keep at it."*
- **C:** *"Perhaps try to do still better."*
- **D:** *"Let's bring this up."*
- **F:** *"Let's raise this grade!"*

For the third group, teachers provided the score and a letter grade, and wrote individualized comments on each paper that corresponded to the teachers' personal feelings and instructional practices. Papers were then returned to students in the customary way.

Page (1958) evaluated the effects of the comments by considering students' scores on the very next assessment given in the class. Students who received the standard comments with their grade achieved *significantly higher* scores than those who received only a score and grade, and the students who received individualized comments did even better. Based on these results, Page concluded that grades can have a beneficial effect on student learning *only* when accompanied by standard or individualized comments from the teacher. Studies conducted in later years confirmed these results (Stewart & White, 1976).

Page's (1958) study is important for two reasons. First, it illustrates that while writing a single score and a grade on students' papers does nothing to improve student learning, grades with comments can enhance students' achievement and performance. Second, and perhaps more important, it shows that these positive effects can be gained with relatively little effort. Even standard comments can have a significant positive influence on students' performance.

A crucial but often missed aspect of Page's (1958) study, however, relates to the nature of the teachers' comments. All of the standard comments included in the study emphasize two important factors. First, they communicate the teachers' high expectations for students and the importance of students' effort. Second, all of the comments stress to students that the teacher is on their side and willing to work with them to make improvements. Note, for example, that the comment is not "*You* must raise this grade!" but "*Let's* raise this grade!" In other words, "*I'm* with you in this!" and "*We* can do it!" Thus, it may not be simply that comments make a difference. The message teachers communicate in their comments may be what matters most.

Grades and Mastery

In his earliest descriptions of mastery learning, Bloom (1968; Bloom et al., 1971) was very clear that students should receive only one of two grades on formative assessments: *mastery* or *not mastery*. When pressed about what he meant by *mastery*, Bloom recognized that any answer he offered was sure to draw criticism. So rather than press teachers to define mastery anew, he simply requested, "Tell me what you expect of students to receive a grade of A." That level of performance then becomes the mastery expectation *for all*.

Bloom (1968) believed different levels of *not mastery* were unnecessary, and he emphasized that this designation must *always* be seen as temporary—or more accurately described as *not yet*. As he stated in his 1968 article, "Learning for Mastery":

> We are expressing the view that, given sufficient time and appropriate types of help, 95% of students . . . can learn a subject up to a high level of mastery. We are convinced that the grade of "A" as an index of mastery of a subject can, under appropriate conditions, be achieved by up to 95% of the students in a class. (p. 4)

Bloom further emphasized that students in the *not mastery* or *not yet* category *must* receive feedback from teachers that is both *diagnostic and prescriptive*. The diagnostic portion identifies for students precisely what they were expected to learn, what they have learned well to that point, and what they need to learn better. The prescriptive portion describes what students need to do next to improve their learning. Hence, Bloom advocated grades *and* comments, so long as both met the criteria he described.

Comments and Motivation

A study by Ruth Butler (1988) focused on the difference between *ego-involving feedback* and *task-involving feedback* on students' interest and motivation. The investigation involved 132 fifth- and sixth-grade students randomly assigned to one of three feedback conditions. The first group received what Butler labeled *ego-involving numerical grades* ranging from 40 to 99 that were based on students' normative performance. In other words, rather than basing grades on specific learning criteria, teachers based students' grades on their relative standing among classmates and assigned grades "to follow a normal distribution" (Butler, 1988, p. 4).

The second group received *task-involving individual comments* related to the students' performance on the learning task. A third group received both the grades and comments. Results showed that students' interest and performance were generally higher after task-involving comments than after ego-involving grades alone or grades with comments. The results of this study were not entirely consistent, however, and revealed what researchers label an *interaction effect*. Specifically, the effects were true *only* for low-achieving students (students ranked in the bottom 25 percent of their class).

High achievers (students ranked in the top 25 percent of their class) who received grades maintained their high interest and motivation. In other words, the influence of grades on motivation varied depending on the grade students received. The fifth and sixth graders who got high grades continued to have high interest and motivation, and those who got low grades based on their normative standing among classmates experienced diminished interest and motivation. The study did not consider whether this is true for students who are younger or older, or for the 50 percent of fifth- and sixth-grade students who ranked in the middle of their classmates.

Similar to the Page (1958) study, an important aspect of this investigation to note is the nature of the feedback students received. *Ego-involving* implies the grades are about the students, and specifically about each student's standing relative to classmates, whereas *task-involving* implies the comments are about the learning goal. If Butler's (1988) study had considered criterion-referenced grades or ego-involving comments such as "You need to work harder" or "This isn't your best work," the results might have been quite different. Thus, it would be incorrect to treat this study as a simple validation of comments over grades. As John Hattie and Helen Timperley's (2007) research review on feedback makes clear, the quality, nature, and content of comments are what matter most. Hence, before making the sweeping recommendation, "No grades; comments only!" we must always consider both the nature of the grades *and* the nature of the comments teachers give.

Factors That Influence the Effects of Feedback

In a large-scale meta-analysis of the effects of offering students feedback through formative assessments, Neal Kingston and Brooke Nash (2011) challenged estimates of the magnitude of influence of that feedback, regardless of the use of grades or comments. Their analysis revealed that the existing research base does *not* support the claim that formative assessments yield average improvements of 25–30 percentile points in student achievement (effect size = +.70 to +.90; Black & Wiliam, 1998a, 1998b; Hattie, 2009). Their review of more than three hundred studies that address the efficacy of formative assessments in grades K–12 found an improvement of only about 10 percentile points (effect size = +.25).

Kingston and Nash (2011) also discovered that the effects of formative assessments varied greatly from study to study, ranging from a decline of 35 percentile points (effect size = –1.0) to an increase of 43 percentile points (effect size = +1.5). Investigating the reasons for this variation, they discovered that the effects of formative assessment feedback differed depending on the following factors.

- **The subject area of instruction:** Generally, formative assessment feedback is more effective in language arts than in mathematics or science.

- **Students' grade level:** Applications in lower elementary grades appear slightly more effective than those in secondary classrooms.

- **The way teachers implement feedback:** Professional development for teachers and computer-based formative systems appear more effective than other approaches.

Their conclusion about the true impact that formative assessment feedback has on student learning was, essentially, "It depends" (Guskey, 2019a).

Factors That Influence the Effects of Comments and Grades

Given these mixed results, there is little we can say with absolute certainty about the effects of grades, comments, or both on assessments. The nature of the grades, the nature of the comments, and contextual factors all appear to make an important difference. The precise nature of these differences, however, has yet to be determined. Factors that appear worthy of further investigation include:

- The nature of the assessments (for example, multiple-choice or completion assessments versus compositions, projects, skill demonstrations, or performances)

- The subject area and content of the instruction (for example, language arts versus mathematics, science, social studies, art, music, or physical education)

- Students' age or grade level (for example, elementary students versus middle, high school, or college students)

- Students' background and previous academic experiences (for example, high achieving versus low achieving)

- Students' economic background (for example, privileged versus economically disadvantaged)

- Individual students' beliefs about success or failure and their sense of self-efficacy (for example, students who perceive their actions can influence the grades or comments they receive versus those who do not)

- The nature of the grades and comments and what each communicates (for example, ego-involving versus task-involving)

- The interaction between grades and comments (for example, the influence of comments may vary depending on the grade)

Lessons From the Research

Given this complexity, what guidance does the existing research offer teachers in their use of grades and comments on student assessments? First, we know that while grades certainly have their limitations, they are not inherently good or bad. Grades are simply labels attached to different levels of student performance that describe in an abbreviated fashion how well students performed. These labels can be letters, numbers, words, phrases, or symbols. They can serve important formative purposes by helping students know where they are on the path to achieving specific learning goals.

We also know that grades should *always* be based on clearly articulated learning criteria, *not* norm-based criteria. Grades derived from norm-based criteria—that is, ego-involving indicators of students' relative standing among classmates—communicate nothing about what students learned or are able to do. Hence, they have no formative value whatsoever. Instead, norm-based grades compel students to compete against their classmates for the few high grades the teacher distributes (Guskey, 2006). Such competition is detrimental to relationships between students and has profound negative effects on the motivation of low-ranked students, as the results from the Butler (1988) study clearly show.

We must also keep in mind, however, that criterion-based, task-involving grades alone aren't helpful in improving student learning. Students get nothing out of a letter, number, word, phrase, or symbol attached to evidence of their learning. Grades help enhance achievement and foster learning progress *only* when they are paired with individualized comments that offer guidance and direction for improvement.

To serve important formative purposes, students and their families must understand that grades do not reflect *who* you are as a learner, but reflect *where* you are in your learning journey—and *where is always temporary*. Knowing where you are is essential in determining what you need to do to improve. Informed judgments from teachers about the quality of students' performance can also help students become more thoughtful judges of their own work (Chappuis & Stiggins, 2017).

Regarding comments, we must remember the four essential aspects of feedback that Bloom initially stressed and later reinforced (1968, 1971, 1976; Bloom et al., 1981).

1. **Always begin with the positive:** Comments to students should first point out what they did well and recognize their accomplishments.

2. **Identify what specific aspects of students' performance need to improve:** Students need to know precisely where to focus their improvement efforts.

3. **Offer specific guidance and direction for making improvements:** Students need to know what steps to take in order to make their product, performance, or demonstration better and more in line with the established learning criteria.

4. **Express confidence in students' ability to learn excellently and achieve at the highest level:** Students need to know their teachers believe in them, see value in their work, and have confidence they can achieve the specified learning goals (Guskey, 2019a).

Summary

Because assessments of student learning provide the primary evidence used to determine grades, teachers must ensure their assessments reliably and accurately measure the learning goals they want students to achieve (Guskey & Brookhart, 2019). Bloom (1968, 1971; Bloom et al., 1971) described how teachers can use assessments as an integral part of the instructional process to enhance student learning. Through a strategy he labeled *mastery learning*, Bloom explained how assessments can become formative sources of information on learning progress for both students and teachers.

But formative assessments alone are insufficient for improving learning, even if they are well designed, meaningful, and authentic. Teachers must follow formative assessments with high-quality corrective instruction that presents the essential concepts and skills differently and engages students in learning differently than the initial instruction did. Checking on students' learning progress and providing feedback on results is just the start. Students also need guidance and direction from their teachers about what to do to get better (Guskey, 2008).

Grades offer students important feedback on their learning progress. They help students identify where they are in their journey to mastering important grade-level or course learning goals. But like assessments, grades alone don't help students improve. Teachers should offer comments that identify what students did well, what improvements they need to make, and how they can make those improvements. Comments provided with sensitivity to important context elements can guide students on their pathway to learning success and ensure that all students learn excellently.

Develop a Systematic Plan for Implementation

Our biggest problem as human beings is not knowing that we don't know.

—Virginia Satir

You made it! You've come a long way to get here, and I hope it's been worthwhile. I know the journey hasn't been easy, and you've undoubtedly struggled along the way. But leading reform efforts in grading and reporting isn't about doing what's easy. It's about challenging traditions that have long outlived their usefulness. It's about recognizing the extensive knowledge base on grading and reporting that researchers have amassed since the early 1900s and putting those ideas into practice. It's about doing what is right and what we know is better for our students.

On this journey, we challenged many "thought-to-be-true" beliefs about grading and reporting reform, the change process, and what actually leads to successful implementation. We questioned ideas promoted by writers and consultants in various books, blogs, and social media chats and disagreed with some of their recommendations. Through it all, I did my best to be honest about the ideas we discussed, admit limitations and shortcomings where they exist, and not argue opinions. Nobody ever wins arguments of opinion. As described in chapter 3 (page 61) on the change process, arguments of opinion serve mostly to harden the perspectives of those involved, rather than to change those perspectives.

This book's approach has been different in that way. In each chapter, I strived to provide evidence to support the ideas presented. When evidence was scant or totally absent, I noted that and identified specific ideas worthy of investigation. With every topic discussed, I did my best to stick with what we know to be true, rather than simply advocate for what I believe. As Jake Tapper, the American journalist and television commentator, frequently says, "There aren't two sides when it comes to the truth. There is only one side: *the truth*."

Hopefully, you are now thinking about these issues in new ways, seeing them in a new light, and considering their consequences for everyone involved in the grading and reporting process: students, families, teachers, school leaders, board members, and community members. With any luck, you have gained new direction in developing reform initiatives that are more purposeful, better informed, and far more likely to succeed. Now, we come to the conclusion: how to put it all together.

> "The ones who are crazy enough to think they can change the world are the ones who do."
> —Steve Jobs

No "Best Practices" and No Perfect Grading System

As with several earlier chapters, we need to begin this chapter with a word of caution. It is simply this: please remember *there are no best practices in grading and reporting*, and *there is no perfect grading and reporting system*.

I know that may be shocking to some and probably unsettling to all. It is surely different from what you might have been told in books, blogs, or chats by writers and consultants who claim to know what is truly "best." And, quite honestly, I wish their claims were true. If they were true, it would make it so much easier for all of us who are struggling to improve grading and reporting systems and trying hard to ensure those systems consistently work in the best interest of students. But, regrettably, it's not true.

Recall our earlier discussion of how Susan Brookhart and I assembled a group of exceptionally talented scholars to analyze and interpret the vast body of research evidence on grading and reporting. We described their brilliant work in our book, *What We Know About Grading* (Guskey & Brookhart, 2019). The conclusion these scholars reached after considering the over one hundred years of research on grading confirms that some practices are clearly *better* than others and provide the basis for making significant improvements. We know, for example, that replacing the unreliable percentage grading scale, which includes 101 distinct performance levels and offers only the illusion of precision, with grading scales that include fewer but more reliably discernible categories of performance would improve grading. We know it is better to base grades on clearly articulated learning criteria than on students' relative ranking among classmates. We know it is better to offer multiple grades that reflect specific product, progress, and process criteria than to combine evidence on these criteria into a single hodgepodge grade that confounds interpretation. Making these changes will greatly improve the communicative value of any grading and reporting system.

What this extensive body of research evidence does not offer, however, are prescriptions for specific policies and practices that we know will work well for *all* students under *all* conditions, which is precisely what *best* implies.

If we implement grading scales with fewer and more reliably discernible categories of performance, for example, we don't yet know the best number of categories to include or the best way to label those categories. If we provide multiple grades reflecting different types of learning criteria, we don't yet know the best criteria to use or the best types of product, progress, and process criteria to consider. Although we can take many important steps to make grading and reporting much better, we still have a long way to go in determining what is truly best.

The major reason we cannot identify best practices and describe a perfect grading and reporting system is because of the powerful influence of context. Research reveals that context matters greatly in grading and reporting, just as it does in almost all aspects of teaching and learning (Llinares & Lyster, 2014; Salili, Chiu, & Hong, 2001). What works best in grading and reporting varies depending on the purpose, the students' characteristics (for example, their age, developmental level, and learning background), the school's culture and other features, and the nature of the communication. These intervening factors snarl effects and complicate implementation.

Nevertheless, not knowing what is truly best shouldn't deter us from using the extensive research evidence we have to take positive steps in the right direction and make grading and reporting much better. As Mark Manson (2016) reminds us:

> Growth is an endlessly iterative process. When we learn something new, we don't go from "wrong" to "right." Rather, we go from wrong to slightly less wrong. And when we learn something additional, we go from slightly less wrong to slightly less wrong than that, and then to even less wrong than that, and so on. We are always in the process of approaching truth and perfection without actually ever reaching truth and perfection. (p. 117)

Our goal, therefore, should not be to employ only best practices or implement a perfect grading and reporting system. We don't have the knowledge or understanding to do that. The nuances of the process and the influence of context make it impossible.

Instead, we should aim to use the knowledge base we have to do things better than we do them now. We need to see grading and reporting more as a challenge in effective communication, rather than one of simply quantifying student achievement. We need to stop using grades to sort and rank students and instead use them to guide students in making improvements in their learning. Most important, we need to help students understand that grades define not who they are as learners but where they are in their learning journey—and where is *always* temporary.

> "The less there is to justify a traditional custom, the harder it is to get rid of it."
> —Mark Twain

These changes won't yield grading and reporting systems that are perfect. But they will make those systems much better—and that alone is significant and valuable.

Essential Elements of Successful Reform Plans

Earlier chapters in this book described a series of essential steps in implementing successful grading and reporting reforms. These include the following.

1. Learn from failures.

2. Form a Coalition for Change.

3. Understand the change process.

4. Clarify the purpose of grading and reporting.

5. Report multiple grades for cognitive and noncognitive outcomes.

6. Get assessment policies and practices right.

7. Develop a systematic plan for implementation.

All of these steps are important and must be approached thoughtfully and purposefully. As discussed in chapter 1 (page 17), the reasons so many grading reform initiatives fail can usually be traced back to misunderstandings in one of these steps or to the complete absence of a particular step in the reform process.

With these crucial steps in place, we now turn to vital elements of the final step: developing a systematic plan for implementation. These elements include (1) surveys of stakeholders, (2) presentations to all staff, (3) presentations to parents and families, and (4) follow-up feedback. In some cases, these elements are practical extensions of earlier steps, while others are crucial additions. We turn to them here because they set forth important details that can make or break the most carefully laid plans.

Surveys of Stakeholders

Success in grading and reporting reform requires a deep understanding of the perspectives of key stakeholders, especially students, teachers, parents and families, school leaders, district administrators, and school board members. What do they value? What makes sense to them? What do they find most useful? What helps them? Broad-based inclusion of these stakeholder groups in the Coalition for Change is an important step in the planning process. Conducting a stakeholder survey can provide even more detailed information and can be extremely valuable in guiding reform efforts.

The best surveys ask questions derived from research on the essential factors of effective grading and reporting practices. Carefully crafted research-based questions help reduce concerns about survey validity. The most useful surveys ask different stakeholder groups the same critical questions in order to determine their concerns and gauge similarities and differences in their perspectives.

Figure 8.1 (page 224) shows an example from GradingRx™ of responses from early elementary (K–2) parents, teachers, school leaders,

Question: Grades and report cards serve a variety of purposes. Based on your beliefs, how would you rank the following purposes from 1 (most important) to 6 (least important)?

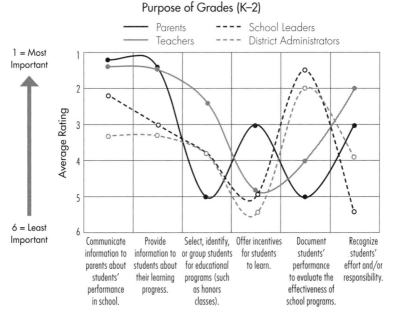

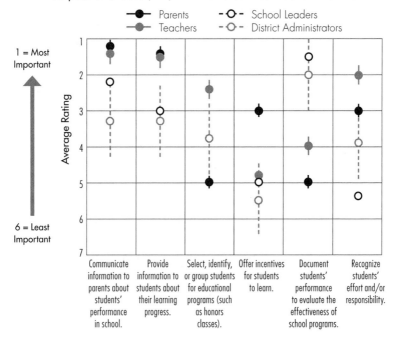

Source: © 2019 by GradingRx @ www.GradingRx.com. Used with permission.

Figure 8.1: Example analysis of a survey question on grading and reporting.

and district administrators to a survey question about the purpose of grades and report cards. The first graph compares the average responses of these different stakeholder groups. The second graph plots confidence intervals around these group averages. The confidence intervals that don't overlap indicate differences between groups' responses that are important and meet the criteria of statistical significance.

A quick review of this survey question's responses reveals important differences in stakeholder perceptions regarding the purpose of grades and report cards. Parents and teachers generally emphasize the communicative purpose of grades, while school and district leaders stress the use of grades to evaluate the effectiveness of school programs. Parents emphasize the incentive value of grades more than educators do. In addition, teachers believe more than others do in using grades to select students for educational programs and to recognize students' efforts and responsibility.

Knowing such differences exist among key stakeholders can help guide improvement efforts. In this case, for example, reform leaders can see they need to work with parents and families to reinforce the communicative purpose of grades rather than their use as incentives or rewards. Distinguishing learning and academic achievement from effort and responsibility also will be vitally important. With these essential data, education leaders, along with Coalition members, are better prepared to identify initial concerns, anticipate difficulties, directly address troubling issues, and guarantee greater success in reforming grading and reporting policies and practices.

Presentations to All Staff

At some point in the implementation process, most districts and schools find it helpful to have a presentation on new ideas about grading and reporting to the entire staff. They often invite board members and parent organization leaders to this presentation as well. The Coalition for Change generally plans the presentation and selects the presenter, but only after Coalition members have had the opportunity to learn about the change process and develop some background on effective grading policies and practices on their own.

Large-group presentations sometimes are discouraged and not considered a useful form of professional learning. Evidence indicates, however, that a well-planned, engaging presentation can serve three key purposes (Guskey, 2000a).

1. **A presentation can provide all staff members with a common knowledge base:** If everyone takes part in the same presentation, and if the presenter tailors the presentation to the issues and concerns most relevant to district or school staff members, the event can establish a baseline of information from which effective reform plans can be developed.

2. **A presentation can focus on the anticipated concerns of stakeholders, help alleviate fears, and dispel rumors:** Teachers and school leaders may believe, for example, that if they no longer consider homework assignments as part of students' academic (product) grades, students will think that homework no longer counts and will have no incentive to do it. Therefore, the presentation must assure teachers and school leaders that:

    • Teachers will still record homework assignments in the gradebook.

    • Parents will receive immediate notifications of incomplete or missing assignments.

    • In addition to their academic achievement grade, students will receive a separate grade for homework on the report card.

    • A summary of homework grades will be included on the transcript.

    With these fears and rumors laid to rest, teachers are much more likely to be receptive to the change. As a result, reform leaders can worry less about misunderstandings that can sabotage reform efforts and move on to addressing other issues more crucial to implementation success.

3. **A presentation can clarify *why* issues:** *Why* should we change the way we grade? *Why* is it necessary to have

consensus among teachers about the purpose of grades and report cards? *Why* is it important to have reasonable and reliable grading scales? *Why* do we need multiple grades that report product, progress, and process learning criteria separately? The district or school must thoroughly address and resolve these *why* issues. Only then will teachers and school leaders be ready to consider options regarding *what* needs to change and *how* to make those changes.

Presentations to Parents and Families

Many districts and schools also find it helpful to plan a presentation of new ideas about grading and reporting for parents and family members. They usually hold this presentation in the evening at a time most parents find convenient. They also keep it relatively brief—typically no more than an hour to an hour and a half—so parents don't have to spend too much time away from home.

Just like presentations to teachers and school leaders, this presentation should focus on *why* issues: *Why* are you changing the way you grade? *Why* do you think the current system doesn't work? *Why* do you believe this new system will be better? Perhaps even more important to address, however, are parents' and family members' highly personal concerns: *How* will this affect my children? *How* will it be better for them? *Are you sure* this won't hurt them in any way, especially when it comes to college admissions? All parents and families care about their children and want them to succeed in school (Henderson & Mapp, 2002; Hoover-Dempsey & Sandler, 1997). But they typically derive their beliefs about education, and especially grading and reporting, from their personal experience (Kohn, 1989). Most have had little or no experience with the grading and reporting reforms the school or district may be considering.

In addition to addressing these *why* and *how* issues, presentations to parents and family members must do the following.

1. **Keep in mind that parents and family members are not moved by philosophical arguments or logical appeals:** They also don't trust the opinions of outside consultants. Parents are particularly skeptical of changes they consider

educational fads, and they want evidence of the reforms' benefits for their children. This means presenters should be prepared to offer parents that evidence and specific resources parents can consult for additional information. They should provide access to reports on college admissions offices' perspectives, like those listed in chapter 4 (page 83). Presenters should also be open to parents' and family members' questions, both during the presentation and afterward as implementation efforts move forward.

2. **Inform parents and family members of plans to gather evidence from different stakeholder groups throughout the implementation process:** As chapter 4 described, parents must be informed of plans to gather evidence from different stakeholder groups throughout the implementation process. Presenters should also explain what plans are in place to gather feedback from teachers, school leaders, and perhaps students themselves. Most important, parents and family members should be assured that this feedback will be used to make revisions or modifications along the way if changes are needed.

3. **Emphasize to parents and family members that the goal in implementing grading and reporting reform is to do what is best for students:** Presenters should stress that the overall goal of these grading and reporting reforms is to improve communication about students' performance in school with parents, families, and students themselves. Perhaps most crucial, presenters need to underscore that improving communication is a two-way street where information flows both ways. Improving school-to-home communication means improving home-to-school communication as well. Educators, parents, and family members are partners in this process, sharing the same important hopes and goals for students.

Follow-Up Feedback

Because there are no "best practices" in grading and no "perfect grading systems," we need to gather evidence throughout the implementation process about what is working and what we may need to revise. This can be done formally through surveys or focus groups with different stakeholders, asking for their honest impressions about the impact of specific aspects of the reform. Informally, Coalition of Change members can gather lots of valuable feedback from stakeholder groups they represent and from others simply by asking, "How's it going?" Additional questions like "What seems to be working well?" or "What problems or difficulties have you experienced?" can help guide efforts to resolve any identified problem areas or trouble spots.

> "As a teacher, what I liked best about parent-teacher conferences is they always made me more forgiving of my students."
>
> —Thomas R. Guskey

Two important issues must to be kept in mind when soliciting this follow-up feedback.

1. **Don't ask for follow-up feedback too soon:** Teachers and school leaders need time to try out new grading policies and practices. They also need time to make subtle adaptations to ensure the new policies fit their particular context and to resolve any unanticipated difficulties. Teachers need time to experience new policies and practices, see how they work in their classrooms with their students, and gain evidence on what benefits they might yield. As discussed in chapter 2 (page 35), *experience shapes attitudes and beliefs*. Most districts and schools wait a few months—perhaps until the end of the first grading period, first quarter, or first semester—to gather follow-up feedback through any formal procedures.

2. **Assure everyone who offers feedback that its primary purpose is to make improvements based on input from *all* stakeholders:** The major audience for follow-up feedback is the Coalition for Change. These are the reform leaders who will take charge of gathering the feedback, interpreting the results, and then planning and implementing any necessary revisions. Grading and reporting reforms must be informed, collaborative efforts. This is the only way to ensure grading and reporting systems are honest, accurate, meaningful, and fair.

Grades as Temporary Labels

Chapter 5 (page 117) discussed the use of labels in identifying student proficiency levels. We described how different labels based on grades are attached to varying levels of student performance through complicated and multilayered procedures that can have confounding effects. On the bright side, labeling can allow students to get the specialized help they need to be successful in school from the adults most qualified to provide that assistance. In many cases, labels also help students gain individualized accommodations or program modifications to facilitate their learning. On the dark side, labeling can create glass ceilings for students that hold them back. Labels may actually limit, rather than expand, students' opportunities.

The real problem, however, rests not so much with the labels but with their permanence and scope. Labels sometimes assign students to fixed categories, and getting out of those categories can be tough. To remedy the potentially negative consequences of labels, we must do two things: (1) ensure that, in most cases, labels describe a temporary situation rather than a permanent condition, and (2) link labels to specific learning goals, rather than consider them immutable characteristics of particular students.

The Permanence of Labels and Grades

A contributing factor to the permanence of labels in education is simply the language we use—that is, English. In other languages, the distinction between permanent and temporary conditions is much clearer. In Spanish, for example, the difference is explicit.

In Spanish, *es* is a conjugation of the verb *ser*, which means "to be." *Ser* is used for things that are permanent or consistently descriptive. *She is a happy person*, for example, is translated, "Ella *es* una persona feliz." This describes a permanent attribute or consistent aspect of her personality. Characteristics of a person or thing that are enduring or unchangeable require *ser*.

Está in Spanish is a conjugation of the verb *estar*, which also means "to be." But *estar* is used to describe temporary conditions like moods or location. *She is happy* is translated, "Ella *está* feliz," which means

"She is happy now, but tomorrow she might be sad." Conditions that are transitory and alterable require *estar*.

The labels we use to describe students should similarly be seen as temporary conditions, not as immutable characteristics. Perhaps if we used Spanish labels with the verb *estar*, that would be more evident. Students are not static in who they are or in what they know and can do. Their knowledge and skills, along with their talents and abilities, are constantly changing. As educators, we must maintain this perspective of the dynamic nature of students, and we must help students develop that same perspective of themselves.

When students face a learning challenge, for example, we want them to recognize that although they may be struggling now, that can and likely will change tomorrow. Everyone struggles with some things at some times. Most important, we want students to know that their teachers are here to help them and ready to offer guidance and assistance when those struggles occur.

We also want students to see grades as dynamic. Granted, education will always include timelines that specify when student performance assessments must be summative for the purposes of certification or assigning grades. But in most instances, we have

> *"Change will not come if we wait for some other person or some other time. We are the ones we've been waiting for. We are the change that we seek."*
> —Barack Obama

flexibility until we reach that time. Some teachers actually share the perspective that assessments should remain formative until students demonstrate mastery, and only then should they become summative.

In university classes, teachers assign grades based on students' performance at the end of each academic term or semester. Professors and instructors must adhere to those specified timelines. But nearly all universities also have the policy that if students retake a course and earn a higher grade, that higher grade replaces the first on students' transcripts. Universities do this because the higher grade is a more honest and accurate descriptor of students' level of performance and accomplishment. Interesting, too, is that the transcript gives no indication as to whether this is the first, second, or third time students took the course. Only the final level of achievement is important.

The Scope of Labels and Grades

In addition to seeing labels as temporary conditions, we must associate labels with specific learning goals, rather than consider them characteristics ascribed to particular students. One student may have difficulty in language arts, for example, but do well in mathematics. Another student may struggle with social studies but excel in science. Even within a subject like language arts, one student may have problems with reading but demonstrate exceptional talent in speaking and giving oral presentations. In mathematics, a particular student may experience difficulties with accuracy in basic computations but have great skill in problem solving.

In other words, the label is *not* attached to the student as an individual but attached to the student in relation to a specific learning goal. The same is true of grades. A student who struggles with one learning goal may be a gifted learner with another goal. As Will Rogers remarked, "Everybody is ignorant, only on different subjects" (Goodreads, n.d.). Whether students are struggling learners or gifted learners can change with every learning goal and every instructional unit.

> *"Ignorance is always afraid of change."*
>
> —Jawaharlal Nehru

A Meaningful Solution

The solution, therefore, is not simply to stop labeling students or stop giving grades. That ingenuous solution to a complex issue might deny students the special assistance they need and deserve. Does anyone really believe that if we simply stop labeling, it will cause all students to learn better and gain more than a year's worth of growth? The labeling itself isn't what matters. What matters is what we do with and about those labels (Guskey, 2018b).

What we must do is change the way we perceive, interpret, and act on labels and grades. We should never use labels or grades to put students into boxes that deny them opportunities and hold them back. Instead, we should use labels and grades to ensure that students receive the individualized opportunities and support they need to become successful learners. In particular, we must make certain the labels and grades we ascribe to students are temporary and targeted to specific learning goals.

Robert M. Hutchins, former president of the University of Chicago, offered this insight regarding programs for gifted students: "The best education for the best is the best education for all" (AZ Quotes, n.d.). The idea is that labels and grades should never pose limitations, but rather prescribe direction in our efforts to provide the best and most appropriate education for all students.

> "Change is the end result of all true learning."
> —Leo Buscaglia

Summary

Although true "best practices" do not exist in grading, and there are no perfect grading systems, much can be done to improve the grading practices used in many schools today. Surveys of stakeholders can provide valuable information for addressing concerns and guiding improvement efforts. Carefully planned presentations to staff members and to parents and families that explain the need for change and the advantages of planned reforms can help soothe the transition to new policies and practices. Planned follow-up activities designed to gather feedback on stakeholders' reactions to reforms, as well as both the intended and unintended consequences of those new policies and practices, can be vital to ensuring implementation success. Finally, changing the way we perceive, interpret, and act on the labels and grades we assign to students, always ensuring those labels and grades are seen as temporary markers rather than permanent characteristics, will help guarantee that they facilitate students' progress and success rather than limit their opportunities.

Significant challenges lie before those who set out to reform grading and reporting policies and practices. But those who approach the process with knowledge, skill, dedication, and thoughtful planning can know uncommon success.

Final Thoughts

So there you have it. We've come to the end of this part of our journey. I'm sure that throughout this book, I didn't answer every question you have about implementing successful reforms in grading and reporting student learning. And as much as I would like to, I also can't guarantee that following all the recommendations described on these pages will result in highly effective and trouble-free reforms no matter where you implement them. What I hope, however, is that you gained important insights into the complexities of implementation and gathered lots of ideas on how to implement reforms well.

I wish I could have told you precisely how to fashion a perfect grading and reporting system and offered you a perfect implementation plan. The problem is, we just don't have that knowledge at this time. And, in all honesty, I doubt we ever will.

Context matters in education. Schools differ drastically, even when located in similar communities serving similar student populations. Adaptations to those contextual differences will always be crucial to the success of any reform effort. I hope this book helps you in making those adaptations, guided by the evidence and knowledge we have of what grading and reporting policies and practices are truly better for our students and contribute to their learning success.

Perhaps this book will inspire you to chip away at all the ways we are doing grading and reporting wrong today so we can do it a little less wrong tomorrow. And if by doing it a little less wrong, we help more of our students see grading as honest, accurate, meaningful, fair, and maybe even helpful in the teaching and learning process, then I will count this book a huge success. I hope that you will too!

References and Resources

Achieve. (2014). *Postsecondary support for competency-based high school transcripts: Lessons from the competency-based transcripts postsecondary convening.* Washington, DC: Author. Accessed at www.achieve.org/publications/postsecondary-support-cbp-transcripts-brief on June 6, 2019.

Airasian, P. W. (2001). *Classroom assessment: Concepts and applications* (4th ed.). New York: McGraw-Hill.

American Educational Research Association, American Psychological Association, & National Council on Measurement in Education. (2014). *The standards for educational and psychological testing.* Washington, DC: American Educational Research Association.

Ames, C. (1992). Classrooms: Goals, structures, and student motivation. *Journal of Educational Psychology, 84*(3), 261–271.

Anderson, S. A. (1994). *Synthesis of research on mastery learning* (ERIC Document Reproduction Service No. ED 382 567).

Armstrong, T. (2000). *Multiple intelligences in the classroom* (2nd ed.). Alexandria, VA: Association for Supervision and Curriculum Development.

Arnold, K. (1995). *Lives of promise: What becomes of high school valedictorians—A fourteen-year study of achievement and life choices.* San Francisco: Jossey-Bass.

Austin, S., & McCann, R. (1992, March). *"Here's another arbitrary grade for your collection": A statewide study of grading policies.* Paper presented at the annual meeting of the American Educational Research Association, San Francisco.

AZ Quotes. (n.d.). *Robert M. Hutchins quotes.* Accessed at www.azquotes.com/author/7112-Robert_M_Hutchins on February 12, 2020.

Balakrishnan, A. (2007, April 23). Edward de Bono: "Iraq? They just need to think it through." *The Guardian.* Accessed at www.theguardian.com /education/2007/apr/24/highereducationprofile.academicexperts on June 6, 2019.

Bandura, A. (1977). *Social learning theory.* Englewood Cliffs, NJ: Prentice Hall.

Bandura, A. (1986). *Social foundations of thought and action: A social cognitive theory.* Englewood Cliffs, NJ: Prentice Hall.

Barker, E. (2017). *Barking up the wrong tree: The surprising science behind why everything you know about success is (mostly) wrong.* New York: HarperCollins.

Barnes, M. (2014, May 19). *7 reasons teachers should stop grading their students forever* [Blog post]. Accessed at www.brilliant-insane.com/2014/05/7 -reasons-teachers-should-stop-grading-their-students-forever.html on June 6, 2019.

Barnes, M. (2018, January 10). No, students don't need grades. *Education Week.* Accessed at https://www.edweek.org/ew/articles/2018/01/10/no-students -dont-need-grades.html on June 6, 2019.

Barton, P. E. (2002). *Staying on course in education reform.* Princeton, NJ: Statistics and Research Division, Policy Information Center, Educational Testing Service.

Belfield, C., Bowden, B., Klapp, A., Levin, H., Shand, R., & Zander, S. (2015). *The economic value of social and emotional learning.* New York: Teachers College Center for Benefit-Cost Studies in Education.

Berg, J., Osher, D., Same, M. R., Nolan, E., Benson, D., & Jacobs, N. (2017). *Identifying, defining, and measuring social and emotional competencies.* Washington, DC: American Institutes for Research.

Black, P., & Wiliam, D. (1998a). Assessment and classroom learning. *Assessment in Education: Principles, Policy & Practice, 5*(1), 7–74.

Black, P., & Wiliam, D. (1998b). Inside the black box: Raising standards through classroom assessment. *Phi Delta Kappan, 80*(2), 139–144.

Bloom, B. S. (Ed.). (1956). *Taxonomy of educational objectives, handbook 1: The cognitive domain.* New York: McKay.

Bloom, B. S. (1968). Learning for mastery. *Evaluation Comment, 1*(2), 1–12.

Bloom, B. S. (1971). Mastery learning. In J. H. Block (Ed.), *Mastery learning: Theory and practice* (pp. 47–63). New York: Holt, Rinehart & Winston.

Bloom, B. S. (1976). *Human characteristics and school learning.* New York: McGraw-Hill.

Bloom, B. S. (1981). *All our children learning: A primer for parents, teachers, and other educators.* New York: McGraw-Hill.

Bloom, B. S., Hastings, J. T., & Madaus, G. F. (1971). *Handbook on formative and summative evaluation of student learning.* New York: McGraw-Hill.

Bloom, B. S., Madaus, G. F., & Hastings, J. T. (1981). *Evaluation to improve learning.* New York: McGraw-Hill.

Blum, S. D. (2017, November 14). Ungrading. *Inside Higher Ed.* Accessed at www.insidehighered.com/advice/2017/11/14/significant-learning-benefits-getting-rid-grades-essay on June 6, 2019.

Boccella, K. (2016, October 30). More top high schools drop out of class-rank system. *The Philadelphia Inquirer.* Accessed at www.philly.com/philly/education/20161030_More_top_high_schools_drop_out_of_class-rank_system.html on June 6, 2019.

Bolster, A. S., Jr. (1983). Toward a more effective model of research on teaching. *Harvard Educational Review, 53*(3), 294–308.

Bonner, S. M., & Chen, P. P. (2019). The composition of grades: Cognitive and noncognitive factors. In T. R. Guskey & S. M. Brookhart (Eds.), *What we know about grading: What works, what doesn't, and what's next* (pp. 57–83). Alexandria, VA: Association for Supervision and Curriculum Development.

Bottoms, G., & O'Neill, K. (2001). *Preparing a new breed of school principals: It's time for action.* Atlanta, GA: Southern Regional Education Board.

Bowers, A. J. (2019). Report card grades and educational outcomes. In T. R. Guskey & S. M. Brookhart (Eds.), *What we know about grading: What works, what doesn't, and what's next* (pp. 32–56). Alexandria, VA: Association for Supervision and Curriculum Development.

Brochu, O. (2013, September 26). Quakertown School District will welcome new grading system next year. *WFMZ News.* Accessed at www.wfmz.com/news/southeastern-pa/quakertown-school-district-will-welcome-new-grading-system-next-year/18825365 on June 6, 2019.

Brookhart, S. M. (1991). Grading practices and validity. *Educational Measurement: Issues and Practice, 10*(1), 35–36.

Brookhart, S. M. (1993). Teachers' grading practices: Meaning and values. *Journal of Educational Measurement, 30*(2), 123–142.

Brookhart, S. M. (2011a). *Grading and learning: Practices that support student achievement.* Bloomington, IN: Solution Tree Press.

Brookhart, S. M. (2011b). Starting the conversation about grading. *Educational Leadership, 69*(3), 10–14.

Brookhart, S. M. (2013). *How to create and use rubrics for formative assessment and grading.* Alexandria, VA: Association for Supervision and Curriculum Development.

Brookhart, S. M., & Guskey, T. R. (2019a). Are grades reliable? Lessons from a century of research. *Education Update, 61*(5), 2–3. Accessed at www .ascd.org/publications/newsletters/education-update/may19/vol61/num05 /Are-Grades-Reliable%C2%A2-Lessons-from-a-Century-of-Research.aspx on June 6, 2019.

Brookhart, S. M., & Guskey, T. R. (2019b). Reliability in grading and grading scales. In T. R. Guskey & S. M. Brookhart (Eds.), *What we know about grading: What works, what doesn't, and what's next* (pp. 13–31). Alexandria, VA: Association for Supervision and Curriculum Development.

Brookhart, S. M., Guskey, T. R., Bowers, A. J., McMillan, J. H., Smith, J. K., Smith, L. F., et al. (2016). A century of grading research: Meaning and value in the most common educational measure. *Review of Educational Research, 86*(4), 803–848.

Brookhart, S. M., & Nitko, A. J. (2008). *Assessment and grading in classrooms.* Upper Saddle River, NJ: Pearson Education.

Bruckheimer, J. (Producer), Flynn, M. (Executive producer), Oman, C. (Producer), Stenson, M. (Executive producer), & Yakin, B. (Director). (2000). *Remember the Titans* [Motion picture]. United States: Walt Disney Pictures and Jerry Bruckheimer Films.

Brumage-Kilcourse, E. (2017, December 1). Opposition to 80/20 grading system not waning amongst parents, students. *Bear Facts.*

Buck Institute for Education. (2013). *6–12 collaboration rubric (CCSS aligned).* Accessed at www.bie.org/object/document/6_12_collaboration_rubric _ccss_aligned on June 6, 2019.

Buckmiller, T. M., & Peters, R. E. (2018). Getting a fair shot? *School Administrator, 75*(2), 22–25.

Butler, R. (1988). Enhancing and undermining intrinsic motivation: The effects of task-involving and ego-involving evaluation on interest and performance. *British Journal of Educational Psychology, 58*(1), 1–14.

Cameron, J., & Pierce, W. D. (1994). Reinforcement, reward, and intrinsic motivation: A meta-analysis. *Review of Educational Research, 64*(3), 363–423.

Cameron, J., & Pierce, W. D. (1996). The debate about rewards and intrinsic motivation: Protests and accusations do not alter the results. *Review of Educational Research, 66*(1), 39–51.

Cannon, W. (1927, December). The James-Lange theory of emotions: A critical examination and an alternative theory. *The American Journal of Psychology, 39*(1/4). 106–124.

Chappuis, J., & Stiggins, R. J. (2017). *An introduction to student-involved assessment for learning* (7th ed.). New York: Pearson.

Chastain, K. (1990). Characteristics of graded and ungraded compositions. *Modern Language Journal, 74*(1), 10–14.

Cizek, G. J., Fitzgerald, S. M., & Rachor, R. A. (1996). Teachers' assessment practices: Preparation, isolation, and the kitchen sink. *Educational Assessment, 3*(2), 159–179.

Claesgens, J., Rubino-Hare, L., Bloom, N., Fredrickson, K., Henderson-Dahms, C., et al. (2013). Professional development integrating technology: Does delivery format matter? *Science Educator, 22*(1), 10–18.

Clarke, D., & Hollingsworth, H. (2002). Elaborating a model of teacher professional growth. *Teaching and Teacher Education, 18*, 947–967.

Collaborative for Academic, Social, and Emotional Learning. (2017). *What is SEL?* Accessed at https://casel.org/what-is-sel on June 6, 2019.

Corcoran, T., Fuhrman, S. H., & Belcher, C. L. (2001). The district role in instructional improvement. *Phi Delta Kappan, 83*(1), 78–84.

Cowan, N. (2001). The magical number 4 in short-term memory: A reconsideration of mental storage capacity. *Behavioral and Brain Sciences, 24*(1), 87–114.

Cowan, N. (2010). The magical mystery four: How is working memory capacity limited, and why? *Current Directions in Psychological Science, 19*(1), 51–57.

Cox, J., Foster, B., & Bamat, D. (2019). *A review of instruments for measuring social and emotional learning skills among secondary school students* (REL 2020–010). Washington, DC: U.S. Department of Education, Institute of Education Sciences, National Center for Education Evaluation and Regional Assistance, Regional Educational Laboratory Northeast & Islands. Accessed at http://ies.ed.gov/ncee/edlabs on November 15, 2019.

Crandall, D. P. (1982). *People, policies, and practices: Examining the chain of school improvement.* Andover, MA: Network.

Credé, M. (2018). What shall we do about grit? A critical review of what we know and what we don't know. *Educational Researcher, 47*(9), 606–611.

Credé, M., Tynan, M. C., & Harms, P. D. (2017). Much ado about grit: A meta-analytic synthesis of the grit literature. *Journal of Personality and Social Psychology, 113*(3), 492–511.

Creemers, B., & Kyriakides, L. (2010). School factors explaining achievement on cognitive and affective outcomes: Establishing a dynamic model of educational effectiveness. *Scandinavian Journal of Educational Research, 54*(3), 263–294.

Cregan, A. (2013, July 7). Class of 2013 says Quakertown's grading system failed them. *The Intelligencer.* Accessed at www.theintell.com/2f728ead -755c-58d4-8c9c-87002a1e4c77.html on June 6, 2019.

Cross, L. H., & Frary, R. B. (1999). Hodgepodge grading: Endorsed by students and teachers alike. *Applied Measurement in Education, 12*(1), 53–72.

Dillon, A., & Gabbard, R. (1998). Hypermedia as an educational technology: A review of the quantitative research literature on learner comprehension, control, and style. *Review of Educational Research, 68*(3), 322–349.

Duckworth, A. L. (2017). *Grit: Why passion and resilience are the secrets to success.* London: Vermilion.

Duckworth, A. L., Peterson, C., Matthews, M. D., & Kelly, D. R. (2007). Grit: Perseverance and passion for long-term goals. *Journal of Personality and Social Psychology, 92*(6), 1087–1101.

Duffy, G. G., & Kear, K. (2007). Compliance or adaptation: What is the real message about research-based practices? *Phi Delta Kappan, 88*(8), 579–581.

DuFour, R., & Mattos, M. (2013). How do principals really improve schools? *Educational Leadership, 70*(7), 34–40.

Duncan, C. R., & Noonan, B. (2007). Factors affecting teachers' grading and assessment practices. *Alberta Journal of Educational Research, 53*(1), 1–21.

Durlak, J. A., Weissberg, R. P., Dymnicki, A. B., Taylor, R. D., & Schellinger, K. B. (2011). The impact of enhancing students' social and emotional learning: A meta-analysis of school-based universal interventions. *Child Development, 82*(1), 405–432.

Dweck, C. S. (2006). *Mindset: The new psychology of success.* New York: Random House.

Elmore, R. F. (1997). The paradox of innovation in education: Cycles of reform and the resilience of teaching. In A. A. Altshuler & R. D. Behn (Eds.), *Innovation in American government: Challenges, opportunities, and dilemmas* (pp. 246–273). Washington, DC: Brookings Institution Press.

Elmore, R. F., & McLaughlin, M. W. (1988). *Steady work: Policy, practice, and the reform of American education.* Santa Monica, CA: RAND.

Emanuele, G. (n.d.). *Disagree and commit or everyone loses.* Accessed at www.shiftyes.com/blog/disagree-and-commit-or-everyone-loses-galen-emanuele-shiftyestribe on December 17, 2019.

Eskreis-Winkler, L., Milkman, K. L., Gromet, D. M., & Duckworth, A. L. (2019). A large-scale field experiment shows giving advice improves academic outcomes for the advisor. *Proceedings of the National Academy of Sciences, 116*(30), 14808–18810. Accessed at www.vit.ly/mentorsimprove on December 5, 2019.

Esty, W. W., & Teppo, A. R. (1992). Grade assignment based on progressive improvement. *Mathematics Teacher, 85*(8), 616–618.

Farrington, C. A., Roderick, M., Allensworth, E., Nagaoka, J., Keyes, T. S., Johnson, D. W., et al. (2012). *Teaching adolescents to become learners: The role of noncognitive factors in shaping school performance.* Chicago: University of Chicago Consortium on School Research. Accessed at https://consortium.uchicago.edu/publications/teaching-adolescents-become-learners-role-noncognitive-factors-shaping-school on July 2, 2019.

Feldmesser, R. A. (1971, February). *The positive functions of grades.* Paper presented at the annual meeting of the American Educational Research Association, New York.

Festinger, L. (1957). *A theory of cognitive dissonance.* Stanford, CA: Stanford University Press.

Festinger, L. (1962). Cognitive dissonance. *Scientific American, 207*(4), 93–107.

Field, K. (2019, April 19). Inside Maine's disastrous rollout of proficiency-based learning. *The Hechinger Report.* Accessed at https://hechingerreport.org/inside-maines-disastrous-roll-out-of-proficiency-based-learning on June 6, 2019.

Foster, E. (2017). As social and emotional learning takes center stage, professional learning plays an important supporting role. *The Learning Professional, 38*(6), 9–10.

Franklin, A., Buckmiller, T., & Kruse, J. (2016). Vocal and vehement: Understanding parents' aversion to standards-based grading. *International Journal of Social Science Studies, 4*(11), 19–29.

Frisbie, D. A., & Waltman, K. K. (1992). Developing a personal grading plan. *Educational Measurement: Issues and Practice, 11*(3), 35–42.

Fuchs, L. S., & Fuchs, D. (2001). *What is scientifically-based research on progress monitoring?* Washington, DC: National Center on Student Progress Monitoring. Accessed at www.readingrockets.org/article/what-scientifically -based-research-progress-monitoring on June 6, 2019.

Fulghum, R. (2003). *All I really need to know I learned in kindergarten.* New York: Random House.

Fullan, M. (2016). *The new meaning of educational change* (5th ed.). New York: Teachers College Press.

Galla, B. M., Shulman, E. P., Plummer, B. D., Gardner, M., Hutt, S. J., Goyer, J. P., D'Mello, S. K., Finn, A. S., & Duckworth, A. L. (2019). Why high school grades are better predictors of on-time college graduation than are admissions test scores: The roles of self-regulation and cognitive ability. *American Educational Research Journal, 56*(6), 2077–2115.

Gardner, H. (2006). *Multiple intelligences: New horizons.* New York: Basic Books.

Gatt, I. (2009). Changing perceptions, practice and pedagogy: Challenges for and ways into teacher change. *Journal of Transformative Education, 7*(2), 164–184.

Gershenson, S. (2018). *Grade inflation in high schools (2005–2016).* Washington, DC: Thomas B. Fordham Institute. Accessed at https://edexcellence.net /publications/grade-inflation-in-high-schools on June 6, 2019.

Gersten, R., Vaughn, S., & Brengelman, S. U. (1996). Grading and academic feedback for special education students and students with learning difficulties. In T. R. Guskey (Ed.), *Communicating student learning: 1996 yearbook of the Association for Supervision and Curriculum Development* (pp. 47–57). Alexandria, VA: Association for Supervision and Curriculum Development.

Gogerty, J. (2016). *The influence of district support during implementation of high school standards-based grading practices* (Unpublished doctoral dissertation). Drake University, Des Moines, IA.

Goodreads. (n.d.). *Henry Ford quotable quotes.* Accessed at www.goodreads .com/quotes/15297-if-i-had-asked-people-what-they-wanted-they-would on December 18, 2019.

Goodreads. (n.d.). *Will Rogers quotable quotes.* Accessed at www.goodreads .com/quotes/19422-everyone-is-ignorant-only-on-different-subjects on February 12, 2020.

Goodson, I., Moore, S., & Hargreaves, A. (2006). Teacher nostalgia and the sustainability of reform: The generation and degeneration of teachers' missions, memory, and meaning. *Educational Administration Quarterly, 42*(1), 42–61.

Goodwin, B. (2018). SEL: Getting the "other stuff" right. *Educational Leadership, 76*(2), 78–79.

Grant, S., Hamilton, L. S., Wrabel, S. L., Gomez, C. J., Whitaker, A., Leschitz, J. T., et al. (2017). *Social and emotional learning interventions under the Every Student Succeeds Act.* Santa Monica, CA: RAND.

Great Schools Partnership. (2018). *College admissions: 79 New England institutions of higher education state that proficiency-based diplomas do not disadvantage applicants.* Portland, ME: Author. Accessed at www.great schoolspartnership.org/proficiency-based-learning/college-admissions on June 6, 2019.

Gullickson, A. R. (1985). Student evaluation techniques and their relationship to grade and curriculum. *Journal of Educational Research, 79*(2), 96–100.

Guskey, T. R. (1985). Staff development and teacher change. *Educational Leadership, 42*(7), 57–60.

Guskey, T. R. (1986). Staff development and the process of teacher change. *Educational Researcher, 15*(5), 5–12.

Guskey, T. R. (1989). Attitude and perceptual change in teachers. *International Journal of Educational Research, 13*(4), 439–453.

Guskey, T. R. (Ed.). (1994a). *High stakes performance assessment: Perspectives on Kentucky's educational reform.* Thousand Oaks, CA: Corwin Press.

Guskey, T. R. (1994b). Making the grade: What benefits students? *Educational Leadership, 52*(2), 14–20.

Guskey, T. R. (1994c, April). *Professional development in education: In search of the optimal mix.* Paper presented at the annual meeting of the American Educational Research Association, New Orleans, LA.

Guskey, T. R. (1994d). What you assess may not be what you get. *Educational Leadership, 51*(6), 51–54.

Guskey, T. R. (1996). Reporting on student learning: Lessons from the past—Prescriptions for the future. In T. R. Guskey (Ed.), *Communicating student learning: 1996 yearbook of the Association for Supervision and Curriculum Development* (pp. 13–24). Alexandria, VA: Association for Supervision and Curriculum Development.

Guskey, T. R. (1997). *Implementing mastery learning* (2nd ed.). Belmont, CA: Wadsworth.

Guskey, T. R. (1998). Making time to train your staff. *School Administrator, 55*(7), 35–37.

Guskey, T. R. (1999). Apply time with wisdom. *Journal of Staff Development, 20*(2), 10–15.

Guskey, T. R. (2000a). *Evaluating professional development.* Thousand Oaks, CA: Corwin Press.

Guskey, T. R. (2000b). Twenty questions? Twenty tools for better teaching. *Principal Leadership, 1*(3), 5–7.

Guskey, T. R. (2002a). *How's my kid doing?: A parents' guide to grades, marks, and report cards.* San Francisco: Jossey-Bass.

Guskey, T. R. (2002b, April). *Perspectives on grading and reporting: Differences among teachers, students, and parents.* Paper presented at the annual meeting of the American Educational Research Association, New Orleans, LA.

Guskey, T. R. (2002c). Professional development and teacher change. *Teachers and Teaching: Theory and Practice, 8*(3), 381–391.

Guskey, T. R. (2003). How classroom assessments improve learning. *Educational Leadership, 60*(5), 6–11.

Guskey, T. R. (2004). Zero alternatives. *Principal Leadership, 5*(2), 49–53.

Guskey, T. R. (2006a). "It wasn't fair!" Educators' recollections of their experiences as students with grading. *Journal of Educational Research and Policy Studies, 6*(2), 111–124.

Guskey, T. R. (2006b). Making high school grades meaningful. *Phi Delta Kappan, 87*(9), 670–675.

Guskey, T. R. (2007a). Closing achievement gaps: Revisiting Benjamin S. Bloom's "Learning for Mastery." *Journal of Advanced Academics, 19*(1), 8–31.

Guskey, T. R. (2007b). Multiple sources of evidence: An analysis of stakeholders' perceptions of various indicators of student learning. *Educational Measurement: Issues and Practice, 26*(1), 19–27.

Guskey, T. R. (2008). The rest of the story. *Educational Leadership, 65*(4), 28–35.

Guskey, T. R. (2009). Grading policies that work against standards . . . and how to fix them. In T. R. Guskey (Ed.), *Practical solutions for serious problems in standards-based grading* (pp. 9–26). Thousand Oaks, CA: Corwin Press.

Guskey, T. R. (2010). Lessons of mastery learning. *Educational Leadership, 68*(2), 52–57.

Guskey, T. R. (2011). Five obstacles to grading reform. *Educational Leadership, 69*(3), 16–21.

Guskey, T. R. (2013). The case against percentage grades. *Educational Leadership, 71*(1), 68–72.

Guskey, T. R. (2014a). Class rank weighs down true learning. *Phi Delta Kappan, 95*(6), 15–19.

Guskey, T. R. (2014b, October 17). *Why the label "exceeds standard" doesn't work* [Blog post]. Accessed at http://blogs.edweek.org/edweek/finding _common_ground/2014/10/why_the_label_exceeds_standard_doesnt _work.html on June 6, 2019.

Guskey, T. R. (2015). *On your mark: Challenging the conventions of grading and reporting.* Bloomington, IN: Solution Tree Press.

Guskey, T. R. (2016a, April 9). *Experience shapes attitudes and beliefs* [Blog post]. Accessed at https://tguskey.com/experience-shapes-attitudes-beliefs on June 6, 2019.

Guskey, T. R. (2016b, October 14). *Standards-based learning: Why do educators make it so complex?* [Blog post]. Accessed at http://blogs.edweek .org/edweek/finding_common_ground/2016/10/standards-based_learning _why_do_educators_make_it_so_complex.html on June 6, 2019.

Guskey, T. R. (2017a, September 7). *Don't get rid of grades. Change their meaning and consequences!* [Blog post]. Accessed at http://blogs.edweek .org/edweek/leadership_360/2017/09/dont_get_rid_of_grades_change _their_meaning_and_consequences.html on June 6, 2019.

Guskey, T. R. (2017b, February 6). New direction in the development of rubrics. *Corwin Connect.* Accessed at https://corwin-connect.com/2017/02 /new-direction-development-rubrics on July 16, 2017.

Guskey, T. R. (2018a, September 9). *How can we improve professional inquiry?* [Blog post]. Accessed at https://blogs.edweek.org/edweek/finding_common _ground/2018/09/how_can_we_improve_professional_inquiry.html on July 29, 2019.

Guskey, T. R. (2018b, May 20). *Labels aren't the problem; it's their permanence and scope* [Blog post]. Accessed at https://blogs.edweek.org/edweek /finding_common_ground/2018/05/labels_arent_the_problem_its_their _permanence_and_scope.html on June 6, 2019.

Guskey, T. R. (2018c, February 4). *Multiple grades: The first step to improving grading and reporting* [Blog post]. Accessed at http://blogs.edweek.org /edweek/leadership_360/2018/02/multiple_grades_the_first_step_to _improving_grading_and_reporting.html on June 6, 2019.

Guskey, T. R. (2019a). Grades versus comments: Research on student feedback. *Phi Delta Kappan, 101*(3), 42–47.

Guskey, T. R. (2019b, February 25). *Let's give up the search for "best practices" in grading* [Blog post]. Accessed at http://blogs.edweek.org/edweek /finding_common_ground/2019/02/lets_give_up_the_search_for_best _practices_in_grading.html on July 2, 2019.

Guskey, T. R., & Anderman, E. M. (2008). Students at bat. *Educational Leadership, 66*(3), 8–14.

Guskey, T. R., & Bailey, J. M. (2001). *Developing grading and reporting systems for student learning.* Thousand Oaks, CA: Corwin Press.

Guskey, T. R., & Bailey, J. M. (2010). *Developing standards-based report cards.* Thousand Oaks, CA: Corwin Press.

Guskey, T. R., & Brookhart, S. M. (Eds.). (2019). *What we know about grading: What works, what doesn't, and what's next.* Alexandria, VA: Association for Supervision and Curriculum Development.

Guskey, T. R., & Huberman, M. (Eds.) (1995). *Professional development in education: New paradigms and practices.* New York: Teachers College Press.

Guskey, T. R., & Jung, L. A. (2011). Response to intervention and mastery learning: Tracing roots and seeking common ground. *The Clearing House, 84*(6), 249–255.

Guskey, T. R., & Jung, L. A. (2013). *Answers to essential questions about standards, assessments, grading, and reporting.* Thousand Oaks, CA: Corwin Press.

Guskey, T. R., & Jung, L. A. (2016). Grading: Why you should trust your judgment. *Educational Leadership, 73*(7), 50–54.

Guskey, T. R., & Link, L. J. (2017, April). *Grades represent achievement and "something else": Analysis of the nonachievement factors teachers consider in determining students' grades.* Paper presented at the annual meeting of the American Educational Research Association, San Antonio, TX.

Guskey, T. R., & Link, L. J. (2019a). Exploring the factors teachers consider in determining students' grades. *Assessment in Education: Principles, Policy & Practice, 26*(3), 303–320.

Guskey, T. R., & Link, L. J. (2019b). The forgotten element of instructional leadership: Grading. *Educational Leadership, 76*(6). Accessed at www .ascd.org/publications/educational-leadership/mar19/vol76/num06 /The-Forgotten-Element-of-Instructional-Leadership@-Grading.aspx on February 12, 2020.

Guskey, T. R., & Link, L. J. (2019c, April). *Understanding different stakeholders' views on homework and grading.* Paper presented at the annual meeting of the American Educational Research Association, Toronto, Ontario, Canada.

Guskey, T. R., & Passaro, P. D. (1994). Teacher efficacy: A study of construct dimensions. *American Educational Research Journal, 31*(3), 627–643.

Guskey, T. R., & Pigott, T. D. (1988). Research on group-based mastery learning programs: A meta-analysis. *Journal of Educational Research, 81*(4), 197–216.

Guskey, T. R., Swan, G. M., & Jung, L. A. (2011a). Grades that mean something: Kentucky develops standards-based report cards. *Phi Delta Kappan, 93*(2), 52–57.

Guskey, T. R., Swan, G. M., & Jung, L. A. (2011b, April). *Parents' and teachers' perceptions of standards-based and traditional report cards.* Paper presented at the annual meeting of the American Educational Research Association, New Orleans, LA.

Hanover Research. (2011). *Effective grading practices in the middle school and high school environments.* Washington, DC: Author. Accessed at https:// njctl-media.s3.amazonaws.com/uploads/Effective%20grading%20 practices%20in%20the%20middle%20school%20and%20high%20 school%20environments.pdf on June 6, 2019.

Hanson, A., Pennington, T. R., Prusak, K., & Wilkinson, C. (2017). PE central: A possible online professional development tool. *Physical Educator, 74*(3), 570–587.

Hargreaves, A. (2005). Educational change takes ages: Life, career and generational factors in teachers' emotional responses to educational change. *Teaching and Teacher Education, 21*(8), 967–983.

Harnadek, A. (1992). *Classroom quickies: Book 2.* Seaside, CA: Critical Thinking.

Harris-Perry, M. (2012, April 19). Let's get rid of grades. *Washington Post.* Accessed at www.washingtonpost.com/opinions/lets-get-rid-of-grades /2012/04/19/gIQAwie5TT_story.html?utm_term=.d63bb0dc2f1b on June 6, 2019.

Hattie, J. (2009). *Visible learning: A synthesis of over 800 meta-analyses relating to achievement.* New York: Routledge.

Hattie, J., & Timperley, H. (2007). The power of feedback. *Review of Educational Research, 77*(1), 81–112.

Heesen, B. A. (2013, May 20). Wilson to drop valedictorian distinction; Latin honors system will include more seniors. *Reading Eagle.* Accessed at http:// readingeagle.com/article.aspx?id=478846 on June 6, 2019.

Henderson, A. T., & Mapp, K. L. (2002). *A new wave of evidence: The impact of school, family, and community connections on student achievement.* Austin, TX: National Center for Family and Community Connections With Schools.

Hill, N. E., & Taylor, L. C. (2004). Parental school involvement and children's academic achievement: Pragmatics and issues. *Current Directions in Psychological Science, 13*(4), 161–164.

Hiner, N. R. (1973). An American ritual: Grading as a cultural function. *The Clearing House, 47*(6), 356–361.

Hoover, E. (2012). High-school class rank, a slippery metric, loses its appeal for colleges. *Chronicle of Higher Education, 56*(15), A1, A5.

Hoover-Dempsey, K. V., & Sandler, H. M. (1997). Why do parents become involved in their children's education? *Review of Educational Research, 67*(1), 3–42.

Huberman, M. (1983). Recipes for busy kitchens. *Knowledge: Creation, Diffusion, Utilization, 4*(4), 478–510.

Huberman, M. (1985). What knowledge is of most worth to teachers? A knowledge-use perspective. *Teaching and Teacher Education, 1*(3), 251–262.

Huberman, M. (1992). Teacher development and instructional mastery. In A. Hargreaves & M. Fullan (Eds.), *Understanding teacher development* (pp. 122–142). New York: Teachers College Press.

Huberman, M. (1995). Professional careers and professional development: Some intersections. In T. R. Guskey & M. Huberman (Eds.), *Professional development in education: New paradigms and practices* (pp. 193–224). New York: Teachers College Press.

Jackson, P. (1986). *The practice of teaching*. New York: Teachers College Press.

James, W. (1890). *The principles of psychology*. New York: Holt.

Jaschik, S. (2017, May 10). A plan to kill high school transcripts . . . and transform college admissions. *Inside Higher Ed*. Accessed at www.inside highered.com/news/2017/05/10/top-private-high-schools-start-campaign -kill-traditional-transcripts-and-change on June 6, 2019.

Jeynes, W. (2012). A meta-analysis of the efficacy of different types of parental involvement programs for urban students. *Urban Education*, *47*(4), 706–742.

Johnson, D. W., & Johnson, R. T. (1995). Cooperative learning. In J. H. Block, S. T. Everson, & T. R. Guskey (Eds.), *School improvement programs: A handbook for educational leaders* (pp. 25–56). New York: Scholastic.

Jung, L. A. (2015). *A practical guide to planning interventions and monitoring progress*. Bloomington, IN: Solution Tree Press.

Jung, L. A., & Guskey, T. R. (2007). Standards-based grading and reporting: A model for special education. *Teaching Exceptional Children*, *40*(2), 48–53.

Jung, L. A., & Guskey, T. R. (2012). *Grading exceptional and struggling learners*. Thousand Oaks, CA: Corwin Press.

Kifer, E. (2001). *Large-scale assessment: Dimensions, dilemmas, and policy*. Thousand Oaks, CA: Corwin Press.

Kim, H. (2013, November 26). School district scraps controversial grading algorithm after outcry. *Q13 Fox News*. Accessed at https://q13fox.com /2013/11/26/federal-way-scraps-controversial-grading-algorithm-after -public-outcry on June 6, 2019.

Kingston, N., & Nash, B. (2011). Formative assessment: A meta-analysis and a call for research. *Educational Measurement: Issues and Practice*, *30*(4), 28–37.

Klecker, B. M., & Chapman, A. (2008, November). *Advocating the implementation of mastery learning in higher education to increase student learning and retention*. Paper presented at the annual meeting of the Mid-South Educational Research Association, Knoxville, TN.

Kohn, A. (1993). *Punished by rewards: The trouble with gold stars, incentive plans, A's, praise, and other bribes*. Boston: Houghton Mifflin.

Kohn, A. (1994). Grading: The issue is not how but why. *Educational Leadership, 52*(2), 38–41.

Kohn, A. (1999). *Punished by rewards: The trouble with gold stars, incentive plans, A's, and other bribes*. Boston: Houghton Mifflin.

Kohn, M. (1989). *Class and conformity: A study in values* (2nd ed.). Chicago: University of Chicago Press.

Kolbert, E. (2017, February 27). Why facts don't change our minds: New discoveries about the human mind show the limitations of reason. *The New Yorker*. Accessed at www.newyorker.com/magazine/2017/02/27/why -facts-dont-change-our-minds on June 6, 2019.

Kotter, J. P. (2012). *Leading change*. Boston: Harvard Business Review Press.

Kourea, L., Cartledge, G., & Musti-Rao, S. (2007). Improving the reading skills of urban elementary students through total class peer tutoring. *Remedial and Special Education, 28*(2), 95–107.

Kraft, M. A., & Papay, J. P. (2014). Can professional environments in schools promote teacher development? Explaining heterogeneity in returns to teaching experience. *Educational Evaluation and Policy Analysis, 36*(4), 476–500.

Krathwohl, D. R., Bloom, B. S., & Masia, B. B. (1964). *Taxonomy of educational objectives, handbook 2: The affective domain*. New York: McKay.

Kulik, C. C., Kulik, J. A., & Bangert-Drowns, R. L. (1990). Effectiveness of mastery learning programs: A meta-analysis. *Review of Educational Research, 60*(2), 265–299.

Kumar, V., Greer, J. E., & McCalla, G. I. (2005). Assisting online helpers. *International Journal of Learning Technology, 1*(2), 293–321.

Lamb-Sinclair, A. (2017, June 16). Why grades are not paramount to achievement. *The Atlantic*. Accessed at www.theatlantic.com/education /archive/2017/06/why-grades-are-not-the-key-to-achievement/530124 on June 6, 2019.

Larson, E. (Ed.). (2002). *Brain stretchers*. Huntington Beach, CA: Creative Teaching Press.

Larson, G. (2017). *An evaluation of standards-based grading in Wisconsin high schools* (Unpublished doctoral dissertation). University of Wisconsin, Oshkosh.

Learning Forward. (2011). *Standards for professional learning.* Oxford, OH: Author. Accessed at www.learningforward.org/standards/index.cfm on June 6, 2019.

Learning Kit Project. (2007). *The learning kit project: Theory and cognitive tools to enhance learning skills and support lifelong learning.* Accessed at www.learningkit.sfu.ca/#disting on April 13, 2019.

Lencioni, P. (2012). *The advantage: Why organizational health trumps everything else in business.* San Francisco: Jossey-Bass.

Lewin, K. (1935). *A dynamic theory of personality.* New York: McGraw-Hill.

Liebowitz, D. D., & Porter, L. (2019). The effect of principal behaviors on student, teacher, and school outcomes: A systematic review and meta-analysis of the empirical literature. *Review of Educational Research, 89*(5), 785–827.

Link, L. J. (2018a). Finding expertise in your own backyard: K–12 educators can collaborate with a nearby university to devise a strategy that serves both partners' needs and interests. *School Administrator, 10*(75), 38–42.

Link, L. J. (2018b). Teachers' perceptions of grading practices: How pre-service training makes a difference. *Journal of Research in Education, 28*(1), 62–91.

Link, L. J. (2019). Leadership for grading reform. In T. R. Guskey & S. M. Brookhart (Eds.), *What we know about grading: What works, what doesn't, and what's next* (pp. 157–194). Alexandria, VA: Association for Supervision and Curriculum Development.

Linn, R. L. (1983). Testing and instruction: Links and distinctions. *Journal of Educational Measurement, 20*(2), 179–189.

Liu, X. (2008, October). *Measuring teachers' perceptions of grading practices: Does school level make a difference?* Paper presented at the annual meeting of the Northeastern Educational Research Association, Rocky Hill, CT.

Llinares, A., & Lyster, R. (2014). The influence of context on patterns of corrective feedback and learner uptake: A comparison of CLIL and immersion classrooms. *The Language Learning Journal, 42*(2), 181–194.

Long, C. (2015, August 19). Are letter grades failing our students? *NEA Today.* Accessed at http://neatoday.org/2015/08/19/are-letter-grades-failing-our-students on July 2, 2019.

Lortie, D. C. (1975). *Schoolteacher: A sociological study.* Chicago: University of Chicago Press.

Lowden, C. (2006). Reality CHECK. *Journal of Staff Development, 27*(1), 61–64.

Maeli, J. (2016, March 28). *The backfire effect: The more your beliefs are challenged, the stronger they become* [Blog post]. Accessed at http://thepolitical informer.com/the-backfire-effect on July 2, 2019.

Mahoney, J. L., & Weissberg, R. P. (2018). SEL: What the research says. *Educational Leadership, 76*(2), 34–35.

Manson, M. (2016). *The subtle art of not giving a f*ck: A counterintuitive approach to living a good life.* New York: HarperCollins.

Martin, J. E. (2020). *Reinventing crediting for competency-based education: The Mastery Transcript Consortium model and beyond.* New York: Routledge.

Marzano, R. J. (2017). *The new art and science of teaching.* Bloomington, IN: Solution Tree Press.

Mastery Transcript Consortium. (2017, February 24). *A broken tool* [Video file]. Accessed at www.youtube.com/watch?v=oxeGGo1e--M on July 2, 2019.

McKibben, S. (2017). Stepping out of rank. *Education Update, 59*(9), 2–3, 6.

McLaughlin, M. W. (1976). Implementation as mutual adaptation: Changes in classroom organization. *Teachers College Record, 77*(3), 339–351.

McLaughlin, M. W., & Marsh, D. (1978). Staff development and school change. *Teachers College Record, 80*(1), 69–94.

McMillan, J. H. (2005). Secondary teachers' classroom assessment and grading practices. *Educational Measurement: Issues and Practice, 20*(1), 20–32.

McMillan, J. H. (2019). Surveys of teachers' grading practices and perceptions. In T. R. Guskey & S. M. Brookhart (Eds.), *What we know about grading: What works, what doesn't, and what's next* (pp. 84–112). Alexandria, VA: Association for Supervision and Curriculum Development.

McMillan, J. H., Myran, S., & Workman, D. (2002). Elementary teachers' classroom assessment and grading practices. *Journal of Educational Research, 95*(4), 203–213.

Medcalf, J., Glynn, T., & Moore, D. (2004). Peer tutoring in writing: A school systems approach. *Educational Psychology in Practice, 20*(2), 157–178.

Merriam-Webster. (2020a). *Coalition.* Accessed at www.merriam-webster.com /dictionary/coalition on January 24, 2020.

Merriam-Webster. (2020b). *Committee.* Accessed at www.merriam-webster .com/dictionary/committee on January 24, 2020.

Miles, K. (2010). *Mastery learning and academic achievement* (Doctoral dissertation). Walden University, Minneapolis, MN. Accessed at https://search.proquest.com/docview/193327442 on July 2, 2019.

Miller, G. (1999). Creating cruise ships with an eye on next generation. *The Cruise Industry News Quarterly, 9*(37), 67.

Miller, G. A. (1956). The magical number seven, plus or minus two: Some limits on our capacity for processing information. *Psychological Review, 63*(2), 81–97.

Mishkind, A. (2014). *Overview: State definitions of college and career readiness.* Washington, DC: College and Career Readiness and Success Center, American Institutes for Research. Accessed at https://ccrscenter.org/products-resources/overview-state-definitions-college-and-career-readiness on June 6, 2019.

Moody, J. (2018, March 22). Albany to change middle school report cards. *Albany Democrat-Herald.* Accessed at http://democratherald.com/news/local/education/albany-to-change-middle-school-report-cards/article_dbbf60b9-6d7c-57b4-9f76-51b8ad54de4a.html on June 6, 2019.

Moran, K. (2014, February 3). What does measuring student growth look like in practice? *Getting Smart.* Accessed at www.gettingsmart.com/2014/02/measuring-student-growth-part-2 on June 6, 2019.

Morrow, G. R. (1979). An almost empirical analysis of committee meetings. *Journal of Irreproducible Results, 25*(2), 22–23.

Nagaoka, J., Farrington, C. A., Roderick, M., Allensworth, E., Keyes, T. S., Johnson, D. W., et al. (2013). Readiness for college: The role of noncognitive factors and context. *Voices in Urban Education, 38*, 45–52. Accessed at http://vue.annenberginstitute.org/issues/38/readiness-college-role-noncognitive-factors-and-context on June 6, 2019.

Nagel, D. (2016, March 15). Panel: Ditch grades now, focus on student learning. *THE Journal.* Accessed at https://thejournal.com/articles/2016/03/15/panel-ditch-grades-now-focus-on-student-learning.aspx on June 6, 2019.

National Association for College Admission Counseling. (2019). *The state of college admission report.* Arlington, VA: Author. Accessed at www.nacacnet.org/news--publications/publications/state-of-college-admission on June 6, 2019.

National Governors Association Center for Best Practices & Council of Chief State School Officers. (2010a). *Common Core State Standards for English language arts and literacy in history/social studies, science, and technical subjects.* Washington, DC: Authors. Accessed at www.corestandards.org/assets /CCSSI_ELA%20Standards.pdf on August 7, 2019.

National Governors Association Center for Best Practices & Council of Chief State School Officers. (2010b). *Common Core State Standards for mathematics.* Washington, DC: Authors. Accessed at www.corestandards.org /assets/CCSSI_Math%20Standards.pdf on August 7, 2019.

Natriello, G., & Dornbusch, S. M. (1984). *Teacher evaluation standards and student effort.* New York: Longman.

Nguyen, T. (2015). The effectiveness of online learning: Beyond no significant difference and future horizons. *Journal of Online Learning and Teaching, 11*(2), 309–319.

Nickerson, R. S. (1998). Confirmation bias: A ubiquitous phenomenon in many guises. *Review of General Psychology, 2*(2), 175–220.

O'Brien, A. (2014, March 26). *Rethinking class ranking* [Blog post]. Accessed at www.edutopia.org/blog/rethinking-class-ranking-anne-obrien on June 6, 2019.

O'Connor, K. (2013). *The school leader's guide to grading.* Bloomington, IN: Solution Tree Press.

Olsen, B., & Buchanan, R. (2019). An investigation of teachers encouraged to reform grading practices in secondary schools. *American Educational Research Journal, 56*(5), 2004–2039.

Page, E. B. (1958). Teacher comments and student performance: A seventy-four classroom experiment in school motivation. *Journal of Educational Psychology, 49*(4), 173–181.

Papay, J. P., & Kraft, M. A. (2016). The myth of the performance plateau. *Educational Leadership, 73*(8), 36–42.

Partnership for 21st Century Learning. (n.d.). *Frameworks and resources.* Accessed at www.battelleforkids.org/networks/p21/frameworks-resources on June 6, 2019.

Perry, N. E., Thauberger, C., MacAllister, K., & Winne, P. H. (2005). *Tasks that extend opportunities for self-regulated learning: A lifecycles learning kit for grade 1 students.* Paper presented at the annual meeting of the American Educational Research Association, Montreal, Quebec, Canada.

Pollio, M., & Hochbein, C. (2015). The association between standards-based grading and standardized test scores in a high school reform model. *Teachers College Record, 117*(11), 1–28.

Pomerantz, E. M., Moorman, E. A., & Litwack, S. D. (2007). The how, whom, and why of parents' involvement in children's academic lives: More is not always better. *Review of Educational Research, 77*(3), 373–410.

Popham, W. J. (2018). *Assessment literacy for educators in a hurry.* Alexandria, VA: Association for Supervision and Curriculum Development.

Putnam, R. T., & Borko, H. (2000). What do new views of knowledge and thinking have to say about research on teacher learning? *Educational Researcher, 29*(1), 4–15.

Rado, D. (2016, June 6). Parents push back against school report cards with no letter grades. *Chicago Tribune.* Accessed at www.chicagotribune.com /news/local/breaking/ct-middle-school-grades-met-20160601-story.html on June 6, 2019.

Rampell, C. (2017, May 11). Why getting rid of grades would help rich students—and hurt poor ones. *Washington Post.* Accessed at www.washington post.com/opinions/why-getting-rid-of-grades-would-help-rich-students -and-hurt-poor-ones/2017/05/11/b038f90c-3683-11e7-b4ee-434b6 d506b37_story.html?utm_term=.925a78f22f7a on July 2, 2019.

Randall, J., & Engelhard, G. (2010). Examining the grading practices of teachers. *Teaching and Teacher Education, 26*(7), 1372–1380.

Raudenbush, S. W., Rowan, B., & Cheong, Y. F. (1992). Contextual effects on the self-perceived efficacy of high school teachers. *Sociology of Education, 65*(2), 150–167.

Rcampus. (2019). *iRubric: Homework completion rubric.* Accessed at www .rcampus.com/rubricshowc.cfm?code=TXB7368&sp=true on July 23, 2019.

Riede, P. (2018). Making the call inside admissions offices. *School Administrator, 75*(2), 26–29.

Rogers, P. (2007). Teacher professional learning in mathematics: An example of a change process. In J. Watson & K. Beswick (Eds.), *Mathematics: Essential research, essential practice. Proceedings of the 30th annual conference of the Mathematics Education Research Group of Australasia* (pp. 631–640). Adelaide, SA: MERGA Inc.

Rose, T. (2016). *The end of average: How we succeed in a world that values sameness.* New York: HarperCollins.

Roth, C. (2017, March 13). Why Henry Ford's most famous quote is dead wrong. *Entrepreneur.* Accessed at www.entrepreneur.com/article/290410 on June 6, 2019.

Rush, L. S., & Young, S. (2011). Wyoming's Instructional Facilitator Program: Teachers' beliefs about the impact of coaching on practice. *The Rural Educator, 32*(2), 13–22.

Russell, J. A., & Austin, J. R. (2010). Assessment practices of secondary music teachers. *Journal of Research in Music Education, 58*(1), 37–54.

Sabers, D. S., Cushing, K. S., & Berliner, D. C. (1991). Differences among teachers in a task characterized by simultaneity, multidimensional, and immediacy. *American Educational Research Journal, 28*(1), 63–88.

Salili, F., Chiu, C. Y., & Hong, Y. Y. (2001). *Student motivation: The culture and context of learning.* Boston: Springer.

Schimmer, T. (2016). *Grading from the inside out: Bringing accuracy to student assessment through a standards-based mindset.* Bloomington, IN: Solution Tree Press.

Scriven, M. (1967). The methodology of evaluation. In R. W. Tyler, R. M. Gagne, & M. Scriven (Eds.), *Perspectives of curriculum evaluation* (pp. 39–83). Chicago: Rand McNally.

Segerstrom, D., & Hansen, A. M. (2014, June 18). *Grading the future: The Illinois State Board of Education's 2014 Student Advisory Council.* Springfield, IL: Author. Accessed at www.isbe.net/Documents/2014-board-presentation.pdf on July 2, 2019.

Shepard, L. A. (2018). Learning progressions as tools for assessment and learning. *Applied Measurement in Education, 31*(2), 165–174.

Sider, S., & Ashun, M. (2013). "My classroom is a bigger place": Examining the impact of a professional development course on the global perspective of experienced teachers. *Canadian and International Education, 42*(1), 1–14.

Signe, S. N. (2016). Advancing work practices. *Interactive Technology and Smart Education, 13*(4), 246–260.

Silver, H. F., Strong, R. W., & Perini, M. J. (2000). *So each may learn: Integrating learning styles and multiple intelligences.* Alexandria, VA: Association for Supervision and Curriculum Development.

Slavin, R. E. (1991). Synthesis of research on cooperative learning. *Educational Leadership, 48*(5), 71–82.

Snyder, R. R. (2017). Resistance to change among veteran teachers: Providing voice for more effective engagement. *NCPEA International Journal of Educational Leadership Preparation, 12*(1). Accessed at https://files.eric .ed.gov/fulltext/EJ1145464.pdf on June 6, 2019.

Spears, V. H. (2017, July 11). This school eliminated extra credit. Now it wants to take "D's" out of the grading scale. *Lexington Herald Leader.* Accessed at www.kentucky.com/news/local/education/article160718814.html on June 6, 2019.

Spehar, B. (2015, June 7). *Guskey's model of teacher change* [Video file]. Accessed at www.youtube.com/watch?v=b8BqMLkeUaQ on June 6, 2019.

Spencer, K. (2017, August 11). A new kind of classroom: No grades, no failing, no hurry. *New York Times.* Accessed at www.nytimes.com/2017/08/11 /nyregion/mastery-based-learning-no-grades.html on February 12, 2020.

St. George, D. (2017, September 17). Report cards: "P" is for perplexing. Traditional grades make a comeback. *Washington Post.* Accessed at www .washingtonpost.com/local/education/report-cards-p-is-for-perplexing -traditional-grades-make-a-comeback/2017/09/17/65a1a2ce-9725-11e7 -82e4-f1076f6d6152_story.html?utm_term=.7f0b81f289ac on June 6, 2019.

Stan, E. (2012). The role of grades in motivating students to learn. *Procedia: Social and Behavioral Sciences, 69,* 1998–2003.

Stanley, T. J. (2001). *The millionaire mind.* New York: RosettaBooks.

Stecker, P. M., Fuchs, L. S., & Fuchs, D. (2005). Using curriculum-based measurement to improve student achievement: Review of research. *Psychology in the Schools, 42*(8), 795–819.

Sternberg, R. J. (1994). Allowing for thinking styles. *Educational Leadership, 52*(3), 36–40.

Stewart, L. G., & White, M. A. (1976). Teacher comments, letter grades, and student performance: What do we really know? *Journal of Educational Psychology, 68*(4), 488–500.

Stiggins, R. J. (1999). Evaluating classroom assessment training in teacher education programs. *Educational Measurement: Issues and Practice, 18*(1), 23–27.

Stiggins, R. J. (2002). Assessment crisis: The absence of assessment for learning. *Phi Delta Kappan, 83*(10), 758–765.

Stosich, E. L., & Bae, S. (2018). Engaging diverse stakeholders to strengthen policy. *Phi Delta Kappan, 99*(8), 8–12.

Stoskopf, M. (2016, November 29). 80/20 disadvantages outweigh advantages. *The Mirror*. Accessed at https://spashmirror.com/3105/opinion/8020 -disadvantages-outweigh-advantages on February 12, 2020.

Sun, Y., & Cheng, L. (2013). Teachers' grading practices: Meaning and values assigned. *Assessment in Education: Principles, Policy & Practice, 21*(3), 326–343.

Swan, G., Guskey, T. R., & Jung, L. A. (2014). Parents' and teachers' perceptions of standards-based and traditional report cards. *Educational Assessment, Evaluation and Accountability, 26*(3), 289–299.

Szamko, M. (2016, April 5). What the paranoid got right: The unlikely legacy of Andy Grove's intel. *The Huffington Post*. Accessed at www .huffingtonpost.com/monika-szamko/what-the-paranoid-got-rig_b _9612326.html on July 2, 2019.

Taketa, K. (2019, October 21). Teachers, experts question traditional ways of grading. *The San Diego Union Tribune*. Accessed at www.sandiegounion tribune.com/news/education/story/2019-10-21/teachers-experts-question -traditional-ways-of-grading on December 5, 2019.

Tolley, J. (2016, May 31). *Valedictorian shocks world with brutally honest graduation speech* [Video file]. Accessed at www.youtube.com/watch?v=a5uq NhfNHL8 on July 2, 2019.

Tomlinson, C. A. (2003). *Fulfilling the promise of the differentiated classroom: Strategies and tools for responsive teaching*. Alexandria, VA: Association for Supervision and Curriculum Development.

Topping, K., & Bryce, A. (2004). Cross-age peer tutoring of reading and thinking: Influence on thinking skills. *Educational Psychology, 24*(5), 595–621.

Trembath, K. (2017, December 1). Teachers react to 80/20 grading policy. *The Mav*. Accessed at https://mavnewspaper.com/2110/features/teachers-react -to-80-20-grading-policy on February 12, 2020.

Tribune. (2013, June 5). *School has 29 valedictorians? Is that too many?* [Video file]. Accessed at https://news.yahoo.com/video/school-29-valedictorians -too-many-121029330.html on December 6, 2018.

Trumbull, E. (2000). Why do we grade—and should we? In E. Trumbull & B. Farr (Eds.), *Grading and reporting student progress in an age of standards* (pp. 23–43). Norwood, MA: Christopher-Gordon.

Usher, E. L., & Pajares, F. (2008). Sources of self-efficacy in school: Critical review of the literature and future directions. *Review of Educational Research, 78*(4), 751–796.

Welsh, M. (2019). Standards-based grading. In T. R. Guskey & S. M. Brookhart (Eds.), *What we know about grading: What works, what doesn't, and what's next* (pp. 113–144). Alexandria, VA: Association for Supervision and Curriculum Development.

Whiting, B., Van Burgh, J. W., & Render, G. F. (1995, April). *Mastery learning in the classroom.* Paper presented at the annual meeting of the American Educational Research Association, San Francisco.

Whitworth, B. A., & Chiu, J. L. (2015). Professional development and teacher change: The missing leadership link. *Journal of Science Teacher Education, 26*(2), 121–137.

Wiggins, G. (1996). Honesty and fairness: Toward better grading and reporting. In T. R. Guskey (Ed.), *Communicating student learning: 1996 yearbook of the Association for Supervision and Curriculum Development* (pp. 141–176). Alexandria, VA: Association for Supervision and Curriculum Development.

Wiggins, G. (1998). *Educative assessment: Designing assessments to inform and improve student performance.* San Francisco: Jossey-Bass.

Wikipedia. (2019). *Vale dicere.* Accessed at https://en.wikipedia.org/wiki/Valedictorian on January 24, 2020.

Wright, J., & Cleary, K. S. (2006). Kids in the tutor seat: Building school's capacity to help struggling readers through a cross-age peer-tutoring program. *Psychology in the Schools, 43*(1), 99–107.

Yaffe, D. (2017, November 15). No more zeros in K–12 education: No-fail grading methods designed to better reflect students' knowledge and abilities. *District Administration.* Accessed at https://districtadministration.com/no-more-zeros-in-k12-education on July 2, 2019.

Yahoo News: Tribune. (2013, June 5). *School has 29 valedictorians? Is that too many?* [Video files]. Accessed at http://news.yahoo.com/video/school-29-valedictorians-too-many-121029330.html on December 6, 2018.

Zimmerman, J. (2006). Why some teachers resist change and what principals can do about it. *NASSP Bulletin, 90*(3), 238–249.

Zins, J. E., Weissberg, R. P., Wang, M. C., & Walberg, H. J. (Eds.). (2004). *Building academic success on social and emotional learning: What does the research say?* New York: Teachers College Press.

Index

NUMBERS

On Your Mark: Challenging the Conventions of Grading and Reporting
Thomas R. Guskey
Clarify the purpose of grades, craft a vision statement aligned with this purpose, and discover strategies to implement effective practices.
BKF606

Proficiency-Based Grading in the Content Areas: Insights and Key Questions for Secondary Schools
Edited by Anthony R. Reibel and Eric Twadell
Discover a clear path for implementing an evidence-based grading system where student growth is at the heart of every classroom, in every content area.
BKF837

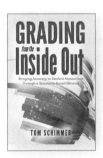

Grading From the Inside Out: Bringing Accuracy to Student Assessment Through a Standards-Based Mindset
Tom Schimmer
The time for grading reform is now. Discover the steps your team can take to implement standards-based practices that transform grading and reporting schoolwide.
BKF646

Assessment Toolkit
Tom Schimmer
Designed by leading assessment experts, this curated toolkit includes 32 books for whole-school professional development.
KTF348